More praise for
The Black Girl Next Door

"A refreshing addition to the written history of the African American experience."
—*The New York Times Book Review*

"Stands out. . . . Forthright and courageous."
—*Los Angeles Times*

"Powerful and provocative."
—*Dame* magazine

"Will move you, enrage you, and ultimately empower you."
—*Essence* magazine

"In elegant prose, Baszile shares enlightening observations throughout. . . . Proud and comfortable in her skin, as well as clearheaded about its hazards, Baszile has written a classic portrait of that girl next door."
—*Publishers Weekly*

"Touching. . . . This poignant autobiography is both a tender coming-of-age story and a strong reminder that the wounds of racial injustice in the United States run deep and are slow to heal."
—*Library Journal*

"This is an absorbing look behind the facade of one black family's striving for integration and the American dream."
—*Booklist*

"Although the memoir is serious and challenging, the book also is packed with offbeat humor and suspense."
—*The Connecticut Post*

"Thought-provoking. . . . Written with heart and gut-wrenching earnestness, Baszile's memoir charts a life of pleasure but tension, confusion tempered with wisdom and hypocrisy with a touch of irony. The result is enough to stop any reader in their respective tracks."
—*Canyon News* (Beverly Hills, CA)

"One of those works that allows people to both find common ground and break down walls."
—Bookreporter.com

"Jennifer Baszile's memoir deftly blends a revealing history of a black girl growing up in an affluent, mostly white neighborhood in the post–civil rights era with an intimate and poignant story of what it was to be simply a girl growing up. This memoir will resonate with those who have felt disenfranchised from the American dream even while working hard to attain it, yet her story will feel familiar to anyone who remembers the moment they realized parents aren't infallible, that life isn't fair, and that growing up is both a curse and blessing. Her eventual triumph makes reading Baszile's journey even sweeter."

—Kim Reid, author of *No Safe Place: A Family Memoir* and winner of the 2008 Colorado Book Award in Creative Nonfiction

"A wonderful book that gives an intimate look at one woman's journey to success. Jennifer's story is powerful, provocative, and at times painful. Her voice is honest and enlightening. A must read!"

—Chrisena Coleman, founder of Just Between Girlfriends Book Club

"Thoughtful, inspirational and timeless. A true tale about the triumph of the human spirit."

—Alan Lawrence Sitomer, author of *Teaching Teens and Reaping Results in a Wi-Fi, Hip-Hop, Where-Has-All-The-Sanity-Gone World*

"Compelling. Thoroughly engaging. An important addition to the African-American story. In *The Black Girl Next Door*, Jennifer Baszile, with youthful innocence and matured reflections invites us to the neighborhoods once forbidden. Through her personal observations, up-close and honest feelings, we experience the inside of the house and the emotional toll extracted as these pioneers set out to mature the American dream. Read this memoir and extend your understanding of the making of America and the maturing of one young girl as she made her way through these uncharted waters."

—Clifton L. Taulbert, author of *Once Upon a Time When We Were Colored*

This title is also available as an eBook

THE
BLACK
GIRL
NEXT
DOOR

{ a memoir }

Jennifer Baszile

A Touchstone Book
Published by Simon & Schuster
New York London Toronto Sydney

Touchstone
A Division of Simon & Schuster, Inc.
1230 Avenue of the Americas
New York, NY 10020

First Touchstone trade paperback edition January 2010.

TOUCHSTONE and colophon are registered trademarks of
Simon & Schuster, Inc.

For information about special discounts for bulk purchases,
please contact Simon & Schuster Special Sales at 1-866-506-1949
or business@simonandschuster.com.

The Simon & Schuster Speakers Bureau can bring authors to your
live event. For more information or to book an event, contact the
Simon & Schuster Speakers Bureau at 1-866-248-3049 or visit our
website at www.simonspeakers.com.

Designed by Mary Austin Speaker

Manufactured in the United States of America

10 9 8 7 6 5 4 3 2 1

The Library of Congress has cataloged the hardcover edition as follows:

Baszile, Jennifer Lynn.
   The Black girl next door : a memoir / Jennifer Baszile.
      p. cm.
   "A Touchstone Book."
   1. Baszile, Jennifer Lynn, 1969—Childhood and youth. 2. African
American women—California—Palos Verdes Estates—Biography. 3. African
Americans—California—Palos Verdes Estates—Biography. 4. Palos Verdes
Estates (Calif.)—Biography. 5. California—Race relations—History—20th
century. I. Title.
   F869.P25B37 2009
   305.48'896073079493092—dc22
   [B]   2008012867

   ISBN 978-1-4165-4327-5
   ISBN 978-1-4165-4328-2 (pbk)
   ISBN 978-1-4165-9449-9 (ebook)

for Caleb

THE
BLACK
GIRL
NEXT
DOOR

{ chapter one }

RUNNING THE RACE

ON AN EARLY AUTUMN morning in 1975, as fog rolled off the Pacific Ocean and covered the Vista Grande School playground, my first-grade girlfriends and I decided to squeeze in a quick foot race before school began. A row of backpacks marked the starting line and, two at a time, we dashed to the chain-link finish. On this morning I ran against one of my closest friends, Tammy, a freckled white girl with auburn hair. I bunched my large hands into fists and pumped my arms and legs in a full sprint to reach the fence well before she did. I could hardly hide my smile, so I knelt down to pull up the knee socks that pooled around my ankles, not wanting to gloat. Tammy trailed after me, pigtails bouncing, the corners of her mouth down turned in defeat. The warning bell announced the beginning of the school day as we collected our belongings and headed for the sprawling complex of single-story brick classrooms. In the din of children's voices, silence fell between us, and I struggled to think of a remark to break it.

Tammy spoke first. It didn't matter that I beat her, she explained. I waited to hear what she had to say, assuming she was trying to be a good sport rather than a sore loser. "My dad already told me," she said, "black people have something in their feet to make them run faster than white people." The claim rang in my ears like an accusation of cheating or cutting in line. Hours of barefooted play at her house and mine had allowed me to observe her feet and my own. My third left toe was shorter than the fourth one, but her toenails were longer than mine. Our feet were different, but I felt nearly positive that I did not have something hidden in mine.

The bickering match that erupted between us had become a full-blown argument by the time we crossed the asphalt and reached the door of our classroom. We appealed to our teacher, Mrs. Branch, a bottle brunette who sported a poor imitation of Farrah Fawcett's hairstyle. She hurriedly declared that my friend's father was right—black people indeed had something in their feet to make them run faster. My breath caught as her words hit me as hard as if she'd given me a slap. I tried to protest. *If black people had special feet,* I thought to myself, *why didn't I know about it?* It didn't sound right. Mrs. Branch ignored the shock on my face and cut across my objections with the order for everyone to take their seats. My jaw clenched. I felt trapped and betrayed. I brooded through the morning and glared at my teacher. Then I scowled at Tammy across the lunch table.

By afternoon play period, I felt desperate to settle the matter of my feet. Almost all of me believed that I would know if something special lurked beneath my skin. But doubt kept creeping into my mind because I had been wrong plenty of times. If Mrs. Branch and Tammy's dad knew something about my body that I did not, then I could retreat from my anger. Mrs. Branch could maintain her authority. When I saw Tammy's dad again, I would swallow my embarrassment that he knew more about me than I did. I could also keep my best friend, even though I might have to give her a head start if we raced again. Ignoring Tammy even for a few hours had made me sad and exhausted. I did not want to have to do it for the rest of the year unless I had to. I wanted to know the truth because the stakes of not knowing had become unbearable. I had to be absolutely sure.

The final school bell droned. I gathered up my belongings and raced through the classroom door to intercept my older sister, Natalie, before we reached the car pool line. Natalie was nine years old, three years older than I, which made her a trusted authority in my eyes. She always seemed to know more than I did, and her routine victories in our is-so-is-too arguments proved her wisdom. She was graceful and well liked and had far fewer playground battles than I did. Children and adults admired Natalie's beauty, manners, and charm. People interpreted her shyness as poise. On the off chance that black feet held a secret, I was sure that Natalie would have known before me. In the same way that Natalie's baby book was thick with pictures of her infancy, and mine was thin and sparse, my sister often had more and better information.

I knew that I had very little time to pose the question. Mom and Dad both worked more than an hour and several freeways away in Los Angeles and couldn't get back to Palos Verdes by the end of school. Any minute our babysitter, Mrs. Molting, the housewife who watched soap operas and babysat kids for extra cash, might pull up in her pea green station wagon. As the seconds passed, Natalie's friend Helen, a British girl who loved Engelbert Humperdinck, chattered on about her middle-aged idol. I broke into their conversation.

"Do black people have something in their feet to make them run faster?" was all I blurted.

"No," Natalie said. I knew that ever since that white boy at our new church had called her a nigger, Natalie hated to discuss the differences between black and white people. The way she whipped her two long braids as she spun her head to look at me made it clear I'd upset her. She focused on Helen and ignored me.

I exhaled in relief that I had not cheated my way into victory. I felt flush as I realized that in another way the situation was as bad as I feared, which drained me of any urge to right the wrong. This was much more than a playground dispute that I could hash out with Tammy. She had to become my enemy. As much as losing a friend hurt, I knew I could do it. But when I told Tammy she was wrong, I'd also be calling her father a liar, which meant that adults were also involved. If Tammy's father was wrong, that made Mrs. Branch a liar, too. I'd never called a grown-up such a thing. I'd already begun to despise my teacher, but she'd have to be confronted and corrected. I would have to tell my parents to set the grown-ups straight, and that seemed scary because I knew they'd be angry. I had to bring home bad news, which both my parents hated.

Bad news disrupted the family routine, they always complained, and I already knew that we could not afford disruptions. Everyone in the family had to do their best to avoid conflicts and "stay on track." Staying on track for me meant that I had to sleep with a pair of clean panties over my head, so as not to mess up the hairstyle that my mother had given me the previous evening, and to get myself dressed in the mornings. I had to pour my own breakfast cereal without spilling the milk. I had to eat whatever my dad packed for lunch, even if the carrots he scraped with a dinner knife and wrapped in aluminum foil turned brown by noon. There were no "sick days"—I had to attend school and take an aspirin with my lunch, unless I could projectile vomit or had a thermometer bursting from my fever.

I brimmed with dread by the time Mom picked us up from Mrs. Molting's house—a house that smelled like burnt margarine and kitty litter—three hours later. I knew how much my mother hated being greeted with bad news, especially after she just finished fighting more than an hour of rush-hour traffic. We loaded into her Pinto and drove home in relative silence. I watched Mom clear her mind. At home, I placed my lunch box on the kitchen counter and went upstairs to change into my play clothes.

I saw the sun drop lower in the sky. I tracked the golden light that bathed the vast field behind our yard from my seat at the kitchen table as I ate my dinner with Natalie and Mom. Dad wasn't home yet; he'd made a late sales call and was stuck in traffic. As I finished my glass of milk, which always signaled the end of my meal, I knew that the time had come.

"Do black people have something in their feet to make them run faster than white people?" I asked. I tried to sound innocent and didn't look at Mom.

"Why would you ask such a thing?" she asked. Mom hated to answer questions with questions and always corrected us when we did it. As soon as she broke her own rule, I knew this was only going to get worse. On top of that, Mom hated any kind of talk about which parts of black people's bodies were good or bad, especially hair and skin.

"Because that's what Tammy's dad said."

My mother put down her fork.

Natalie sat perfectly still and just watched Mom.

"That's ridiculous," she declared. She narrowed her eyes in close inspection of my face to make sure that this was not one of my pranks.

"That's what I said," I began, "but when I asked, Mrs. Branch said it was true." I braced for my mother's reaction.

Mom's entire demeanor soured. The red undertones in her skin emerged as the muscles in her jaw clenched. The vein in her forehead—the one that bulged when she got really angry or drank red wine—appeared. Mrs. Branch had gone and done it.

My mother, the person who had decided to move our family to Rancho Palos Verdes in the first place, then cajoled and berated my father into agreement, had chosen the upscale and predominately white community for two reasons: the clean, smog-free air and the top-ranked schools. She feared that the orange chemical cloud that hung over our old house in Carson, the all-black suburb built near a refinery, might kill us. She was an elementary schoolteacher to black and Latino kids in Los Angeles. She knew the state rankings of each school district and the entire elementary school curriculum by heart. I never heard her complain as she rose before dawn each morning to beat the traffic. Whenever I asked Mom why she never met me after school, she explained that she was willing to work in the city and drive for hours so that Natalie and I had the best, the Palos Verdes schools. She celebrated the day that I began first grade and told me that I had become a big girl. She saved the money she used to budget for my private preschool and kindergarten tuition to buy real estate. Mrs. Branch's comment revealed a crack in Mom's plan, a crack that had to be repaired immediately. I read her disgust and disappointment in her narrow eyes. My mother worked too hard to allow some teacher, especially a white woman, to ruin her daughter because she peddled some bit of madness as truth.

"What in the world!?" Mom said. She pursed her lips to reveal the feathery traces of rust lipstick that still rimmed her mouth. Then she made her face blank, as if dropping a curtain, and part of her disappeared. Mom could escape inside herself and conceal her feelings from everyone, especially if she got angry or sad. In those moments, Mom became more than just silent; she became impossible to read. Natalie and I didn't know what she was thinking, but we knew that Mom's expression meant trouble—real trouble. We watched her and waited.

"Girls, clear the table," my mother said. Her voice sounded too sweet, like June Cleaver or Carol Brady, though it barely concealed her fury. We both scurried to obey. If the place mats, Wish-Bone dressing bottle, and our plates didn't disappear instantly, her anger might focus on us. I could almost hear the gears turning in my mother's head as she considered the situation and plotted her next move. When we'd finished, Natalie went to her room to practice her violin. I hung around the family room and listened to the silence. Then, even though I did not yet receive homework from school, Mom gave me a math worksheet to keep me quiet and busy.

In a little while, I heard my father raise the door as he pulled into the garage. Then I listened to him kill the engine on his pumpkin-colored Mercury sedan. His fat ring of keys clinked as he opened the door, and finally he whistled to announce his arrival. He wore a starched white dress shirt and his perfectly knotted tie. Dad looked particularly dashing. His praline-colored skin flashed against the dark wool of his suit. He set his briefcase by the door and dropped his keys on the entry table. Then he sang my name when he saw me, which always made me giggle. Not even my worry about my feet, Tammy, and Mrs. Branch could erase my delight at seeing Dad. I loved the way he used his sweet baritone and beautiful phrasing to shape my name into a song that felt warm. Seeing him always made me feel special. I gladly received his kiss and grinned.

But my mother ordered me upstairs, and I knew that Dad's good mood would not last. I felt sorry that I had something to do with it. I hung around the top of the stairs trying to hear what they said, but Mom had lowered her voice and Dad had taken her cue. Dad didn't hide his anger or sadness like Mom did, and the slamming cabinets and rattling drawers first told me that Dad had gotten the news. He was as upset as I'd feared. In another second, a flood of curse words poured from Dad's mouth. Standing at the top of the stairway, I couldn't remember the last time I'd heard get Dad this angry. When everything got quiet again downstairs, I crept back to my room and tried not to make any noise.

Near bedtime, I still hadn't seen Dad again. I changed into my gown and brushed my teeth in silence. I was too afraid to go downstairs and kiss Dad good night. When she came upstairs, Mom said very little as she unbraided my hair and brushed it.

But the way she pressed the plastic bristles of the brush into my scalp and made me wince told me all I needed to know. Even when she tucked me in and turned out my light, I could not find the courage to ask her anything else about my feet.

The next morning seemed normal on the surface. I awoke to the sound of the news radio my father listened to as he dressed. I removed the clean panties protecting my hair, put on my dress, and watched *Yogi Bear* as I ate my cereal. Dad was subdued as he drove the usual route to school, but he wouldn't look at me and didn't smile. When we arrived at the front of Vista Grande, Dad swung the car into the parking lot rather than into the car pool line. When he killed the engine and opened his door, I knew instantly that his getting out of the car had something to do with my feet, the race, and my teacher. Dad took his suit coat from the hanger in the backseat and put it on in a single fluid movement. He walked us past the administrative office and into the school. Natalie and I scurried to gather our backpacks and keep up. The heels of Dad's polished Johnston & Murphy shoes echoed in the corridor. Natalie, armed with her backpack and violin case, kissed Dad and then headed for the playground. A door away from my classroom, my father finally turned to me.

"You play out here. I need to speak to your teacher," he said. He strode to my classroom, knocked on the door, and entered when Mrs. Branch answered. I could not see my teacher's face but knew that my dad was about to ruin her day.

I turned cartwheels on the grass in front of the classroom. Then I sat on the metal rail where we lined up for lunch or trips to the library and felt the cold metal on the backs of my knees. I looked for worms. I peered at the tinted windows of my room and wondered what my father was saying. Finally, the door opened.

I trotted up to Dad as he closed the door. I looked for the easy salesman's smile that usually warmed his face and could not find it. I noticed but could not understand the anger in his eyes, his faint but tight grimace, and his otherwise vacant expression. I listened as he hastily told me that he had taken care of the matter of my feet. This was the first time he'd mentioned the incident to me, and I wondered why he offered no details, why he seemed so subdued. I did not understand the balance my father had struck to assert himself as an informed and concerned parent and not simply a big, dangerous black man in a first-grade classroom. I never knew exactly what he said or what it had cost him to defend my victory.

A few minutes later the bell clanged and hundreds of kids surged off the playground. Mrs. Branch called Tammy and me over to her. I watched Mrs. Branch's face flush and her eyes blink wildly. She looked down into my thin, brown face as the words "I am sorry" choked in her throat. An apology from an adult was utterly new to me, so I took a cue from my father's demeanor and said little. I held my breath and made my face still. I watched Mrs. Branch turn to Tammy. "Your father was wrong," she said to Tammy as her voice cracked from tension. "Black people do not have something in their feet to make them run faster." Red splotches rose on Tammy's face and I savored her shame. But neither the apology nor the correction could get back what I had lost in the incident: a friendship, respect for my teacher, and my belief that school was a safe and open place. I hated that teacher, Tammy's father, and my former friend. My victory felt tainted and diminished.

I didn't realize it at the time, but the fact that I could run on a playground against a white girl whom I considered a friend and the fact that my father could confront a white woman behind a closed door without risk of lynching marked tremendous strides in my family's history. An early boyhood in Louisiana had put my father on a first-name basis with Jim Crow. He entered elementary school at the same time he began to work in the rice and cotton fields. By the time he started high school in Port Arthur, Texas, my father had already received more formal education than any of my grandparents. My victory, dents and all, signaled a kind of progress that no earlier generation of my family could experience.

I hated Tammy. We sat apart at lunch. I beat Tammy in dodgeball whenever I could. I never picked her to play on my team, and she never chose me for hers. We barely spoke, but we argued all the time. The school principal had to settle our disputes because neither of us trusted Mrs. Branch, and she steered clear of our constant battle. By the Christmas holidays, I was ready for a break from my siege with Tammy. Then my parents announced that my father was about to open his own metals distribution business, the first black-owned distributorship in the country. I didn't understand his achievement. But when they explained that we were moving to a bigger and better house right after the New Year, to live among aerospace executives and law partners instead of engineers and legal associates, the change became a bit clearer. I felt proud of Dad and thrilled at my good luck. I wished that I could change schools as well as houses. Mom told me I'd have to finish the year at Vista Grande and transfer for second grade. As far as I was concerned, I couldn't leave Tammy, my ignorant teacher, or my old playground fast enough.

There was plenty about my life on Verde Ridge Road that I knew I would miss. I would definitely miss the backyard field that I considered my real playground and the place where I experienced my greatest sense of freedom. I'd passed the best hours of many days in that twenty-acre expanse of wild fennel, weeds, and other brush that towered two feet over my head. I'd skipped joyfully through a sea of green and brown. When I grew thirsty from running, I'd stripped down the wispy leaves, sucked the stalks, savored the juice that tasted like licorice, and then gnawed them like sugarcane. I'd rubbed the budding flowers and fronds in the palms and inhaled the peppery sweetness on my hands. I'd crossed a drainage ditch by walking over a two-by-six board with my arms outstretched to plunge deeper into that wilderness. I'd carried a stick to probe some mound here or there or to whack a path through the brush. Hawks circled over my head, their cries making the only sound besides the trickle of water. I'd never felt afraid. I'd loved to watch the sunset from out there and see the sky turn orange. I would miss being able to see the Pacific Ocean from the field and from every room in our house.

Our new house on Chelsea Road was a block from the

ocean. We moved in January 1976. I could stand on the balcony overlooking the street and always smell the Pacific, hear the surf crash and foghorns wail, but I couldn't see it. The house had a wrought-iron gate, rather than a picket fence, that separated the driveway from an inner courtyard dense with ferns and calla lilies. Instead of the cookie-cutter tract houses on Verde Ridge Road, every house on the new street was distinct—French chateau, English country, colonial, or Italian. Home owners had to abide by the rules of the local architecture board, which approved all exterior changes to a house, including the rooflines and paint colors. Our stucco house had a clay tile roof and was fashioned to resemble a Spanish villa. We had moved into a neighborhood so exclusive that it had neither sidewalks nor street lamps. We moved up to live among new neighbors, dressed in golf shirts and tennis whites, who took their purebred dogs for after-dinner strolls. We all hoped that, with a move to the more exclusive town of Palos Verdes Estates, we had outrun race. We were sorely mistaken.

February mornings on Chelsea Road often dawned with a soaking, thick fog that saturated everything. We had settled into something of a routine in the new house. The smells of fresh paint and wallpaper paste lingered in the air because Mom was still redecorating the house one room at a time. She had just resumed her work around the house after taking a break to complete all of the new Black History Month posters and displays for her classroom. After dinner she just reviewed her new lesson plans and made new dittos for the next day's projects.

One morning shortly after we moved in, I awoke to find my new house far too quiet. It was a Thursday morning. Tension replaced the usual percussion of our weekday mornings. Natalie was in the bathroom getting ready as usual, but I knew something felt wrong. I entered the master bedroom where my mother, dressed and made up for work, stared through the window into the courtyard. *Why hadn't she taken me into her bathroom to brush my hair before she went to work?* I wondered.

"Are you staying home today?" I asked.

At the sound of my voice, Mom drew the curtains and turned her back to the window. She walked toward me but did not give me a hug.

"No," she said, taking her blazer off the chair.

I heard the door that led down to the garage open and my father call out, "Janet, you've gotta go." There was too much force in his tone. His feet fell too heavily on the stairs. I knew something was very wrong before I saw his face.

"Get dressed," Dad barked at me as he followed my mother back down the stairs.

I withdrew to my room feeling confused and put on a white blouse, a navy blue sweater with red apples around the waist, and blue pants. I pulled up my knee-high socks and tied my shoes.

As I descended the spiral staircase and saw through the window that my parents remained in the driveway, my concern deepened. *Why hadn't Mom left yet?* She never missed work. I could not hear their discussion through the closed window or over the warming car engine. Mom's defiantly raised hands told me that my parents did not agree on something. But after Dad took my mother in his arms, she got into the car. He stood aside while she backed away, then he walked to the end of the driveway to watch her drive up the street. He did not move. A few seconds later, the black-and-white police cruiser emerged from the cotton bale of fog like a phantom. I panicked. *What were the police doing at our house?*

My father squared his shoulders. He moved toward the cruiser and waved them down. As a former probation officer, Dad knew how to talk to the police. He had never called them for help before. I became even more confused when I realized that the police had not turned on their lights or sirens. My father waited for the white officers to emerge from the car and position the clubs on their belts. Dad had summoned them, I finally understood. *What was so bad that he needed their help?*

My mind raced as they exchanged words at the curb. Dad and the officers looked stiff. I pressed my nails into my palms as he led them up the driveway toward the iron gate. I ran into the living room and peered through the sliding glass door but dared not open it. They all bent their heads. I could not see what they saw even as I stood on my toes and craned my neck. The officers returned to the car and talked on their radio. My father, in the same place, sensed my presence and looked up at me. The hardness in his face made me back away. I had never seen that particular combination of anger and distress in his eyes.

I found Natalie upstairs making her bed. She did not know what had happened either, which made me even more anxious. Another police cruiser had arrived by the time I returned to the window. I had no sense of time and forgot about Frosted Flakes and *The Flintstones.*

Finally, Dad came inside. We stood on the glazed adobe tiles in the entry that always made the downstairs feel cold.

"Dad," I whispered, "what's happened?"

"Last night, someone wrote something on the front walk," he said. "Get your backpack or you will be late for school." Whatever had happened outside had made my father even more determined to keep our family on track.

"What did they write?" I asked, trying to imagine what words could bring the police to my house so early in the morning.

"Go home, niggers." He spat the words out of his mouth like sour milk. Disgust and fury mingled in his eyes as his brow furrowed. His jaw twitched.

"Mr. Baszile," an officer called from outside. Before I could say anything else, Dad descended the steps two at a time and was gone.

The fog had lifted and the sun rose higher in the sky when I hurried through the garage. I needed to see the words for myself and walked around the pink bougainvillea bush to the place where the officers and my father had been standing.

Every letter was capitalized. "GO HOME" the top line insisted. "NIGGERS" sat centered and underlined below it. The uneven, thick brushstrokes showed all the times they had stopped midletter to dip the brush back into the bucket. The enameled lines and curves glistened in the light, and the paint seeped in the crevices of the concrete.

My head felt heavy; I could not take my eyes from those words. *I* had been called nigger. Sometimes boys whispered the word as I walked by them at school. But I had never experienced hatred in this way: plural, intimate, and anonymous at the same time. Fear seized my empty stomach and my eyes stung. My parents had taught me that people who used those words were white trash, rednecks, or crackers. Until that moment, I thought that they lived somewhere else. "Prejudice," as my parents called it then, was the product of ignorance. Executives, doctors, engineers, and lawyers lived on our street with their families. I knew how long my parents had worked to put miles and money between our family and white trash. I kept rereading the message and shivering; everything but the words seemed out of focus.

I puzzled over the instruction, "Go Home Niggers." We *were* home. There was no place else to go. This house, nestled in a town so remote and exclusive that residents drove twenty minutes to the nearest freeway, was supposed to provide a sanctuary from our striving. This refuge, with its garden courtyard and wrought-iron gate, was meant to make me safe. This home was supposed to remind us, and everyone else, how much we had overcome. This was the house where I was just supposed to be the black girl next door.

But it hadn't been that way for the past two weeks, and the words meant that I couldn't deny that fact anymore. On another foggy morning, Mom had discovered that someone had defaced the recessed tile fountain in the courtyard of our house. They had walked through the iron gate and painted the playful cherub who spouted water through its mouth black. Mom and Dad had minimized it. But I was upset because I loved that fountain. As soon as I heard about it, I had run outside in my pajamas to see what had happened. I had fumed and stared at the bow-shaped lips, perfectly round eyes, chubby cheeks, and tousle of hair that all seemed so animated in white stone dripping with distortion. On that earlier morning, Dad had tried to play down the incident. He and Mom had tried hard to convince all of us that it was a prank. I tried to believe them. As I had stood there staring at the black enamel that dribbled from the cherub's chin like spit and made him come alive, I let Dad convince me that it was no big deal.

Dad had agreed to let me help him scrub the paint off the cherub and drain the fountain. With bunches of steel wool and paint thinner, we had scrubbed black paint from its hair, skin, eyes, ears, and lips. At first, I peppered Dad with questions about why anyone would paint the cherub black and what it meant. But he had directed me back to the task of cleaning the cherub and avoided the answers I so desperately wanted him to provide. Cleaning the cherub was a big job, and we worked until nearly dark. The combination of enamel and paint thinner had penetrated the soft stone and turned it gray. By the time we'd drained the fountain of its brackish water, wiped down the tiles, and filled it again, I'd given up asking Dad questions. In the days after the attack on the cherub, I had tried to forget what had happened. I couldn't, so I had just pushed it to the far corner of my mind. We had gone about our business. We had barely talked about it among ourselves and hadn't complained to anyone else about it.

But "Go Home Niggers" cast a new shadow on the gray cherub and changed it into a minstrel. It also proved that my parents' decision to remain silent had been a mistake. Dad had been wrong about my cherub, and that made me all the more worried about the words. For the first time in my life, I didn't trust him. The police standing beside their cruisers told me that Dad stopped trusting his own judgment. *What would happen next?* I wondered.

Dad left the huddle of policemen, walked up the driveway, and stood by my side.

"Who did this?" I asked him, my voice flat with despair.

"I don't know," my father answered. His voice sounded as flat as mine.

"Why did they do this?" I asked.

He had no answer to my question. "It's time for school," he responded. Dad could not confront the people who attacked us, so he sought disruption instead.

I longed to remain close to my father. The thought of leaving that spot in front of the gate seemed impossible. The westerns I watched on Sunday afternoons told me that this was the time to hunker down and circle the wagons. Dad urged me back inside.

"What if something happens while I'm at school?" I asked my father. I needed to know what to do. The words *to me* stuck on my tongue. School felt like a perilous place where bad things had already taken me by surprise. Things seemed like they were getting worse. I knew Mrs. Branch wouldn't protect me. Our new house was my retreat from a bad teacher and a mean girl, but "Go Home Niggers" made my hold on it feel slippery. Right then I realized how much those words had stolen from me. I didn't feel safe in my own yard or on my own street. I began to wonder if there was anyplace where I could escape from these problems. Where could we go? Nowhere seemed to be the answer, and that frightened me.

"Nothing is going to happen," he said and seemed to know what I was really asking.

Even though I needed to hear exactly those words, I doubted them as much as I doubted Dad. He did not know the answer. None of us knew, but I prepared to leave anyway. Natalie had only glanced at the words for a second before getting in the car. We didn't talk about what had happened on the way to school. Dad made no promises of safety as he dropped us off at Vista Grande. I drifted through my day in near silence and didn't tell anyone what had happened. I didn't raise my hand a single time in class. I even avoided Tammy because I couldn't bear to fight on two fronts. I skipped lunch. "*Go Home Niggers.*" Those words were stuck in my mind.

Mom burned up her brakes as she raced home from the babysitter's house. As we pulled into the driveway, my empty stomach lurched, afraid of what else I might find. I jumped out of the car and ran over to the message. Mom and Natalie followed me, and the sight of the words made us all very quiet.

I was surprised but relieved to hear Dad pull into the driveway a short time later. I hurried into my shoes and ran outside. I stopped in my tracks when I saw Mr. Shorter, our only black neighbor, greet my father. Mr. Shorter lived two houses down from us and had the prettiest roses and the greenest lawn on the block. Friendly but not friends, our families had a lot in common. Mr. Shorter had a doctor wife and two teenaged daughters. Although my father was younger by a generation, both men hailed from the South. Years of California living had mellowed the accents of their boyhoods. The men conferred at the curb, standing close together, their bodies rippling with tension and frustration. Something in their stillness told me that I would not be welcome. It was as though they stood in dark space reserved for black men. As much as our neighbor's presence gave me comfort, it also deepened my worry. *How had Mr. Shorter and his family avoided this assault?* I wondered. *Why were we attacked and not them?*

From the instant Dad came inside, I trailed him like a cub. He changed out of his suit into an old blue warm-up jacket with white piping on the sleeve, an old pair of pants, and a worn-out pair of his Johnston & Murphys. These were the exact same clothes he'd worn two weeks ago when we'd rescued the cherub. I could still see the black splatters on his pants and jacket. When I figured out that he was preparing to remove the words, I asked if I could help. Working with Dad to clean the cherub had made me feel safer, closer to him, and I wanted to feel that way again. He said no.

His refusal hurt, but I was grateful that Dad did let me stand beside him. I understood that he wasn't rejecting me. We had left the realm of pranks and couldn't deny the meaning or the message any longer. He didn't want someone else's fury to stain my hands or ruin my life. He didn't want me to have to clean up someone else's mess. As he removed the hate from our house, I stood and watched. The sharp smell of paint thinner stung my nostrils. The wire brush flicked diluted paint onto my dad's hands, the scraping bristles echoed in the yard. Dad knelt on one knee beside a pile of rags and scrubbed the message away one letter at a time. When he wiped, rinsed, and scrubbed, the fog rolled back in and the sun began to set on the two of us. Dad didn't stop until even the faintest trace had disappeared. I stayed out of his way but remained by his side until we both went inside together at nightfall.

Saturday morning, Dad rose even earlier than usual to meet the paperboy instead of the police. He had called the news desk at the *Palos Verdes Peninsula News*, the newspaper that covered the four towns of the peninsula, after the police left. I looked over his shoulder as he opened the paper. Above and below the fold, my father stared out of the photograph as he pointed down at the three words that leaped off the front page. My eyes skipped to the place in the article where Dad said he feared for our safety. He and Mom didn't like to hear me talk about how hard it was being the only black kid in my class, so Dad's admission that we were attacked because we were black really terrified me. Just to ensure the local police and our neighbors knew he was serious, Dad had called the FBI field office after he'd called the newspaper. The FBI agents had spent the morning going door to door questioning our neighbors.

Even though three days had passed since she'd discovered the message, Mom still seemed shocked, if not surprised. But I didn't know much more than that about her reactions because she hid the rest of her emotions from us. No one had ever called her a nigger, she'd explained the first time it happened to me at Vista Grande. She couldn't say that anymore and she must have hated it. I sat in the backseat while Mom drove from one newspaper dispenser to the next. She placed three nickels, the price for a single paper, into the news racks and pulled out stacks of paper. Mom had spent her own Detroit girlhood on the cusp of hardship and learned early not to waste money. She wanted to mark the moment and planned to put one copy in our own family scrapbook and then send the other clippings back east and down south to our relatives. She wasn't proud of the attack, yet she refused to be isolated by it. But Mom planned to do something in the neighborhood first.

When we returned home, she gathered the remnants of her Black History Month materials—scissors, poster board, glue, and a thick marker. Sitting at the family table, she cut out the article and pasted it on the poster. In Mom's teacher-perfect penmanship she wrote "These Are Your Neighbors" above the article. Then Mom taped her project on our mailbox for all the twilight dog walkers and evening strollers to read. As always, my mother wanted to have the last word. The paint was gone, but she wanted the community to bear the shame she refused to feel.

For the next three evenings, I hid in the corner of our living-room and watched our neighbors looking at the poster. From the slump in some of their shoulders, I guessed that Mom's tactics succeeded in spreading the shame around to more people than just us.

A week of fog and sunshine warped the poster board and yellowed the newsprint, but the incident remained sharp in my mind. As carefully as my mother controlled her emotions, I lost control of mine. First thing each morning I looked out of my parents' window and checked the courtyard for new messages before I even went to the bathroom. Each afternoon, I braced myself for a newly blackened cherub. I looked over my shoulder more often when I walked or rode my bike in the neighborhood. In the early evening, I watched my neighbors from our balcony. Although I feared something else might happen, I also longed to hurt the people who had hurt me. The coward still lurked in my neighborhood and part of me wanted to coax him from the shadows. I was one of the youngest and smallest people on the block and could not force anyone to do anything. I could not tell off adults because I could not use the swear words I knew or yell at them. I practiced mean faces in the mirror. I glared at my neighbors and hoped to provoke a confession. It never worked. Still, I thrilled each time my unwavering stare forced an adult to look away first. I patrolled our driveway like a cop. Everyone needed to know that I was mad. Everyone needed to know that I was watching and would not be fooled again.

The Saturday following the newspaper article, I emerged from the garage and noticed a sharp smell tinged the briny air. The smell was familiar but out of place so early in the morning. It was fuel, probably lighter fluid. As I mounted my bike at the end of the driveway, I recognized the faint aroma of smoke and realized that something had burned. My nostrils flared instinctively. I did not hear fire engines. Still, I felt anxious. *Someone had burned something, but what? Why?* I pedaled slowly down the driveway and sniffed again and again. A quick look up the block assured me that everything behind me was fine. I looked from one side of the street to another, scanning chimneys, looking for smoke. The first house seemed okay. Then I passed the vacant lot. No one had thrown a cigarette into the weeds by mistake.

The smell grew stronger as I got closer to Mr. Shorter's house, and my nose confirmed the source before my eyes processed the scene. I nearly lost my balance as I stared in disbelief and rested my toes on the curb. I leaned my forearms on the handlebars of my bike. A perfectly symmetrical cross smoldered right in the center of the Shorters' immaculate lawn. The sharp outlines of the profane symbol and the carefully controlled burn identified it as the handiwork of the same people who had attacked us. The patch of turf was as charred as the cherub and reignited my anger. No one else was on the street or had done anything about it, so I guessed I was the first to spot it. I had not been watching carefully enough. Fear flooded me again as I wondered who might be watching me. I went back to our house and told my parents what I'd found. My father and Mr. Shorter met on the curb later that morning.

Week after week, I watched Mr. Shorter coax new grass to sprout from seed. As those tender blades emerged, I wondered whether the neighbors who tried to torch his pride still wore hoods. I gave up scowling even though I wanted to know who had done this to us. I wanted them to stop hiding so that I could feel safe.

As much as I doubted my neighbors, I still ached to believe in my parents. My father had set Mrs. Branch, Tammy, and her father straight. Even though Dad had called the police and my home felt like less of a sanctuary, nothing else happened to our house. So every time my parents insisted that we were not going anywhere and we would be fine, I tried to believe them. But it was still hard. As they would tell me often in the days after the attack, as children my parents longed for the chance to compete. Integration was a form of competition. We would stay, they insisted, because our every victory was a test and a testimony: a test of our endurance, a testimony to the will of our entire family. I just wanted to be normal. I wanted to disappear. I knew I could do neither.

I didn't completely understand it then, but I was part of a family running and fighting for more than just ourselves. My parents, sister, and I ran to redeem grief and unspeakable humiliations that no one named. My every victory not only proved my talent and my skill but also bore witness to the strength of my entire family. But along the way, we were collecting too many pictures that captured the trouble we were facing. The race we were running in Palos Verdes was getting tougher by the day. I was just beginning to understand that some things were impossible to outrun.

{ chapter two }

SHACKS AND MOONSHINE

AROUND NINE O'CLOCK ON summer nights, neighborhood kids knew to make for the streets, stepping beyond the glimmering porch lights and into the bluish yellow sheen the moon cast on the street. The day's sweltering heat had disappeared with the setting sun, and everyone in the know knew it was time to get a move on. Natalie and I scuttled alongside the gutter to our standing appointment at Bunny Schoal's mailbox.

The summer had been full of surprises. Whatever problem the attackers were having with us, it didn't carry through to the kids who played outside on our block. I'd never heard of the game kick the can until the neighborhood kids turned me on to it just after school had ended. The game combined the speed of tag with the thrill of hide and seek. In actuality, kids on our block didn't kick a can—they tagged a mailbox—but they'd inherited the game from their older siblings and no one was going to argue with tradition.

The neighborhood kids didn't have to ask us twice to play that first time. Natalie and I were eager to make friends before we enrolled at our new school. The trick was convincing Mom and Dad. We brought seven or eight kids with us for backup when we asked their permission. They had never allowed Natalie and me to play in the street after dark, and we were convinced that they would say no. But our excitement about the game cast the same spell on Mom and Dad that it cast on all the parents. They agreed, maybe relieved that some neighborhood kids were being nice to us. No matter how late we played, adults never interrupted the game, and even the grumpiest neighbors didn't complain about the noise we made.

Games took place on the top of our street at the gigantic octagonal intersection called Margate Square. The sprawling front yards of four houses sat catty-corner and streets filled the other sides. One house belonged to Bunny and another house across the street belonged to a family who owned a local funeral home. I refused to hide in the undertaker's yard. It looked like any other house, with its white shingle siding and blooming flowers, but I didn't trust people in the death business. The wooden street signs, with names like Chelsea, Chiswick, and Dalton, proclaimed the community's fake English airs. When the Olmstead brothers, the sons of the famed landscape architect responsible for Central Park, designed the community of Palos Verdes Estates as a beach haven for movie stars, I bet that they couldn't have imagined how many generations of kids would make this their nighttime playground.

Kick the can had become a streetwide obsession and the games were serious. We played a few times a week. By the end of the summer, we knew all of one another's best tactics and favorite hiding places. We had to plot new strategies, hide deeper in the bushes, climb onto thinner branches of the ash trees that could barely support our weight—anything that would give us an edge. We had to do whatever it took to keep the game exciting.

Eight kids huddled around a mailbox as we set the boundaries of the game. We were the core group who always played. No one was older than fifteen. We dressed for the game—jeans and long-sleeved shirts or dark hooded sweatshirts—more clothes than we'd worn all day. Sneakers and socks were a speed requirement. As one of the youngest players, I took extra care in this department. In our uniforms for the places beyond shadows, we all looked the same. We were all dark in the darkness.

Bunny's house always served as home base. I didn't know how he got his nickname, but I did know he was two years older than me. His blond hair fell over his forehead and ears into gentle waves. His cheeks were always deeply tanned and peeling from the hours he spent at the beach with his older brothers. Though he seemed shy, Bunny had a friendly, mischievous smile that gave him away. He was a bigger kid but deceptively quick and often scampered to the mailbox to win the game. Since his dad's recent transfer and his house being put on the market, Bunny had been quieter than usual. He knew it was his last summer in the game.

George and Dwight Nager, two brothers who lived in a white Cape Cod house three doors up from us, were regulars as well.

The first time they introduced themselves to me and I heard their last name I flinched, unable to conceal my shock. "Nager" sounded too much like "nigger," and I thought they were making fun of me. But they weren't. In fact, George and Dwight, in a cool and sort of goofy way, reminded me of Heckle and Jeckle, the cartoon crows. They were always pulling pranks and arguing. Their parents looked like they'd stepped straight out of the L.L.Bean catalog. Catsy, their mother, was nice but sort of quiet and spoke with a blueblood, thin-lipped New England accent. She wore her red hair in a pageboy that curled up at the end, with bangs. Their father, CJ, made all the neighborhood kids nervous. He reminded me of Richard Nixon with his black hair, bushy eyebrows, and square jaw, and I didn't think he had much of a sense of humor. One night, when he came home from work, none of his three boys looked up from the television to greet him. So CJ threw the television away and refused to buy a new one. After that George and Dwight came to our house, and we all watched *The Rockford Files* and *Barnaby Jones* together in the afternoons.

They were the first white boys I'd ever played with. They went to Margate, the local intermediate school. I'd never known boys like these at my former school. They were cool and nice at the same time, and they proved it when they told Natalie and me about the older boys, our neighbors it turned out, who were the ones who'd attacked our house. I'd never met them. I guessed the attackers hated us enough to stay out of our way. George and Dwight told us how they heard the older boys bragging about what they had done. Something in the way that they stared at their shoes as they described what they knew made me know that they really felt badly about what had happened to us and wanted us to know that they hadn't been part of it. But they didn't get all mushy or make a big deal about what they'd done, even after Natalie and I told Dad what they'd said and Dad confronted the attackers' family. Dad never told us what he'd said or done.

Natalie and I were the only black kids in the game, but I wasn't afraid of these white guys. They were nothing like my old schoolmates who always wanted to fight me. When we played together, no one accused me of cheating or stashing something in my feet. Besides, I wasn't nearly as fast as they were. Prowling through the night, everything about my life seemed clearer. In the dark, we were all the same. I was just another kid in the pack. I wasn't the new black girl next door. I was just Jennifer.

Most of the time, only two other girls besides Natalie and me played kick the can. Betsy Langer was the second youngest kid and only girl in her family of six. She was tough; she watched out for her little brother Drew and didn't let the older boys push her around. Our families went to the same church, and she always seemed annoyed to have to put on the skirts her mother insisted she wear. She looked more relaxed in her summer uniform: a one-piece bathing suit and denim cutoff shorts. Boogie boarding and swimming had bronzed Betsy's skin, and her head full of thick tangled curls were sun-bleached and bouncy. She ignored her hair most of the time, preferring to leave it pulled back into a ponytail.

Betsy's best friend Leigh also played. Like Betsy, she was two years older than me. Leigh's bone-straight bangs hung to her eyebrows, her long brown hair brushing her shoulders. She came from an even larger family than Betsy's and she had lots of older brothers. Leigh lived around the corner and had the only indoor fishpond and fountain I'd ever seen. But we never played at her house. We only swung by there to get her if her phone line was busy. Leigh spent lots of time on our block.

One night we plotted a conspiracy, a game within the game. The target? Johnny Stone. I don't know what he did to get on the wrong side of so many kids in the neighborhood, but he was clearly the outcast in the group. All the boys said he was a wimp and they treated him like a tagalong. They called him by his last name—"Hey, Stone"—and it always sounded like a shove. I could see why they treated him badly. Johnny's house was near ours, and I often heard him whining through the bushes in his yard. He was skinny and pale, and something about the way he rounded his shoulders and let his arms flop around made him look weak and vulnerable. A couple of times every week he showed up to play kick the can and seemed not to notice people snickering. (That's the thing about kids: we sensed his desperation, and the more he showed us he wanted to be part of the game, the more we made him work for it.)

We decided to let everyone else tag themselves safe except Stone. He'd get tagged out, which would make him the counter. Then we would take forever to hide and make him count to one hundred over and over again. When we had hidden ourselves, we would creep out of our hiding places and ditch him, leaving him searching the square while we all abandoned the game.

So we began kick the can, and everyone but Stone knew there were two games being played. Dwight volunteered to count, and before he'd buried his face in his elbow and leaned against Bunny's mailbox, everyone scattered. As I bolted across the square and dove into the ivy, I heard Dwight counting: "thirty-six, thirty-seven, thirty-eight." Still panting, I lifted my head just enough to see his figure creeping across the square. Dwight knew all the best hiding places, but on this night he didn't manage to find anyone. Even though Dwight was super-fast, everyone except Stone jumped out of the most obvious spots and beat him to the mailbox. He was the only kid still out there, and it didn't take Dwight long to find him. "One, two, three on Stone behind the Daniels' car," Dwight yelled. They sprinted to the mailbox and the rest of us cheered at the sight of their lean figures coming toward us out of the dark. Dwight slapped the mailbox with the palm of his hand, making Stone "it" for the next round. We stole glances at one another and gave our secretive nods. The plan was working.

Stone leaned over the mailbox and counted aloud to a hundred. When, as the rules required, he called, "Apple, peaches, pumpkin pie, who's not ready holler I," we all yelled back "I" in unison. We never did that to anyone else, and Stone should have known something was afoot. He didn't. So he counted to a hundred again, and we shouted "I" all over again. He'd counted to three hundred at this point, and our snorting laughter echoed in the night because he couldn't start looking for us until we'd stopped yelling "I." We'd all selected hiding spaces on the far side of the square. Stone tried so hard that he didn't notice that no one *ever* had this much trouble finding a hiding spot.

Natalie and I crouched behind a camellia bush and waited until Stone stopped counting. He looked in everyone's usual hiding places. Someone tossed a rock to throw Stone off our trail. As Stone wandered off in the direction of the sound, we crept out of our spots, then took off running down the street and around the corner. The sound of him calling our names carried through the night, but we didn't stop running until we were at the bottom of the street. We laughed so hard we could barely speak. How long would it take him to figure out we were all gone?

It was still early, just past ten, and no one had a curfew. We were all pooped from the running but high from the trick we'd pulled. Someone suggested we go back to our house, and Natalie and I agreed. Ice cream floats and some television seemed like the perfect way to celebrate our caper.

For the first time all summer, maybe since we'd moved to Palos Verdes, ditching Stone gave me my first taste of how it felt to be an insider. As I walked down the street in this gaggle of laughing, chattering kids, a thrill coursed through me. No one felt sorry for Stone, least of all me. It was a relief not to be on the receiving end of the cruelty. For once, the practical joke wasn't on me. Besides, Stone had it easy. No one ruined his house with paint or hurt anything but his feelings. He was on the outs because of what he *did,* not because he was white. He'd survive. Eventually he'd figure out we ditched him and might even discover where we'd gone. A week from now, all would be forgotten. I fell into bed exhausted, but I couldn't help replaying the sound of whiny Stone chasing shadows in the square.

The next day stretched out like taffy—sticky and endless. Late summer days felt like a burden with too many hours of daylight and no way to fill them. I was bored. I went to the high school pool every weekday for lessons and free swim, but I was weary of water and didn't even want to take a bath at this point. The beach had lost its magic—another trip meant another losing battle with the sand. I hated sand. It invaded my snacks, crunched in my teeth, slipped into my bathing suit, and seeped into my braids. I never understood why white kids loved to lie in the sand and bake.

Dad didn't need my help with the Sunday cooking because the chicken and fish were already in the backyard smoker and the rice was simmering on the stove. It was too hot to help Mom cut back the spindly stems of the impatiens that had become flowerless and pale with the drought. Mom and Dad rarely sat down before sunset. They were always doing some kind of chore around the house. That's why they always acted insulted if I said I was bored. On this Sunday, as with any day really, I knew if I sat in front of the television much longer, Mom would accuse me of having too much time on my hands. Then I'd find myself cleaning a bathroom or folding laundry. I couldn't stay inside.

I ambled down the driveway and hung a right back up the street. I stretched my arms out and made the curb into a balance beam. Two doors up the street I passed the witch house. It was a two-story blue colonial, but we called it the witch house because an old widow lived there. This place was straight out of a Grimm fairy tale. The windows were always dark and the branches of the towering pine tree looked like grasping arms. The yard was a blanket of dead pine needles and graying pinecones. The witch only emerged from the house once each week to check her mailbox and always wore a filthy pink robe, a face full of powder, and red lipstick.

The sound of a bouncing ball drew my attention, and I looked up the street. There was Drew Langer, his sister Betsy, and her friend Leigh, three kick the can regulars from the previous night. Drew was six and looked like Mikey from the Life cereal commercial, with a pert nose and freckles that covered his face like merit badges. His two much older brothers were in high school, and during the school year, I'd see them ambling down the street with surfboards tucked under their arms. Drew chased the basketball to the edge of his driveway while Betsy and Leigh sat on the curb and stretched their tanned legs into the street. Two skateboards lay flipped over like turtles stranded on their backs while Drew bounced the ball against the garage door.

Betsy and Leigh looked up, saw me coming, and waved.

"Last night was fun," Betsy said, and we exchanged knowing looks.

"How long do you think Stone looked for us?" Leigh asked.

I shrugged. "Two hours probably. I bet he was out here all night."

I took a seat next to them on the curb and we just sat there for a while, baking in the heat. It was so hot. I felt like my eyelids were melting, but sitting out here was still much better than going back home and risking Mom putting me to work. Finally, Betsy suggested we go inside. I gladly followed. Drew rested the ball against the garage door and scampered behind us.

From the street, the house looked like a modest single-story ranch, but once inside, you discovered that it was actually two stories built on a hillside so that the kitchen, living room, dining room were all upstairs, with two bedrooms and three other rooms downstairs. The house smelled like kitty litter and damp bathing suits, chlorine and suntan oil. At the back of the living room an enormous picture window opened onto a panoramic view of the Pacific Ocean and all the cities along the coast. On days like this, you could see every beach from Torrance all the way up to Malibu. The Pacific was deep blue and there must have been a hundred sailboats sprinkled on the water. But Betsy, Leigh, and Drew had seen all this before and ignored the view. They stepped over Mindy, the family's basset hound, who dutifully galloped down the stairs after us.

A long hallway led to three kids' bedrooms. But before we reached Betsy's room something made her pause at a door leading to the space under the stairway. She pulled the door open. The smell of damp dirt was strong, and the air was cool and comforting in contrast to the heat outside. Betsy yanked a string cord and the naked lightbulb illuminated the dark space. I could see the house's bones—copper pipes and stair joists, the concrete foundation and electrical wires. This was the room where the Langers stored everything they planned to give to charity—snow gear and musty sleeping bags, knickknacks and old Christmas decorations.

While the other kids fingered old toys, I wandered back toward the neat stack of cardboard boxes. As I unfolded the top, the sharp smell of mothballs hit me. In a minute I was up to my elbows in knit gabardine and slick polyester, dresses in burnt orange and avocado plaids, mustard yellow floral, red and brown paisley. These were fragments of an older woman's life. The need to escape my boredom overwhelmed the fact that I was touching a stranger's things. I discovered an old black leather handbag with a short handle and a pair of white gloves I placed on my hands. In the corner of the box, I grabbed a salt-and-pepper wig with short bangs that was cut into a punch bowl. I propped it on my head and tucked my braids beneath it. The hard hair brushed my bare neck. From a vast stash of costumes and other random items in the box below, I dug out a pristine white dress with a fringe on the bottom. I had no idea where it had come from and could not imagine Betsy wearing the dress: it was too girly. I slipped it over my head and it stretched to the floor. I placed a few strands of orange beads around my neck and then topped off the outfit with a wide white shawl.

Betsy and Leigh stopped picking through the camping equipment in another corner. Drew gave up trying to make ski poles into spears. They'd never seen me like this. All three of them laughed at my getup, and their gawking told me that I'd stumbled onto the richest score. I was going to make the most of it. First, I hunched my shoulders, putting my hand in front of me as though leaning on an invisible cane. I took a few shaky steps as an old woman. The kids hooted. I soaked up the laughter like a thirsty rag. I commanded a new kind of attention. I didn't play dress-up much anymore, but I liked my pals' laughter and attention.

Next, I folded my lips inside my mouth to make it seem like I didn't have teeth. I started speaking in a shaky, high-pitched voice, dropping my final consonants. Some kind of bastardized drawl formed in my throat. Words like "lawdy" and "whipper-snapper" tumbled from my lips. My audience seemed to like my old lady and wanted more, as much of her as I would conjure. I shuffled behind Betsy, Leigh, and Drew bent over like I had a hump in my back. I hobbled into Betsy's room where the afternoon light illuminated her horse collection that sat on the shelves lining the walls. Betsy closed her bedroom door enough so that I could inspect myself in the mirror. I laughed as I studied my reflection.

Something within me turned. I'd spent too much time exiled as the new black girl. I wanted these kids to be my friends. I wanted more of the warm feeling I got when we rode our bikes around the neighborhood together or played kick the can. I wanted to feel like that all the time. But if I didn't do something to hold their attention, those good feelings would evaporate. I wouldn't have anything to balance out the lonely days. So I began to lie.

"This is what my grandmother looks like," I said.

"Really?" Drew asked. Betsy and Leigh stopped laughing.

The truth was much more complicated than that. My paternal grandmother was not a familiar presence in my life. We didn't have any pictures of Dad's mom displayed in the house, and I rarely spoke to her on the phone. Every Christmas she sent a big box of homemade pecan pralines and peach preserves from Louisiana, but only Dad ate them. Grandmother had visited shortly after we moved into our house, so I knew she looked nothing like this. But these kids didn't know that.

On this sweltering summer afternoon, the bedroom became my stage. As the spotlight shined on me, I walked into the middle of the floor, but when I spoke this time, I added a new element— the Southern dialect that I'd heard black actresses employ to portray benevolent maids in old Hollywood movies. There was no sass or attitude in my accent, no Florence from *The Jeffersons* or Mammy from *Gone with the Wind,* but still the voice was unmistakably black. "Chile" replaced "whippersnapper." I called Leigh and Betsy "honey" and shook their hands.

I performed on the edge of anger and desire, but neither feeling had much to do with my grandmother. It was me and the ball of loneliness and longing I'd carried all year. Deep down, I shouldn't have felt as lonely as I so often did. Making friends shouldn't have been as hard as it had been for me. I wanted these girls to like me, for us to become tight. I wanted them to really become my friends. I dipped into the well of their ignorance about black people that I knew existed—Natalie and I were probably some of the few black people they knew or invited into their houses—and took full advantage. I thrilled at my own power to hold their attention. This was my feeble attempt to bring the stupid questions and shock of white kids under my control. I could turn their ignorance against them. But I also had to turn it against myself.

"I's makes my own moonshine and drinks it."

Six wide eyes stared at me. I could see Betsy and Leigh getting more interested. I unfurled the lie like thread from a spool.

"I's lives in a shack," I said.

Their mouths gaped. I wove their surprise into my lie.

"I's smokes a corncob pipe."

All three of them gasped and then burst out laughing.

For as long as I could remember, Dad had always described himself as a "country boy." Whenever I asked him about his boyhood or what being a country boy meant, he'd sing, perform actually, the chorus of a song he'd learned when he was a boy.

"I'm just a plain old country boy," Dad always began. When he sang, his voice was loud and drowned out any other conversation in the room. He sang about simple food and hard work. He'd stand up and smile broadly, sweeping his arms wide and using hand gestures to punctuate his lyrics. "Look over that old gray mule when the sun comes up on Monday," he'd say with an extra twang. It was a whole routine, and he'd sing the song over and over again until I stopped with my questions. I'd heard the song so many times I knew it by heart, even though it never told me what I most wanted to know. The song was never an answer. It was always an evasion.

I knew the song, but I didn't know Dad's story. I didn't know the names of his friends or his school. I didn't know what games he played or his favorite hobby. I didn't know about his chores around the house, his best birthday, or his favorite holiday. I didn't know the details of his life in Louisiana, which meant I didn't know much about his mother, my grandmother. We hadn't been to her house since I was an infant. Dad described himself as a country boy, so she must have been a country grandmother. But for all that he didn't say about his childhood, I guessed that country and poor were closely related in Dad's memory and that it was easier to keep the pain of that fact from view. Country also had something to do with being black, but exactly what I wasn't quite sure. I had asked over and over again, but Dad wouldn't tell me. All I ever got was his stupid song.

I heard soft, uneven steps in the hallway. Betsy recognized her mother's polio-weakened gait and pushed the door open again.

"Hey, Mom," she said, "come see this."

Mrs. Langer's tall, solid frame appeared in the doorway. She was the coupon-clipping homemaker who drove a paneled station wagon. She and Mom were friendly but had too little in common to be friends. She made Chex mix from a magazine recipe and served it warm on special occasions. Everything about this woman seemed practical and efficient. She wore variations of her standard uniform—a short-sleeved shirt, permanent-press slacks, and a pair of low-heeled espadrilles. Her thick wavy hair was trimmed to her neck. "Well, well," Mrs. Langer said, smiling. She eyed my costume.

"Do it, Jennifer," my friends urged me. They wanted to see the routine all over again. They were hooked now.

Suddenly I didn't want to perform. My country grandmother didn't seem so funny anymore. Mrs. Langer hearing the voice I'd conjured seemed like a bad idea. My face felt flush and my body prickly hot in all of these clothes as I felt the situation slipping away from me.

"Let me get my camera," she said. "Go into the living room."

Leigh, Betsy, and Drew thought this a great idea and hurried up the stairs.

But not me. I lingered in the hallway for a minute, trying to find an excuse to stay downstairs. *Stop this now,* I thought as I trudged up the stairs. A picture would make this permanent. *Just don't ask me to perform again,* I prayed. I lumbered up the stairs and stood rooted on the top step clutching the banister.

Mrs. Langer came into the living room, advanced the film in her slim rectangular camera, and popped on a fresh flashcube. She arranged Betsy and Leigh on one side of the fireplace and Drew on the other. She kept a spot in the center open for me. Their impatience and excitement pulled me. Finally, I walked over stiff-legged and stood awkwardly. The kids gathered around me. I mumbled "cheese" as the flashbulb flared.

I couldn't bear to show my teeth and instead pulled my lips into more of a wince.

Then the other kids stepped away from me so that Mrs. Langer could take a picture of me alone. Nothing about this felt good until someone cracked a joke and I smiled through my bunched mouth in spite of myself. But my fear returned as the blue light finished dancing in my eyes. *When would this moment end?* Pressure built in my head and my thigh muscles began to tingle with a new feeling overwhelming me. Panic. *Just take off the dress, scarf, and the wig,* I thought. *Return them to their resting place and go home.*

Suddenly Mrs. Langer had a brilliant idea. "Jennifer, why don't you show your parents?" she asked me.

"Yeah," chimed Betsy and Drew.

"No," I stammered. "Thanks, but I'll just take this all off and bring all this stuff back downstairs."

"Don't worry about that," Mrs. Langer said, reassuring me. "I'm sure that your parents will get a kick out of seeing you."

Somehow, I doubted that. Dad would hate what I'd done to his country boyhood and his mother. Mom would hate the fact that I'd lied and been "clowning"—that was the word she always used to describe showing off to get attention. My own fear of my parents' anger suddenly dwarfed any worry about Mrs. Langer or these kids. Lying to these kids, lying on my grandmother, this was the kind of thing that would earn me a bare-bottomed, leather belt spanking, maybe the longest one ever. I had to get out of this house.

Only one thing could make this moment worse: someone blabbing to Mrs. Langer about the lies I'd told about my grandmother. I stared wild-eyed at Leigh, Betsy, and Drew, willing them to stay silent. But as we headed for the door, Drew piped up, "Jennifer's dressed up like her grandmother. She lives in a shack. She drinks moonshine. She smokes a corncob pipe."

The kids laughed.

For a split second Mrs. Langer looked horrified, afraid that maybe her son mocked me. She searched his face for irony and found none. Then she turned to the girls. I watched her eyes grow wide with uncertainty as she forced her own faint smile. Finally she looked at me. The discomfort in Mrs. Langer's eyes met the discomfort in mine. There was a part of me that recognized this moment as my chance. All I had to do was speak up and admit that I'd made the whole thing up. But the words caught in my throat. I hunkered down in my fear-filled silence and didn't admit to Mrs. Langer that I'd lied to her kids. I couldn't break the spell of my deception. I was a coward, afraid of the kids' disappointment and their rejection. So when Betsy threw the front door open and the kids marched back out to the driveway and down the street toward my house, I followed.

Outside in the blazing sun, my lies beat down on me and I began to sweat. Leigh, Betsy, and Drew walked in the middle of the street like they owned it as I strayed toward the curb. My dress dragged on the ground. I concentrated on the asphalt to avoid thinking about the mess I'd made. The wig smothered my scalp and made it itch.

Tell the truth, I thought. *Stop them here in the street and explain that the only things I know about shacks and moonshine I learned from my favorite television show,* The Waltons. I wasn't even thinking about grumpy live-in Grandma Walton. I was thinking about apple-doll-faced Martha Corrine Walton, the great aunt and scrappy family sage who lived high on the mountain and made the Waltons seem sophisticated. But as I tried to force the words from my mouth, the words just wouldn't come out. I didn't want to be the new Stone in the neighborhood, the butt of everyone's jokes.

We were approaching my house. Drew became positively frisky with excitement. I led them between the parked cars in my driveway and walked into the darkened garage. Betsy and Leigh remained composed, but I could tell they were waiting for the whole show to begin again. My fear tightened around me as we climbed the stairs and I opened the door that led into my house.

As we walked into the family room, I noticed that Dad wasn't in his usual Sunday spot. For some reason he was sitting on the opposite side of the room in a Queen Anne chair, his bare feet propped on the matching ottoman. He wore a short-sleeved shirt and shorts. His old dress shoes, with the backs bent down, were tucked underneath the ottoman. He glanced away from the television.

By now Betsy, Leigh, and Drew knew I was shy about my costume and didn't even wait for me to explain this to Dad. "Look, Mr. Baszile," they said as I stood there. "Look at Jennifer."

"What's all this?" he asked.

I knew he meant me, and why I was dressed up, but I didn't say a word. The sportscaster's commentary persisted, but otherwise the room was silent. Dread surged inside me. Calamity came straight toward me. In my silence, by not offering a made-up excuse, I had closed all of my escape routes.

"Jennifer's dressed up like her country grandmother," Drew said.

I could no longer process what was happening. I felt, rather than heard, the words spoken as the kids repeated them. Corncob pipe. Moonshine. Shack. I cowered inside my mind because everything felt so bad. I couldn't focus.

It was only when the kids turned to me and nearly yelled, "Do it, Jennifer, do it," that I emerged.

I couldn't look at anyone as I drowned in my own shame, too pained to cry. I shook my head. Dad sat motionless in his chair.

"Come on, do it just like you did it a minute ago," they begged. They felt in on the joke, like it was theirs as much as mine, and so they explained the scene for Dad.

"Jennifer was showing us how her grandmother talks, how she walks. It was really great." Drew kind of bent at his waist and started trying to do his own imitation. He tried to make his voice faint and drawling like mine, but the impression fell flat.

Dad looked at me as if the other kids weren't even here. Even though I'd denied him the performance, he'd seen enough to feel its impact. His eyes filled with disappointment. He held my gaze and called me a liar without even saying a word. He turned all his attention back to the television and dismissed us with his silence. The other kids were too frenzied to notice Dad's dismissal because he had said so little since we'd walked into the house.

I hustled everyone out of the family room and back into the garage. I couldn't stand to wear the clothes for another minute. I didn't care if I never made these kids my buddies. At the bottom of the steps, I nearly ripped the wig off my head and tore off the gloves and purse. My hands fumbled with the zipper and I struggled to strip myself of the dress. Then I bundled everything together and handed it back to Betsy. It wasn't her job, but I had to get away from these kids. I didn't want them around when Dad got mad at me.

When my friends left, I skulked back into the house, certain that I was in the biggest trouble of my life. I climbed the stairs to my room and lay on my bed, waiting for Dad to call me. The looping sound of my lies trained my ear for the prelude to the spanking I was sure was coming. I knew the routine. First, the question, "Jennifer, what were you thinking?" I was feeling worse by the second.

I grew tired of waiting for the prelude to begin. Dad hadn't talked to me all afternoon. He had stared through me at dinner and had kept his eyes on the television. He had spoken very little to anyone. He didn't say a word to me. The sequence of punishment turned into both a dream and a nightmare that made the backs of my knees tingle. By nightfall, the silence became unbearable. As I sat on my bed, my scorching liquid fear turned molten and then into a solid block of resignation. The exact date and time of my punishment became irrelevant. I knew it was inevitable.

In September 1976, I began second grade at Lunda Bay School and received the first part of my punishment. The kids I met on my first day of second grade seemed very different from the kids I'd known at Vista Grande. When the teacher asked about our summers, one person after another described exotic vacations. These were the blondest kids I'd ever seen, their hair bleached by days spent boogie boarding on local beaches or surfing in Hawaii. I had never met an eight-year-old surfer before. Other kids acquired their deep tans and freckles from the hours they spent on their private tennis courts taking lessons from coaches who made house calls. At recess, I played soccer rather than dodgeball. These boys and girls wore Vans sneakers for skateboarding or Rod Lavers for tennis rather than cheap, all-purpose Keds that the kids in Rancho Palos Verdes had favored.

A few weeks into the new year, the morning we took class

pictures, I arrived at school determined to keep my hands out of my newly braided hair and keep my dainty pink and white dress with the puffed sleeves clean. I locked my two-wheeler in the bike rack and walked onto the playground. Before I could find my friends, I felt Andy, the boy from my class who had been threatening to "string me up" for weeks, staring at me. He had dirty blond hair and skin the color of bile. He still pissed his pants. I called him Piss Boy in my mind because he constantly reeked of drying urine. He always seemed sour, even more so since the day I outpedaled him as he chased me part of the way home. Although I had not yet heard the word *lynching,* I felt the menace in his threat and had nightmares. Piss Boy intercepted me as I walked onto the playground. I saw that he was not alone. Buck Tooth, a new Southern boy whose thin lips never completely covered his gigantic teeth, stood behind Piss Boy's left shoulder. Fat Boy, a pudgy, short-legged jerk who rolled up his Toughskins jeans, stood on the right. I remained silent and tried to keep moving.

Before I knew it, children gathered and then surrounded me.

"Oooh, it's a fight," a voice called out from behind me, "a nigger and a white." There was that word again. *What had I done to them? Why did that term make white people so giddy? How did they know there would be a fight?* Piss Boy must have been bragging all morning, plotting to beat me up because he could not string me up.

Other children sensed the tension and joined the rising chorus of voices. Crowded together like Red Vines, the children encircled us. Piss Boy and his fellow goons stood on one side whispering, and I stood alone on the other side of the grassy ring. There was no way to break through and find Natalie on the vast lower playground where the older kids gathered. I was the only black girl in my class, my grade, and my school besides my sister. Mom and Dad had already left for their jobs downtown. My few new friends were nowhere in sight. I didn't even bother to hope that a teacher might intervene. I could not outrun this fight.

As I spread my feet apart and braced my legs, I felt the dew seep through the stitches of my shoes. Maybe the chanting that sounded like clapping made the three boys feel brave. It only made me slightly dizzy. I hadn't known that so many kids had been waiting for a chance to call me nigger. My stomach cramped. Piss Boy bounced up and down in anticipation. There was not much time. I tried to drown out the children and ignored the taste of metal on my tongue. Spit flooded my mouth and made me swallow hard and often.

I tried to concentrate on the two instructions my father had given me about fighting. First, never throw the first punch. But if someone else starts a fight, he said, "Kick their ass."

More children gathered and joined the surging chant. Excitement built for everyone but me. I let my arms hang at my sides and waited. I tried not to blink or take my eyes off the three boys. Piss Boy crouched low and ran at me first. He tried to tackle me, but I moved out of his way to dodge his body and his blow without much struggle. The crowd groaned with disappointment in their champion. A few kids shouted encouragement to him. No one cheered for me.

The children jeered and yelled louder, but I could barely hear them. Buck Tooth opened and closed his hands. He rushed toward me and raised his fists. I was breathing hard by now. As he cocked his arm, I ducked when he tried to make contact with the side of my face. Buck Tooth had thrown the first punch.

Something feral rose within me. Maybe it was the realization that help was not coming. The perimeter of onlookers faded. Piss Boy, who had remained behind me, jumped on my back and caught my neck in the crook of his elbow. I acted before I could think. I flipped him over and he hit the ground with a thud. I knew that I had messed up my hair. *What about my picture?* Mom would be upset.

Fat Boy grabbed the backpack I had forgotten to remove. Buck Tooth grabbed the other side. I struggled to remain upright as they tried to yank me to the ground. *Why did they want to get me on the ground?* I heard either my dress or my backpack rip. If they pulled me down, I knew I would get up bloody. Whatever it took, they would not sit on my stomach, hold my arms, and beat me to a pulp. They would not make my flowered panties show. *Don't let them take you down,* I screamed inside my head. I stopped fighting their force and let the backpack slide down my back. Buck Tooth let go.

I spun Fat Boy around and then released him and the backpack. Then I unleashed my fists, elbows, and knees. I caught Piss Boy in the diaphragm and he gasped for air. My own lungs burned by now. I popped Buck Tooth in the mouth the next time he came at me. Fat Boy still had my backpack and did not approach me. So I walked over and kicked him as hard as I could anyway. He did not seem to want any more of me. The three boys bent over and rubbed the body parts I hoped I had bruised with my bony limbs. I did not know when the spectators had stopped chanting. I had no idea how many minutes had passed. I was too busy trying not to cry. It was over, but it was another unsatisfying victory.

"Do you want any more?" I demanded, hoarse and huffing.

None of the three boys answered my question. Where were their voices now? I snatched my backpack from the grass. I felt for the white satin ribbons that Mom had tied at the ends of my three braids. I only spied one mashed in the grass. I was missing my pink barrettes and could feel one of my braids unraveling. I had ruined my hair. The silent chanters looked at me both frightened and amazed. They had expected my defeat and anticipated my beating. The circle parted, and the children stood out of my way to let me pass. No one used that word anymore. No one said anything. None of my friends appeared. The bell rang for school.

I knew that these people would never really be my friends. They had shown me who they were—cheerleaders for bullies. And they had kept calling me a nigger. It was like they had been waiting for a chance to use that word. Anyone could see how unfair the fight had been—three against one. No one had spoken up, tried to help me, or run for a teacher. They'd just chanted, "Oooh, it's a fight, a nigger and a white." I didn't want kids like those to be friends of mine. What was the point? By the end of the fight, I was too exhausted and too many kids were standing around for me to memorize the chanters' faces or try to distinguish any voices. They'd shown me how alone I really was. I hated all of them.

Through the Pledge of Allegiance, morning attendance, and the short walk to the cafeteria, my sense of dread deepened as I realized that the fight had already ruined my picture. If my new teacher noticed how rough I looked, she didn't say anything to me or offer any help. As I stood in line waiting for my picture to be taken, I felt the disaster on top of my head—hairs stood on end and sweat kinked my entire hairline. I had ruined hours of Mom's finest work with the straightening comb. I was not allowed to leave the house with a brush, so I tried to rake my fingers through the defiant strands of hair, which only made me look worse. My braids had begun to swell like bruises. I felt the ripped shoulder of my dress and hoped that it would not show. The neck of the dress gapped and the bow at my waist was untied. When I sat in front of the horrified photographer, I widened my eyes in anticipation of the blinding flash. I had done what my father told me. I had remained standing. I had fought and won. I grinned at the camera in relief.

I never told my parents about the fight. I'd taken care of the kids just like Dad told me to, so there was nothing to tell him. I didn't want to upset him or make him take another morning off from work. The three boys had laid off me since the fight. I never said anything to Mom, because she always insisted that girls shouldn't fight, and I didn't want her to be mad at me. Sure, I was worried about my picture, but warning Mom about my picture would have meant disclosing what had happened. So I just prayed that the picture wasn't going to be too bad.

When I handed Mom the proof pages, her exclamations of horror told me that it was worse than that. I remained quiet when she expressed her disappointment with my sloppy picture. My mother ordered the smallest package of pictures and never put my photo on display. She kept it out of the family room that was crowded with trophies, certificates, and plaques because it was not an artifact of uplift. The picture never made it back east or down south to relatives who had hauled, cooked, and washed my family through hard times and were always anxious for news of our success. Dad didn't say anything to me about the picture. But I was about to find out just how much my shacks-and-moonshine stunt had affected him.

{ chapter three }

THE OTHER ONE

When I first visited my father's home state, Louisiana, in the spring of 1970, I wasn't yet walking. One evening near the end of the trip something made me cry. My diaper dry, my belly full, and free of fever, Mom tried all of the usual ways to console me— bouncing, burping, rocking, singing, laying me down, and sitting me up—nothing worked. I bawled until my whole body became hot and then broke into a sweat. I cried for hours until I nearly ran out of tears. Nothing could quiet me.

Until that visit, Dad had been a pretty patient father. He already knew that babies cry the way that adults speak. But that night Dad couldn't stand my crying. Maybe it had nothing to do with me. Maybe the fact that I wailed in his mother's house, the place where he'd shed his own boyhood tears, made him feel something unbearable: maybe helpless.

Out of patience and desperate for quiet, Dad got an idea. He took out a fifth of whiskey and poured some in the screw cap. My head thrashing, Dad held the cap to my moving mouth. Liquor spilled over my lips and most ran down my neck. Enough of it seeped down my throat for me to register the burn and the bitter taste. I shrieked, helpless.

He should have drunk the whiskey himself.

No one knew why I cried beyond consolation that night.

The next morning brought quiet but little peace. I didn't yet speak but held my first grudge against Dad. I knew he'd burned my mouth, and I didn't trust him. I wouldn't leave Mom's arms or go to anyone else in the house. I whimpered every time Dad came near me. I refused his touch and all of his cooing. All day, I turned my head away from him and refused to look in his direction.

Dad told me this story every now and then in California. Mom always got quiet as he recounted it, maybe because she hadn't stopped him from burning my mouth. I hated that story because it made me feel distant from Dad. I wished he'd stop telling it, but I never told him so. By the time I was seven years old, that episode had become a kind of family legend. Dad was the only one who kept the story alive. I hated hearing the story because it made me feel mistrustful of Dad in a way that I found too frightening.

Christmas Eve 1976 fell on a Friday and we'd been traveling all day. Dad sped the rental car down Louisiana Highway 190 into

Jefferson Davis Parish. It was a two-lane road, straight and empty. He clutched the steering wheel at ten and two and hunched his shoulders close to his ears. He never drove this way. Usually, Dad rested his right hand at the base of the wheel and hung his left arm out the window. We rode in silence as the sun dropped behind the green fields that stretched for miles. Dad locked his eyes on the road. Mom glanced over at Dad every few minutes but didn't say anything. She spent most of the ride looking out her window, but I knew she worried about Dad. I did, too.

This was the place that made Dad a country boy, but it felt more eerie than quaint to me. We had arrived in Cajun country, southwestern Louisiana, just across the Texas border. We hardly passed another car. Dad's frantic pace smeared the landscape green and gray. This was the strangest, most solemn Christmas Eve of my life. It had neither the bright confection of a California holiday nor the white Christmas of my fantasies.

Finally, Dad removed his foot from the gas pedal and the car glided as hulking metal structures came into view. The silos loomed over the highway ahead of us and seemed like they were more suited for outer space than the middle of nowhere. When I asked what they were, Mom called them rice dryers. We moved more slowly into their shadows, and I could see the dents and grooves in the towers. I didn't know the way to Dad's hometown and wasn't sure how much longer we'd have to stay in the car, but the tense silence made it clear that it was not a good time for questions.

A white metal sign, no larger than a license plate, read Elton. Rust blistered the smaller black letters on the next line and made it impossible to read the three numbers after the abbreviation for population. I couldn't imagine too many people lived here.

Between the fields and the thick woods, little room remained for houses. A single row of buildings squatted on the opposite side of the highway and stretched less than a quarter of a city block. Everything was painted white. A two-pump gas station, shut for the holiday, marked the end of "downtown." This place felt too small and too deserted to be a town.

A single set of railroad tracks ran parallel to our side of the highway. I didn't know how long the thick brush beside the road had concealed them. These tracks, unfettered by flashing signals or the yellow and black signs I saw at Los Angeles crossings, sat a few feet above the road. The people of Elton who lived beyond the tracks had to cross them without the benefit of a signal to get everywhere they wanted to go—to get food or gas, to pick up their mail, or to go to a bigger town. In this nearly forsaken place there was little protection from the train.

I clenched the door handle and listened for a train whistle as our car mounted the slight ridge. Dad looked both ways before he rolled across the track and down the other side. A decrepit feed store nearly backed onto the railroad tracks. Burlap sacks lined the entrance, and I wondered what kept people from stealing after hours. But something did.

We entered another part of Elton. The sputtering sound of tires on loose gravel and our bouncing car told me we had left the world of paved roads. We turned left and created a cloud of dust even as we inched along. The sight and sound of the car announced our arrival.

It was no more than forty degrees, but Dad rolled down his window and leaned his forearm outside. People, whose complexions ranged from taupe to pitch, sat on their porches. They remained as motionless as owls perched on branches, tracking us with their eyes. They stared without shame, barely blinked, and never averted their gaze. To me, their expressionless faces all posed the question *Do you belong here?*

Dad rested his right hand on the base of the wheel for the first time all day. He waved out the window to no one in particular and nodded his head to those who couldn't see his hand. He understood the protocol. He knew you didn't drive among these people without speaking or at least waving a hand and showing respect. The owls seemed satisfied. They nodded back or simply blinked, all small gestures. Dad knew Elton's rules.

Dad's waving also answered a question I'd had for a long time. Back in LA, he drove through South Central Los Angeles or any other black neighborhood in the same way. He acknowledged nearly every black person he encountered, including complete strangers. It never mattered whether the person swept the floor, parked a car, or just passed us on the street, if they were black, Dad made a point to acknowledge them with a nod or a wave. I finally understood that Dad learned that lesson on this side of the tracks.

Mom kept her window up and applied a fresh coat of lipstick.

Halfway down the street, Dad slowed to a crawl as we approached a one-story house. A deep gully filled with nearly frozen water separated the front yard from the gravel road. Like all the other houses on this side of the tracks, this one was tiny but not a shack, twice as long as it was wide. This house was the color of banana pudding. White wrought-iron bars nearly enclosed the porch. The trunk and bare branches of a tree three stories tall dominated the small yard and explained the patchy grass. A column of smoke rose from the oil drum–turned–barbeque rig in the vacant lot next door.

Dad pulled into the driveway behind a lopsided blue Crown Victoria and a rusty Ford pickup. He chuckled for the first time all day. A wide smile spread across his face. Recognition. He opened the car door and leaned on the roof as he waited for Mom, Natalie, and me to emerge.

My grandmother's stout body remained motionless like her neighbors', seated beside the open front door. Her raspy voice filled the yard.

"I've been wondering when y'all'd get here. I've been waiting all day."

Grandmother's cashew-colored skin wrinkled around her deep-set eyes. Her large square glasses overwhelmed her face. Her skin hung loosely on her jawline. The deep creases on either side of her mouth made her seem stern and made her jet-black Shirley Temple ringlets even more confusing. The tortoise barrette clipped at her temple made her seem like some ancient girl. White powder clung to the inside of the nearly empty glass Coca-Cola bottle she held in her hand. Her stockings, rolled just above her knees, peeked from beneath the hem of her skirt. She dabbed her top lip with a well-worn tissue. She looked nothing like the costumed figure I'd created back home.

Dad bounded across the patchy grass-covered yard and climbed the steps to the porch. He leaned over to kiss and hug his mother. Grandmother looked tiny as Dad bent down; her arms couldn't even encircle his back. The man in my dad receded as the boy, eager to embrace his mother, emerged.

"How are you today, Mother?" he said as he stepped back.

For a moment, I wondered what had made Dad so sullen all day if seeing his mother could make him this delighted. Then I recalled my lying stunt that mocked Dad and his mother with tall tales about corncob pipes and moonshine. Since the day it happened, the incident never left my mind, but I had focused more on my anticipation of a Louisiana Christmas than on the decision to make the trip this year. Seeing the two of them together and remembering the months since then when Dad never mentioned it, I got a new kind of sick feeling. I was the reason we were here—my impersonation of Grandmother explained the timing of the trip. Right then, I knew that Dad wanted me to know who my grandmother really was and to teach me a lesson. I thought about Dad's surly mood. I wasn't sure whether he'd spent the day replaying my mockery over and over in his mind, or if something else about coming to this town made him uncomfortable. Either way, I hated the burden I'd put on Dad.

"I'm alright, LeRoy," she said to Dad.

LeRoy? Who is LeRoy? I didn't know my dad by that name. It was strange to hear him respond to his middle name like it was his first. But then again, Grandmother named him Barrow, not Barry, at birth. He was born at home and didn't have a birth certificate, so Dad changed it when he enlisted in the army. Maybe calling her oldest son by a name she gave him, even the middle one, made Grandmother feel better.

"Where's Daddy?" Dad asked.

"He's around here doing something or another," Grandmother said as she waved her hand in dismissal.

Daddy? It sounded strange for me to hear Dad use that word. Daddy was actually Dad's stepfather, a man named Tom. Dad's biological father had died before I was born. Even though he wasn't related to me by blood, I called Tom Grandfather, just like I did my mother's stepfather, Grandfather Al.

"Well, hello, Miss Rose," Mom said as she stepped forward.

She clasped Grandmother's outstretched hand. They were never very warm toward each other, but at least this time, the chill between them matched the day.

"Janet," she said with a regal nod. "How you feelin, baby?"

It was such a strange question, like everything else here.

"Fine," Mom said. "We're just so glad to be here." I knew it wasn't quite true. Mom had struggled not to snap at us since we'd been traveling.

I remained frozen on the second porch step as Mom greeted Grandmother. I stared at Grandmother but didn't dare to walk onto the porch without an invitation. I was afraid that Dad had already disclosed my lies. I was even more terrified that he or Mom would make me confess to Grandmother on the spot. Not even my very best behavior felt like it would be enough here.

"Well, hello, young ladies," Grandmother said. Her speech sharpened with each word. "Come and give Grandmother some sugar." I hugged Grandmother after Natalie. Her body was soft and warm, but her cheek was cold. I inhaled the clean floral scent of her Camay soap.

I stepped back and stood beside Natalie.

"Janet," Grandmother said to Mom, "they're just like perfect little white girls."

I stared at Grandmother in shock. *What did she mean, "perfect little white girls"?* I thought. Her voice sounded so warm and full of praise, but no one had ever said those words to me before. I didn't know how to react. It didn't make sense. I looked over to Mom, relieved that Grandmother didn't expect a response from me.

Mom's shoulders became rigid and her expression clouded. She stretched her lips taut and she smiled the fake way that she did whenever someone offended her but she didn't want to show it.

"Thank you, Miss Rose," Mom said.

Mom's response made me feel even more confused. In a thousand small ways, my life in Palos Verdes had shown me I was *not* a white girl. At least Mom must have known this. Her hard, flat voice told me she was annoyed, but she didn't correct Grandmother. She usually blasted people who said "the white man's ice was colder," that white was better. I didn't know Grandmother well enough to know what she meant. I *did* know Mom well enough to know that she wouldn't have tolerated the comment if she thought Grandmother was trying to insult us. So I just assumed it was a strange sort of compliment.

I'd been too lost in my shock to focus much on the man who rose from the porch swing and spread his legs into a wide stance. The man had a red Afro and sallow skin, like Grandmother. His black horn-rimmed glasses had thick lenses that magnified his bulging gray eyes. His shirt barely stretched over his potbelly. He kept his arms folded across his barrel chest. He rooted himself like a tree, trying to seem taller as he stood before Dad.

"Hey, Brock," Dad said.

"Hello, big brother," the man said in a voice that sounded as rough as sandpaper. The two men shook hands first and then embraced for a moment. In their own way, each man resembled Grandmother, but they couldn't have looked more distinct from each other.

"Jan Jan," he said as he swept Mom into his arms.

Mom, who hated nicknames, grimaced and held her body stiff at the embrace.

"Sonny," she said as she steadied herself.

Brock? Sonny? I was still trying to figure out why Dad and Mom called the same man by two different names when he spoke again.

"My my," he said to Natalie, "don't you have pretty hair."

I thought it a strange greeting for Natalie. Mom had let Natalie get a perm and feathered bangs at the beginning of the school year. Her long, thick hair passed her shoulders, but the damp had made her hair slightly more frizzy than usual. Natalie hadn't worn braids a single day since.

"She sure does," Grandmother agreed.

Then he turned to me and stared without admiration.

"Hello, Niece," he said.

Sonny's formal greeting caught me off guard. He didn't speak my name or compliment my two braids.

"Hello, Uncle," I said, not knowing whether to call him Sonny or Brock.

He roared with delight, even though I didn't mean to be funny. Still laughing, he nearly pulled me off my feet and into a hug.

Christmas Eve night was strange for lots of reasons. Dad had spent most of the evening outside. He leaned against the porch rail for a while. Then he dragged Natalie and me down the street to his aunt Dell's house so that we could visit with her. He lingered in the yard when we got back and went inside a minute only to get some dinner. No matter how many times Grandmother urged him, Dad refused to sit down at the table or put his plate on a television tray. He leaned beside the kitchen counter while he ate.

We all had gone to Golden Chain Baptist Church, the place where Dad worshiped as a boy. The sanctuary was as small as everything else in Elton, but I loved it. I loved singing the carols. We sang the same lyrics as in California, but instead of being set to harps, violins, and a cello, jaunty gospel melodies played on a Hammond organ backed our voices. I couldn't help but sway to the music, and even Mom bobbed up and down. Not Dad. He shifted in his seat the whole time and frowned. It seemed that he grew more tense by the minute. Sitting among my twelve first cousins, five aunts, and four uncles made me feel part of a pack—warm and protected. Grandmother told me that most of the seventy or so worshipers were relatives of mine. I couldn't believe it.

I saw my first black Santa. Black Santa spoke with an accent as thick as gumbo, had a gold tooth, and wore dusty cowboy boots. But most of the kids squealed when he teetered on a cane up the center aisle. They cheered and called to him the way that kids did at home. They believed it was really him. He didn't look anything like the blue-eyed Santa that frequented the mall near our own house every Christmas. But inside Golden Chain, I ignored the fact that Black Santa weighed half as much as mall Santa. I wanted to believe he was the real Santa, and so he was for me that night.

By the time we returned home from church the temperature had dropped another ten degrees. All the cousins gathered inside to open our presents. That's the way Grandmother did it, so Mom didn't object. All fourteen kids sat on the worn living room carpet, the color of red velvet cake, and opened our presents in a mad frenzy. I couldn't believe that Mom had allowed us to join the fray because at home we waited until Christmas morning and opened presents one by one. Mom, Grandmother, and all the aunts watched us, while Dad poked his head inside only a few times. I couldn't understand why he was so agitated and aloof. He acted as though staying in the house too long might make it impossible to leave again. I stayed out of his way and asked neither him nor Mom for an explanation. The rest of the night, Dad stood down by the smoker where my grandfather cooked chicken and pork until late into the night. He didn't visit with his sisters in the family room or tuck me into my strange bed.

I awoke Christmas morning in the bedroom with Pepto-Bismol-colored walls, just to the right of the front door. I'd spent the night tossing on a mattress that felt stuffed with lumpy oatmeal. Even though it wasn't even light out yet, I couldn't go back to sleep and didn't know how Natalie rested in the twin bed beside mine. The hiss of the kerosene heater made the only sound in the house and filled the air with the faint smell of noxious gas. I looked through the window beside my bed to the front yard and the empty street beyond it. I knew I couldn't leap out of bed and start screaming "Merry Christmas" like I did at home every year. So I waited.

An hour later, Dad stood in the doorway that joined the room where he and Mom had slept to mine. He didn't look at all rested. He spoke to us in a flat voice that carried none of its usual chime. He told us "get dressed" rather than "Merry Christmas." The grimace he had worn all the previous night had returned to his face. Meeting Grandmother, greeting her so politely, and being on my best behavior should have shown Dad I had learned my lesson. I finally realized that something other than my stunt was upsetting Dad.

I passed Grandmother on my way out of my parents' room where Mom had just brushed my hair to make it perfect for the day's pictures. Grandmother kissed my forehead and wished me a Merry Christmas. She was fully dressed and looked as though she'd been awake for hours. None of my aunts, uncles, and cousins lived in Elton, but we were the only ones who had spent the night in Grandmother's house. I couldn't wait for my cousins to return so that I could really get to know them.

In the middle of the morning, more people began to fill the house. Neighbors, church members, and friends arrived with pots and plates of food. I had no idea so many people lived in Elton. Steam dripped from the windows, and all of the people crowded into the house. Only a narrow path remained through the house. Children waiting for dinner dodged corrections and reprimands.

By noon, with the house bursting, all attention shifted to the preparation of Christmas dinner. The smells of smoked pork,

cayenne pepper, vinegar, onions, bell pepper, and celery penetrated every porous surface in the house. In the kitchen, a torrent of food engulfed me. A coconut cake, trays of homemade
hand pies, and pralines covered the round table that stood in
the center of the kitchen. Plates of barbequed and smoked ribs
and chicken were piled high and tented with foil. Mayonnaise
jars of pickled pig's feet, a cast iron skillet of glistening golden
corn bread, and a bowl heaped with long-grain rice crammed the
counters. A cauldron of collard greens sat on the front burner
of the stove. A curly bit of pork fat floated in every serving. Pink
rounds of andouille sausage and shreds of chicken bobbed in the
murky brown gumbo. Ground sassafras powder, white vinegar,
and the hot sauce rested beside the stove. The dirty rice—with
bits of seasoned ground beef and chicken livers mixed with long-
grain rice and spices—simmered on the other burner.

For all of the Christmas cheer, Dad was sullen and again
stayed outside on the porch. He talked to everyone, but his nerves
seemed flimsy like tinsel. Whenever he saw one of his cousins,
he called Natalie and me outside to meet them. He held us up
like shields to these people and put us on display. I knew Dad
was proud of us, but it felt to me like a distraction even more
than pride. When I wasn't being paraded out to meet people, I
mostly sat on the edge of the bed where I had slept, out of the
way. I didn't want to meet anyone else. I didn't want another
kiss on the cheek, another stranger's hug, or another person's
comment about my "funny" California speech. My brain couldn't
retain any more names. I wandered to the back of the house.

Tired of sitting for so long, I stood in the archway at the end
of the hall and tried to decide whether I should pass through
the kitchen and go into the family room or go outside. I heard

Sonny's croaky voice as a blast of cold swept into the front room. He sounded excited.

"Come on, man, you won't believe it," he said. Sonny strode along the plastic runner, sweeping his head from side to side.

"Okay, okay," another man said. He sounded hurried but didn't appear for a long moment.

"Hurry up," Sonny urged as though whatever they sought might scamper away. My uncle ignored my slight frame as I clung to the archway. He passed into the kitchen. In the swarm of people, I was easy to miss. As much as I thought I liked it that way, Sonny's failure to greet me didn't feel like a relief.

As the other man ambled into view, I understood Sonny's frustration. He greeted every person tucked in the corners of the front rooms. The stranger's short legs barely supported an enormous sagging belly. He moved his arms in stroking motions as if trying to gain momentum for the next step. A khaki button-down shirt and matching pants draped the stranger's body. A gold star shield glistened on his breast, and a flashlight, handcuffs, and pistol crowded his black belt. He leaned on the wall beside me and looked happy for the rest. He stared at me with cow eyes and flashed a weary smile. If this guy was a cop, I knew that he'd never caught anyone in a pursuit on foot.

"Hey, Brock," the stranger called.

"What, man?" Uncle Sonny said, irritated at having to backtrack.

"Is this the one here?"

I didn't understand the question, but it was clearly part of a conversation that the men had started outside.

Sonny settled his eyes on me and shook his head.

"Naw," he said, exasperated. He flicked his fingers and wrist as if swatting a fly in front of me. "This here is the other one. My pretty niece must be in the back."

The Other One.

Sonny had called Natalie pretty since we'd arrived. Whenever he saw Natalie enter a room or pass by, he'd just call it out. I hadn't given it much thought. I'd assumed he called her pretty because he forgot her name, not that he meant it as a compliment. In that moment, I realized that Sonny remembered Natalie's name but chose not to use it. "Pretty" had become Natalie's nickname, a proper name, just like "Jan Jan." I also realized that Sonny had given me a nickname of my own, the Other One. Even though I'd just heard it for the first time, I knew that the Pretty One and the Other One must have emerged in his mind at the same instant.

I hadn't given much thought to being pretty. People always fawned over Natalie, so I thought I was used to it. I had convinced myself that I could be pretty in my own way, although not as pretty as Natalie. But my new nickname told me something different. I wasn't pretty in my own way or less pretty than Natalie. I wasn't pretty at all. I already knew the name for the absence of pretty: ugly.

I must be ugly.

The smile I had plastered on my face in anticipation of another introduction faded and my whole being burned with shame. Everything crumpled. Sonny's statement felt nothing like the crazy compliment Grandmother had offered the day before. Besides, she had referred to both Natalie *and* me. Even if the words "perfect little white girls" struck me as strange when she said them, her tone told me Grandmother meant well. She hadn't meant any harm. No praise hid in what Sonny had just said.

I found Mom seated on the family room couch beside Aunt Mary, the wife of Dad's brother Charles. Mom stopped her conversation when I approached her with my stricken expression. I felt on the verge of tears and knew that a huge sob lingered in my throat. I tried to stay calm as I asked Mom to speak privately. She sensed trouble and took me in the guest bedroom where we could be alone. Behind the door she'd closed, I explained what had just happened and Mom didn't interrupt. She looked exhausted, not at all surprised or outraged. It was almost as if she always expected such a thing would happen here. She took my hand and led me through the room where I'd slept and out the front door.

Dad was leaning on the porch rail laughing with some of his cousins but stopped as he looked from my tight face to Mom's and back again. He asked what was wrong. Mom prompted me to tell my story in front of everyone. My description of Sonny's comment uncorked Dad's temper. When I had mocked Grandmother, Dad retreated into a brooding silence and had protected me from his anger. He hadn't even defended his own mother that day. But the throbbing vein in Dad's temple told me how much Sonny's insult infuriated him. He felt my hurt which made me frightened and happy all at once. He believed me instantly. Even though I'd lied to my friends about his mother and the house in which we stood, Dad didn't question my version of Sonny's remark. He flew into a rage and began cursing despite Grandmother's warnings to everyone to watch their language. Dad threw the storm door open and called my uncle by both his names. He hunted his brother in every room of the house and asked everyone if they'd seen Sonny.

Sonny mounted the porch as Dad came around the right side

of the house. Dad asked Sonny if what I'd said was true. Sonny said yes, and Dad demanded that Sonny apologize to me. These raised voices silenced every other conversation in the crowded yard, and all eyes rested on Sonny and Dad. Sonny refused to apologize. Deep hatred for Sonny welled up inside me. Any schoolkid knew that what he said to me was mean, and I couldn't believe he wouldn't take it back. I felt as mad as Dad. Sonny didn't have to tell me I was as pretty as Natalie, but the fact that he wouldn't apologize for hurting my feelings made me wish I could punch his lights out.

Dad told Sonny to keep his mouth shut and turned his back on his little brother. Sonny muttered something about Dad thinking himself a "big shot." *Why won't Sonny just apologize?* I thought.

I'd noticed the way that Sonny had rolled his eyes every time Dad had described our life in California. I guessed that he was jealous and thought Dad had been boasting. But ever since we'd arrived, people had just kept asking Dad about his business and the big new house we lived in. What could he do but explain? Besides, I knew how hard Dad and Mom had worked for our life; he had every right to be proud. In that moment, I realized Sonny had been nursing a grudge against Dad for a long time and had grown tired of standing in his older brother's shadow.

For all the fights we'd had, I couldn't imagine ever making Natalie this angry. Then again, I couldn't imagine saying anything so rude to my own niece. Dad spun around and stood nose to nose with Sonny. He threatened to make Sonny shut up. Sonny stepped down into the yard, raised his fists, and invited Dad to try.

Terror froze me where I stood.

Dad leapt from the porch and stood centimeters from Sonny.

My cousins stopped playing and retreated to the safety of the looming tree. Word of trouble spread like fire, and in an instant, men converged and women streamed out of the house. I hoped some adult would intervene in this impromptu squared circle. The cow-eyed stranger, even with the law on his side, didn't step between the men. He just shook his head and looked down. Grandfather and the rest of my uncles watched in fascination. Men laughed, but nothing felt funny to me. Someone might really get hurt.

Dad and Sonny stood chest to chest.

I knew the fighting was about to begin, and I couldn't have felt worse if I were about to fight. Hurt and fear swirled inside me, and I regretted repeating Sonny's words. I felt as though I carried the stink of trouble wherever I went. My lies were what had made a California Christmas impossible. My mischief was the reason we were at this house, around people who seemed to make Dad so tense. But Sonny had pushed Dad too far. I cowered beside Mom, looking for comfort, but she'd turned to stone. As much as I wanted to hide, I couldn't stop staring at Dad. I'd never seen him this angry about *anything*. I'd never seen Dad on the brink of a fistfight. I was terrified but mad at Sonny. I hoped Dad would win.

Dad and Sonny circled like bulls. Then Sonny shoved Dad. Contact. Ignition. The men locked their arms and wrapped their hands around each other's collarbones. Shoving and huffing, they kicked up lots of dust and began to perspire despite the chill.

My cousins, Anthony, John, and Kurt, cheered for their dad. Sonny's daughter Dana, who attended a "special school," stood mute, drifting oblivious in the separate world she always occupied. She hadn't uttered a complete sentence since we'd arrived, but that was normal for her. Sonny's wife, Leanna, just shook her head.

No one cheered for Dad, even though we were related to nearly everyone there and he was right to defend me. I couldn't figure out why. Natalie and Mom remained silent. I was too frightened to make a sound and couldn't do anything except watch. People called Sonny's name as though he was the hometown hero. Suddenly I felt the way I often did in California, like it was the four of us against everyone else. I didn't expect to feel such a thing among all these relatives.

Grandmother burst through the front door, shaking a long metal spoon and shouting at her two sons to stop ruining Christmas Day. But she intervened too late. Everyone who'd followed her instructions all morning ignored her now. Her ringlets jiggled as she shrieked and sounded as if she was crying. Over and over again, she called Dad and Sonny by their full names and ordered them to stop. She urged Charles and June, her other two sons, to break their fighting brothers apart, but neither listened to her. She didn't leave the porch but just kept screaming.

I wanted to scream, too.

Dad and Sonny continued to wrestle. Dad's moves were mostly defensive, but when Sonny finally tried to choke Dad, he put Sonny in a headlock. Sonny punched Dad in the side to loosen his hold. It seemed like a cheap shot, and Dad pushed Sonny to the porch railing. They fought like brothers and understood all the other's moves. Sonny tried to execute a full nelson but couldn't get a grip.

I glared at Grandfather, who smirked and grinned. At that moment, I hated him. I had seen him make more of an effort to end a dogfight than this confrontation between his two sons. I didn't know what he found so funny. But Dad was Grandfather's stepson and Sonny was his biological one. I wondered if that had something to do with why he was so passive. If Grandfather knew what Sonny had said to me, I wanted to think that he would have demanded an apology and told Sonny he was wrong, but I couldn't be sure. Grandmother glared at Grandfather and declared him "full of the devil." Grandfather only laughed more. I knew Grandmother was right.

Sonny and Dad wrestled all over the yard trying to strangle each other into submission. Through a clenched jaw and with flared nostrils, Dad kept demanding Sonny apologize. Sonny just shouted no. Neither man maintained the upper hand for long. The fighting persisted. Finally, Dad and Sonny unlocked in exhaustion. It was a stalemate, a draw, and each man retreated. Dad stalked out of the yard, slammed the gate, and disappeared down the street. Mom, Natalie, and I stood there and people began to whisper. No one said anything to us.

"Go and get you something to eat," Grandmother muttered over and over again. Grandmother looked as though she had fought. She kneaded her hands like dough, paced the porch, and shook her head. My aunt Vicie, Dad's youngest sister, disappeared into the house and then reemerged with a Coke. She handed it to Grandmother along with a little packet about the size of a stick of gum. Grandmother thanked her daughter and said that her nerves were "real bad." Grandmother sat back into the chair and tumbled the white powder—which Dad had whispered to us earlier was a sedative called "Stan Back"—into the bottle. It created a huge foamy head on the soda, and Grandmother gulped it like medicine.

Mom grabbed Natalie and me by the hand and led us inside

without a word. I had no clue where we were headed; I didn't ask any questions. I didn't care. My mind raced, but I wasn't thinking clearly. All I could do was maintain my grip on Mom—I couldn't afford to have my other parent disappear around these people.

I didn't feel at all hungry, but there was nothing else to do. I took a plate and got a chicken wing and a forkful of greens. I created a well in a little mountain of rice and ladled a bit of gumbo. Then I walked into the family room and sat beside Vicie's daughters Antoinette and Michelle. They were eating quietly and told me where to find another television tray. We talked about school and our hobbies every now and then, but mostly we just sat in silence. No one mentioned the fight.

I listened to Sonny's booming voice on the porch cracking jokes. He strutted through the house like he was the winner. But he kept out of my way and he stopped calling Natalie "Pretty." Mom wore her plastic polite face, but I didn't think anyone found it convincing. Dad stayed out of sight for so long that I really began to worry. Even as some people began to leave, Grandfather kept smoking meat in the barbeque outside. Grandmother nursed one Coca-Cola after another, each one accompanied by the powder.

New neighbors and relatives appeared. The officer, like many other people, lingered and ate into the early evening. Just before sunset, my remaining uncles, Charles and June, called the kids into the yard to light firecrackers. Sonny's kids got the most excited, but I stayed on the porch, out of their way, afraid of what I wanted to do to them. The magic had disappeared for me. This had been a strange and terrible Christmas, maybe the worst one ever. I wanted to go to bed and then back to California.

At about nine o'clock, Dad finally returned. He conferred with Mom for a minute and then walked straight to the telephone in the family room. We were supposed to stay for another three days. But I heard Dad talking to an operator about exchanging our tickets for the earliest flight back to California. When the lady told Dad we'd missed the last flight, he slammed the receiver back into place. He and Mom called one airline after another trying to find the earliest flight. They ordered me to bed, but I couldn't sleep.

Dad roused me before dawn. The house was silent, the street and yard nearly black. He told me it was time to go, that we were leaving right then. I leapt onto the cold floor and into clothes, shoes, and my coat. The warming car hummed in the driveway. Grandmother and Grandfather remained asleep. Dad nearly threw the suitcases into the trunk. Before we could even buckle ourselves, Dad gunned the engine, drove down the street, and back onto Highway 190, away from the past.

In 1952, three years before the murder of Emmett Till, my Dad was fifteen, the oldest son of parents who struggled to make ends meet. Dad gave Grandmother most of his wages to enable her to say what she would to her dying day, that her family "was poor but never hungry." Dad had held a job since he was seven years old— he picked cotton and rice and even worked as a houseboy. So his work as a gas station attendant was an improvement. Even with Dad's help, shoes were a luxury his family could not afford. Dad attended school and church and even worked in his bare feet.

The station owner, Mr. Donald, never used Dad's name; instead he called Dad "Little Tom." In addition to pumping gas, Dad chauffeured Mr. Donald wherever he wanted to go. Every day, Dad drove

Mr. Donald home for lunch in his black 1951 Ford pickup. Mr. Donald had a son around Dad's same age, but he didn't work at the station or drive his father's car. On these lunch trips, Mr. Donald sat in the passenger seat. Rex, Mr. Donald's hunting dog, sat in the middle. When they reached the house, Mr. Donald and Rex walked through the front door and into the house. Since Dad wasn't allowed in the house, he walked through the yard to reach the back porch.

As soon as she served her husband, Mrs. Donald opened the back door without speaking to Dad. She placed a plate of food on the porch, and Rex trotted out to eat his lunch. Then, Mrs. Donald handed another, identical plate to Dad. Dad and Rex ate together and waited until Mr. Donald was ready to return to the station.

Mr. Donald always told Dad the same joke on the drive back to work.

"Little Tom," Mr. Donald said. "Do you know the two most stupidest people in the world?"

"No, Mr. Donald, sir," Dad said.

"A nigger man and a white woman." Mr. Donald howled every time he told Dad that joke.

Dad escaped the afternoon heat by sitting in the garage where the mechanic kept a barrel of Liquid Rubber, used to patch holes in the inner tubes and tires. The Liquid Rubber stench always hung in the air. Sometimes Dad slept in a chair, with his feet propped on a box or a crate, until the service bell summoned him back outside.

One day, Mr. Donald's son snuck into the garage with a few of his pals. They coated a brush with Liquid Rubber and painted the thick skin on the soles of Dad's feet. Then they lit a match and stood back to watch Dad's feet burn. The boys doubled over with laughter as Dad awoke, his feet on fire. Dad scrambled and hopped to put out the fire, much to the delight of Mr. Donald's son and his pals. This prank of theirs became a regular pastime known as "hot foot."

For Dad, it was no game. But he knew better than to complain to Mr. Donald or strike Donald's son. Dad was a country boy and a Southerner who, unlike Emmett Till, knew better than to challenge the conventions of segregation. Dad never told his parents about hot foot. He just put out the fire, swallowed his feelings, and went back to work. Dad kept the job because the family needed the money, but he dreamed of leaving Elton forever. He saw the train tracks from the gas station and thought about taking the train out of town stashed with the cargo. Grandmother, who didn't know about hot foot, refused to help him. So instead, Dad spent his working hours and his little free time dreaming of California, writing his name and an imaginary California address on scraps and sheets of paper. Whenever Dad got a hot foot, he would just repeat his California address over and over again in his mind.

In late 2006, as I prepared to write this chapter, I asked my father about the Christmas trip and he told me this story for the first time.

{ chapter four }

EIGHT MILE ROAD

THE FIRST SUNDAY AFTERNOON of summer felt more relaxing than any Sunday I could remember. Around three o'clock, as I sat in an old oak chair beside the stove with a towel wrapped around my shoulders, I thought about the school year that had just ended. I had survived second grade without getting beaten up, cleaned out my desk, and said good-bye to the teacher who always disappeared when bullies cornered me. The summer ahead had to be better than the year just past, I told myself. Every ten seconds or so, I chased another stream of water that dripped from my hair. It was a cool June afternoon, and I couldn't keep up with the dripping water. My shirt collar already felt soaked and made me shiver. But nothing could ruin my first summer weekend.

Once a week we made the kitchen into a beauty parlor, the domain of women and girls. Dad cooked most of our family meals. Mom only cooked hair. But as long as we did hair, Dad didn't so much as get a glass of water until we were finished. The four-hour saga unfolded the same way every Sunday and was far too involved to use the bathroom. Dad knew what to expect. He'd just sit in the family room watching television with the volume turned up loud.

Just getting to the chair had taken an hour. I had shuttled up and down the stairs gathering hair grease, shampoo, conditioner, an Afro pick—with the Black Power fist—and a wide-toothed comb. I also carried a plastic bristle brush molded into a steel back and handle. We called it the steel brush, and I'd never seen another one like it. Mom had owned it since she was a teenager.

My hair grew out of my head, but it did not belong to me. As far back as I could remember, I had heard stories about the complicated nature of my hair—the special care it demanded, the challenges it presented, what it said about our entire family. Black girls didn't ever wash our own hair, our mothers did. Black girls didn't control our own hair in virtually any way. Brush or comb it? Mom did that. Choose my own hairstyle? Never. I had to abide by Mom's strict three-braid rule because she thought that any more than three braids made me look too much like a "ghetto girl." Most weekdays, Mom woke me up before she left for work, braided my hair, tied a scarf on my head, and sent me back to bed for an extra hour of sleep. I couldn't carry a comb or a brush to school like my white friends. My only and most important job was to keep my hands away from my hair. If I didn't, I got in *big* trouble.

That Sunday, I'd managed to sit still in the chair long enough for Mom to remove my ribbons and ponytail holders and unbraid my hair. Next came the wash. I climbed onto the counter like a pro, stretched out my legs, and reclined into the kitchen sink. Mom held my head in her hand and shampooed and rinsed my hair three times. I kept my eyes closed as she applied the conditioner and rinsed again. I winced but didn't complain as Mom ran the wide-toothed comb through my hair to remove the last tangles.

Mom flipped on the blow-dryer to its highest setting and it roared to life. It blasted my hair and scalp with so much heat that I began to sweat, even under the damp shirt. Mom trapped a section of my hair between the steel brush and the dryer and worked from my scalp to the ends of my hair. Smoke billowed. My ears rung. By the time she'd finished, my hair felt light and bushy, and it moved and bounced. I couldn't help but shake my head with wonder like the ladies in the Breck shampoo commercials.

Mom was too short to reach the high cabinet where she stored the most precious tools she owned. So every Sunday I'd stand on the chair to retrieve the metal pressing comb and the curler. They were relics, seasoned with years of use. The comb had stubby metal teeth set close together on a rounded barrel spine. A faded blue wooden handle wrapped around the shaft of the comb. It smelled like charcoal, and a black notch marked the spot where the stove had burnt the wood. The curling iron was all black metal and as slick as a skillet. Its straight handles crossed like scissors, and a screw held them together.

As soon as I sat back down, Mom turned on the front burner of the electric stove. In an instant, the coils glowed red. She placed the pressing comb on the center of the coil and balanced it on the burnt notch. Mom sectioned my hair. She unscrewed the jar of Hair Food, the fluorescent yellow hair grease that looked like electric Vaseline and smelled like lemon furniture polish. She spread a glob into her palm to melt it, ran her hands through my hair and then through the exposed parts of my scalp.

"You are going to wear your hair down for the trip," Mom said.

I couldn't believe what I was hearing because Mom so rarely spoke these words. With tightly coiled hair like mine that curled elaborately and tangled in the presence of moisture, straight hair marked special occasions. Pressed hair remained a precious treat that meant fancy party dresses, buckle shoes, and white tights. It meant I got to wear my frilly poncho and carry my very own purse. Pressed hair meant Shirley Temple cocktails ordered with extra maraschino cherries, just the way I liked them. Long hair meant lobster with drawn butter at the Palm, the Los Angeles steakhouse where sawdust covered the floor. Long hair was Christmas morning, an Easter egg hunt, and my best birthday party all rolled into one. Long hair made me feel pretty.

The fact that I'd be wearing my hair down clarified everything that had puzzled me about the next day's trip to Detroit, Mom's hometown. It made sense of Mom's frantic washing, ironing, and packing our best outfits into the suitcases. It also shed light on why Mom had bought us new play clothes even though we hadn't outgrown the ones we had. For the first time since I'd learned of it, my hair made me excited about visiting Detroit. If I had the chance to wear my hair long, some very special people must be there, even though I knew hardly any of them and hadn't been there since I was a toddler. My long hair finally told me how much going home to Detroit meant to Mom, and in that moment, my hair made it a big deal for me.

The magic began when Mom picked up the pressing comb. She positioned her hand an inch below the notch. Smoke spiraled. Mom set the comb on a folded stack of toilet paper squares to test the heat. It scorched the tissues and left a brown imprint. In another minute Mom licked her index finger and grazed the comb to retest. It was perfect. She grabbed a section of hair on my crown and pulled it straight into the air, then pressed the comb as close to my roots as she could.

Both Mom and I were too busy to make conversation. She judged the heat and tension of the comb. I concentrated on remaining perfectly still. As the teeth of the comb met my hair, the sweat on my scalp sizzled, and steam burnt me. It seemed like I had the easier job, but it took a lot of effort to suppress my natural reflex to flinch when a burning piece of hot metal passed millimeters from my skin. Mom almost never burnt me and she kept the butter beside the stove just in case she slipped. I still feared the comb, but I hardly blinked even when Mom straightened the shortest baby hairs that framed my face. Second by second, I combated my instinctive desire to flee. The fake lemon aroma of the hot Hair Food couldn't cover the stench of my own burnt hair. I held still and tried not to fidget.

Mom reduced the heat on the stove and set the comb down on the eye. She placed an old cloth diaper in the palm of her hand and picked up the comb again. This time, she rotated the comb so that the teeth faced up and the spine rested on my hair. She ironed my hair into the cloth. It yielded instantly and became straight.

Another hour later and Mom was done. I couldn't believe that the flowing mane that skimmed my shoulders belonged on my head. My hair moved with the softest shake of my head and felt nearly weightless. I had hair like the models on television. I stroked my silky tresses with the palm of my hand and could barely control my delight. I felt like the newest member of an elite club. All I needed to do was swipe my lips with Chap-Stick and swish down a mountain like the blond skier, "Suzy ChapStick."

"Can I brush it?" I asked, positive Mom would refuse.

"You may," she said as she placed the steel brush in my hand like a scepter. "Just a little."

I walked over to the double ovens that became my mirror. I tilted my head to the left and let my hair hang on my shoulder. The brush glided freely and I grinned. My hair made me feel free and Mom hadn't stopped me. So I did what I saw older white girls do all the time. I bent at my waist and brushed the underside of my hair. Then I whipped my head up so fast that the room spun for a second.

"Okay, Jen," Mom said, "that's enough." She held out her hand. I could've played with my hair all night but knew I had to surrender the brush. My nearly singed hair could break with too much brushing.

"Sit down and let me curl your bangs," Mom said. She picked up the curling iron and clanked the barrel and the shaft together. More smoke rose. The clapping metal and squeaking hinge made a strange music. Mom made a horizontal part in my hair to create the bangs, caught the end of my hair with the curling iron, and rolled back toward my head in a single under-handed motion. I was too thrilled to even fear a burn, which seemed like a small price to pay for such good luck. Now I had bangs and felt just like a Rose Parade Queen.

Mom, Natalie, and I landed in Detroit the next afternoon, while Dad stayed in California to work. But our arrival felt far from a pressed-hair moment. When we stepped onto the Jetway, the muggy heat hit me. I walked into the terminal and spotted my grandmother immediately. I hadn't seen her in three years, since she'd stayed at our old house for a few days, but I recognized her immediately. Grandmother wore casual clothes—green double-knit pants, a short-sleeved shirt, and laced oxfords. Her skin, the color of milky tea, stretched tightly across her perfectly round face and the backs of her arms where it sagged on other women her age. A lifetime of healthy eating had kept her lean and strong. Grandmother had a round, broad face that I searched for a resemblance to my mom. I could not find one.

I looked up at Mom, her bouncy, relaxed hair curled off her

face, her freshly applied makeup. She smiled with all of her teeth and stepped in front of us.

"Hello, Mother," Mom said. Even as she flooded her voice with warmth and embraced my grandmother, who was even shorter than she was, the formality of Mom's greeting surprised me.

"Janet," Grandmother warbled. It was the voice that I remembered. I smirked as soon as Grandmother spoke. Grandmother had the strangest voice I'd ever heard. She began her sentences in a screeching soprano. Then midway through the sentence, a raspy alto emerged from deep within her throat, almost like a huge burp. She used the words *yeah* and *hmmmm* like commas and periods to rest her voice. Natalie and I suppressed giggles every time the floor dropped out of her voice. A voice like Grandmother's was unforgettable, no matter how little of it I'd heard.

It felt strange to think of Mom as somebody's daughter.

Then Mom moved over and urged Natalie forward to say hello.

"Hello, Grandmother," I said when it was my turn.

"Jennifer," she said. Grandmother was short and thin, but her embrace was strong and her skin stretched over the muscles on her arms. Her eyes danced as she gave me a wide, closed-lipped smile. A longish salt-and-pepper Afro crowned her head. I thought of my own hair, pressed into submission, and felt awkward.

"Hi, Jan," I heard Grandmother's husband, Al, say in a soft, shaky voice. No one called Mom Jan.

Al wore a cream-colored shirt, burgundy plaid slacks, and a straw hat. He wasn't my mom's father, but he responded when I called him Grandfather. He spoke more slowly than anyone I'd ever met and loved to tell sad stories that took forever. His eyes watered all the time and he seemed so glum. He had flabby lips and always gave slobbery kisses. But he was kind.

"Well, Mr. Howard," Mom replied as she forced the warmth into her voice. She held out her hand for a shake as she pressed her cheek to his but didn't kiss him.

"Hello, Grandfather," I said as he planted a wet kiss on my cheek.

We gathered our brown Samsonite suitcases from the baggage claim conveyor belt. My sister and I trailed behind Al, who carried the matching bags.

We arrived at Grandmother's Monopoly-sized house on Monte Vista Road, a nondescript street in a working-class north Detroit neighborhood. Grandmother and Al welcomed us, but there was no fuss—no special meal, just a bland but healthy dinner and fruit for dessert. Mom braided my hair. We watched Al's favorite show, *Wheel of Fortune*, and went to bed. I slept in the front bedroom crammed between Natalie and the wall, listening to the sounds of the Detroit summer night and thinking about my hair.

The next morning, after a bowl of bran flakes and a piece of dry toast, Mom swung the car onto Eight Mile Road, the bustling street that marked the northernmost edge of Detroit. I got my first real look at the city and its residents. It was like a parallel universe compared to Los Angeles. The low-slung skyline made the day seem dingy. Rust-pocked American cars cruised the streets like tugboats. I didn't see a single one of the Japanese imports that crowded the freeways at home. I didn't see a single white person either. Black people walked down the street and waited at the bus stop. Almost every older black man I saw sported either a jaunty straw fedora with a feather or a baseball cap to match his factory uniform. Some women fanned themselves against the crushing heat as others tried to contain screaming kids.

All I saw were the liquor stores, pawnshops, convenience stores, and barbershops, but Mom saw much more. She chattered about all the fun she'd had on Eight Mile and pointed to storefronts that remained the same. She described the pack of cousins who used to roam this strip for adventure. None of my own cousins lived close enough to roam the streets. Eight Mile, Mom explained, was the main drag of her early life.

I'd never seen Mom this excited. At home, Mom never told stories about Detroit or her childhood, no matter how many times I asked her what she was like as a girl. Mom usually focused so intently on the present that the past seemed irrelevant. Only when I really persisted did Mom relent and tell me something she liked as a girl, but it was always trivia and never a story. She never talked about this place as fondly as she just had, which made me confused.

We swung into the far lane and turned left down a street called Westview.

"Girls, this is the Township," Mom said. "It's aged a bit, but this is where I grew up. This is it."

Natalie and I craned our necks looking for *it*. The houses on this side of Eight Mile Road were older, two or three stories instead of just one, built from bricks rather than vinyl siding. Some houses looked rundown, with overgrown grass and weeds in the yard. Trees lined the streets and their roots buckled the sidewalks. Hunting dogs howled, and then I saw packs of them pace behind chain-link fences. Even though these lots were twice the size of the ones on Monte Vista, they seemed too small to contain these dogs that appeared agitated in the city. They were fierce, well muscled, and alert, anxious to get off the leash and track a fox or a raccoon through the woods.

Mom pulled the car into the driveway of the biggest house on the block. The two-story brick house looked like several others I'd seen but felt more formal, better tended than any other one. Heavy curtains covered every window. The edged and perfectly trimmed grass matched the tailored shrubs beneath the porch. Next door I saw grassy space that seems like a private park. Peach and cherry trees bloomed. A picnic table rested beside a grill along with scattered lawn chairs.

Mom turned around to inspect me, licked her thumb, and motioned for me to come closer. She wiped stray toast crumbs from my cheek. Then she slanted the rearview toward her face, fluffed her hair, and pressed her lips together. She stepped out into the heat and Natalie and I trailed behind her like ducklings.

"Okay, girls," she said. "Let's go see Aunt Frenchie."

I'd already met all of Mom's sisters, so I wasn't sure how this woman I'd never met was supposed to be my aunt. But by then, I'd learned to follow Mom's hopscotch logic in silence. Since we'd arrived she'd become annoyed every time I asked her to clarify someone's relationship to me. At Grandmother's house, Mom acted like she had spoken of these people millions of times and that I had not paid attention. But I knew that at home Mom never talked about Detroit relatives, people with peculiar names like Frenchie and Cree, Barnum and Bailey, Sonny Boy and Standish.

Mom rang the doorbell and then smiled at us. This was all very peculiar.

A moment later the door opened and a hummingbird of a

woman stood before us. She was short, just over five feet tall. She and Mom shared the same beak of a nose. Her ageless mahogany skin shone like lacquer. Her thick wavy hair hung down her back and nearly reached her Barbie-sized waist. Her perfectly manicured hands gleamed with gold rings. She resembled Mom more than anyone I had ever met, even Grandmother. She was probably in her sixties and was the most elegant woman I had ever seen. She wore a robe and still looked regal. I immediately understood that Mom had pressed my hair to meet Aunt Frenchie. I couldn't take my eyes off her.

Mom and Frenchie embraced in the darkened vestibule of the house, rocking back and forth for a moment. The strong bond between the two became more obvious as the seconds passed. They kept holding hands. Mom acted less formal and more affectionate than with her own mother.

They inspected each other as they continued to hold hands.

"Janet," Frenchie said. "It's so good to see you."

"Aunt Frenchie," Mom said, hugging the woman again, "you haven't changed."

"I still have my twenty-four-inch waist," Frenchie said as she gathered her hands around her middle "and I still weigh one hundred and twenty-four pounds."

They chuckled exactly the same way. Frenchie and Mom both shared the same crisp diction and intonation. I marveled at this slightly smaller, older version of my own mother.

Aunt Frenchie threw her arms open to Natalie and me and said, "I'm your aunt Frenchie." I loved how she staked her claim as she embraced me with surprising strength. I could feel her thin bones. She held me in her arms as though she already knew and loved me.

We were standing in the living room then, just beyond the vestibule, and I squinted against the dark cool air that filled the house. The dim lights bounced off the cherry dining table, matching buffet, and china cabinet. My eye caught the yellowing plastic that covered every sofa and chair in the living room to my right. Aunt Frenchie only needed a few velvet ropes to make the room into a museum. We walked through an archway into the kitchen that looked straight out of *Leave It to Beaver*, with white metal cabinets and a black-and-white checkerboard floor.

We passed into the den, bookcases crowding the walls, but photo albums rather than books lined the shelves all arranged by style and size. Frenchie perched in a club chair as if she sat on a throne. Mom sat closest to Frenchie on the coordinating leather sofa, with Natalie in the middle, and me on the end.

She handed Mom the album on the coffee table.

"Janet, this is your book," Aunt Frenchie said.

Tucked inside the front cover, I recognized Mom's handwriting and realized that she had been sending Easter cards and Christmas letters for years, each one enclosed in its original envelope, arranged by postmark. On the first page, I saw Mom, Dad, Natalie, and me standing in front of our old house on Verde Ridge Road. The four pictures were stuck to the adhesive on the page and covered in plastic. I saw our school pictures and finally understood why Mom usually ordered the deluxe package of school pictures every year—to send them to relatives like Frenchie. On the next page, a perfectly trimmed magazine article announced the creation of Baszile Metals Service, Dad's new company.

"I keep a book for everybody," Aunt Frenchie explained to Natalie and me. "Our family is really doing some great things."

Frenchie named one person after another and described their recent high school graduation, college degrees, or job promotion. Mom didn't explain these people's relationships to Natalie or me, but I could follow the trail of accomplishment even if I still didn't recognize the names. Frenchie knew all of the family firsts, all of the milestones, and every distinction everyone had earned. She flipped through this catalog of family achievement in her mind like a Rolodex. She was so proud.

"But," Frenchie said to Mom, "you know our family has always had it together."

I was confused. There was so much to talk about, I couldn't figure out why Mom had been so quiet at home, why we hadn't made trips to visit Frenchie and meet our other relatives before. Frenchie's version of our family was so dazzling, so upbeat. I couldn't figure out why Mom had chosen to let us live in such a lonely way in California. *Why had she moved to California at all?* I'd assumed that we just didn't have much family on Mom's side, but the albums told me I'd been wrong. We had plenty of family.

Mom nodded eagerly.

"Can the girls see the basement?" Mom asked.

I had no idea what could be so interesting about a basement. No one in Southern California had a basement, and I'd never seen one before. At the bottom of the stairs, Natalie and I entered a place that looked like a saloon. The room seemed ready for a party. Red leather booths decorated the perimeter wall. A Wurlitzer jukebox, filled with 45s, stood in a corner. Rows of liquor bottles lined the shelves of a mirrored wall enclosed by a red leather bar. The wood countertop gleamed as did the matching bar stools. I bent down on my knees to look more closely at the metal specks inlaid in the floor. They were silver dollar pieces. I couldn't figure out why anyone would have destroyed money to decorate a floor.

At the back of the room, I opened a door and smelled cedar. Rack upon rack of hangers draped with plastic bags crowded the room. It was like Frenchie's private costume closet and she could play dress-up whenever she liked. Broom skirts, in every shade of the color wheel, spanned an entire rack. With their tiny waistbands and the folds of fabric at the hem, I understood how these favored Frenchie's figure. I also understood why Frenchie wore a robe around the house—choosing an outfit from this collection could take all morning.

I wondered where Frenchie had worn all of these clothes and the kind of life she led to need all of them. There were too many outfits and combinations for any single person to wear in an entire lifetime. The collection was its own kind of clock, and I could tell it marked seasons, years, and even decades. She'd devoted one rack to slacks in winter white, gray, and black, navy blue, powder blue, and red. Coats of every conceivable length and weight hung on another rack. Fur jackets and stoles drooped on another rack. Full-length mink, fox, and beaver rested in another section. Although the styles varied, the size of the clothes did not. This was the most immaculate collection of clothes I had ever seen.

Frenchie's wardrobe also told me something new about Mom, who had always worried about how things looked. If Frenchie hadn't invented the three-braid rule, I was sure she understood it. With Frenchie as an aunt, Mom had grown up in a world where clothes and hair—appearance—were an obsession. Mom fussed about my "look," as she called it, because pressed hair, like immaculate clothes, told stories as much as pictures did for Mom and Frenchie.

Frenchie's clothes clarified the pattern I'd seen in her scrapbooks. Every photograph captured a dazzling moment. Not a single person scowled or frowned in her world. She had sorted and
preserved only the pictures of composed delight. Women wearing
mink coats, sparkly jewels, and pointy heels clustered together.
Dapper men leaned on the hoods of gleaming cars. Well-scrubbed
children stood still and displayed toothy smiles. Everyone was
perfect on the pages. No one was upset or even mildly troubled.

I didn't know anybody who lived that way; we certainly didn't.
Even though we had our own album, and I recognized our smiling faces, I knew how much effort it took to get us to look picture perfect. Most days our life in California felt confusing and
hurried; sometimes even frightening. Thinking about the tense
and scary parts of our experience made me think about what was
missing from our album. For all of the clippings, the "Go Home
Niggers" article was absent. I began to wonder what Frenchie
had left out of the other family albums. How much were her
albums and photos a mirage?

I still thought about the albums as Natalie and I left the
basement and went back into the study. Mom and Frenchie
lowered their voices as we reached the top step of the basement staircase and stopped talking altogether as we entered the
study. Their silence told me that they had been having an adult
conversation.

"What did you think of that basement, girls?" Mom asked.
Her voice, just a little higher than usual, was the one she used to
try to divert us or when she wanted to change the subject.

"It was really neat," I replied, looking from Mom to Frenchie,
hoping to detect a thread of conversation or sense the mood.
But Frenchie had turned her face to stone in the exact same way

Mom did when she wanted to hide her thoughts and feelings. Frenchie sat perfectly still. Without knowing what Frenchie was concealing, I knew where Mom had inherited her ability to drop the curtain on her face. When Dean women wanted to keep a secret, they kept it.

"It was really neat," I said, again keeping my eyes on Aunt Frenchie. "It looks like you could really have fun."

"We had some grand times down there. Didn't we, Janet?" Aunt Frenchie said.

I headed over to the couch, excited to hear about the grand times. Even though I'd seen lots of pictures, I wanted to hear stories.

"We sure did, Aunt Frenchie," Mom said as she rose from her seat before I could get to mine. "Girls, it's time to go."

Leave? What about the stories? I wanted to stay and listen. *Why couldn't we stay longer?* We were on vacation. But I looked at Mom's face. Her eyes looked sad, as though the adult conversation had upset her. Even though I'd never seen Mom cry, I wondered if this was the way her face looked just before she cried. Maybe Mom really meant that the time of the grand basement parties and high times in Detroit had ended. Mom was ready to go. We were leaving.

Frenchie didn't try to change Mom's mind. She smoothed her robe as she stood, put her arm around Mom's waist, and they headed through the kitchen for the door. Frenchie was the smaller of the two women, but she looked as though she was supporting Mom. I saw my confusion reflected on Natalie's face. She'd wanted to hear the basement stories as much as I did. But, like me, something in the moment had told her to follow instructions. We walked behind Mom and Frenchie in silence.

When we got to the door Mom and Frenchie lingered in their embrace, and I thought I heard Mom sniffle. Frenchie gave Mom another big hug, then walked over to Natalie and me.

She hugged me and then took my face in her hands, as though holding a treasure.

"Be good," she said to me.

Then she did the same to Natalie. We said good-bye to Frenchie and left her alone with her clothes and her albums.

As we drove along in the car, I mulled over the same questions. *If girlhood had been so sunny for Mom, if she belonged to such a proud and wealthy family here, why had she left to go to California? Why didn't we spend more time here? Why hadn't she shared any of the great stories that the pictures and scrapbooks suggested?*

Mom killed the car engine in front of a neat house that felt less like a showplace. Aunt Eva opened the door before we knocked and greeted us warmly, in her tender and good-natured way. I instantly recognized Eva's resemblance to Frenchie. They shared the same red mahogany skin and beaklike noses. Eva was fuller-figured with an ample bosom and wide hips, like Mom. She wore her hair in a short bouffant that flipped up at the back. Eva's hands were exactly as I recalled them, large and free of rings. Her nails were unpolished.

Besides Grandmother, Aunt Eva was the only Detroit relative I could remember visiting our old house. It had been three years ago, when she came to Los Angeles for a massage therapist convention. *Masseuse* was such a funny word, and I had pestered Aunt Eva with questions until she offered to show me what she did. I'd stretched out on my bed and she kneaded my limbs with ease and knowing. Her firm but gentle pressure had forced all the tension from my body, and I felt as though I'd slipped into a dream.

We gathered at Aunt Eva's dining room table. There was much less plastic here, and the furniture looked inviting and comfortable. Aunt Eva disappeared down a hallway and returned a few moments later with a bulging photo album of her own. This album looked nothing like the ones I'd just seen. The edges of the photographs stuck out at all angles, and Eva struggled to make sure none of them dropped to the floor.

"Come here, girls," Eva said to Natalie and me. "Do you recognize anyone in this picture?"

I stared at the bent photograph that rested on the tablecloth. It was a black-and-white image of some kids. These boys and girls didn't pose; they sat and stood on wooden steps looking in all different directions as though almost ignoring the camera. All these kids shared nearly the exact same glistening dark skin tone and looked enough alike in various ways for me to guess that most of them were somehow related. My eyes rested on a little girl, maybe four years old, who stared off into the distance with slightly sad eyes. She had a broad forehead that she had wrinkled as if she were deep in thought. Her crooked half-smile made her look funny and a little naughty, as though she tried to hide trouble or a secret from the camera. She wore three braids, a thick one leaning over her left side, and the two back ones mostly concealed by the collar of her heavy coat. Underneath, it looked like she wore a sweater and a pair of pants—play clothes. She looked as though she had as much trouble as I did keeping clothes clean. I liked this girl.

Natalie guessed that the girl was Mom first. Aunt Eva confirmed it. I marveled, astonished. It wasn't just that I'd never seen this particular picture of Mom as a girl, it was that I had never seen a *single* picture of Mom as a child. No pictures of family hung on the walls of our house or decorated mantels or bookshelves. Grandmother didn't display pictures of her own children in her house either. Mom seemed amused by the picture, but our shock at never having seen her as a girl embarrassed her a little bit. I couldn't believe it, even though I knew it was true. But it wasn't just the pictures, it was the silence that surrounded Mom's girlhood. At home, I'd always assumed that she hadn't told stories because there were none to tell, but this picture corrected me. There were plenty of stories. *Why hadn't Mom shared them with me?*

Aunt Eva started reminiscing about Mom playing marbles with her cousins, wandering through open fields on her way home from school, and running to the corner store for candy. She even recalled Mom's love of old clothes and the way that she always tried to sneak and wear her favorite things that Grandmother had put into the rag bag. It all sounded great, but Mom's mischievousness puzzled me as much as her sadness.

I continued to stare at the Little Janet. She looked like my kind of girl, someone who would share an ice cream cone or dig for worms. Little Janet seemed spunky. I knew that if we'd met back then, we'd have been buddies. But my introduction to Little Janet also made it even harder for me to understand Mom's frustration about my messy room. I wanted to know where Little Janet had gone.

"Janet, have you seen these pictures?" Eva asked as she laid out more pictures. "I just found them in my trunk."

Mom's gasp answered the question.

The first picture was sepia more than black and white, older than the ones of Little Janet. A man in a double-breasted pinstriped suit, a crisp white shirt, and a perfectly knotted tie stood at a slight angle. He barely smiled, but his eyes had a relaxed grin in them. His profile showcased the strong chin formed by his underbite. The man's trousers broke perfectly at his shins, and the cuffs skimmed his glistening dress shoes, just the way that Dad's always did. The man in the picture clasped a white bowler hat. He stood straight but easily in his suit, proud and delighted.

"That's Daddy!" Mom exclaimed. "I've never seen this picture."

Daddy? It was just a word, but I'd never heard Mom refer to her father at all, let alone speak of him in such an intimate and lively way. Mom's father had been a phantom until this moment. I didn't even know his name. I didn't ask, because Mom's voice sounded so different—smaller, tender, and younger—as if Little Janet might emerge any second.

"That's Mammon," Aunt Eva said, looking from Natalie to me.

Mammon. *What a strange name,* I thought as I repeated it over and over again in my head so that I could remember it. Where had it come from? Mammon looked just like his sisters, Eva and Frenchie, but he and Mom resembled each other even more closely. I finally had found the source of all of Mom's features. I recognized Mom's long forehead in him. I found Mom's eyes in his face. Seeing my grandfather for the first time shocked me even more than meeting Little Janet.

"That was taken probably a few years after Mammon came to Detroit," Eva said. "Maybe ten years before the accident."

Accident? What accident? My mind felt as though it might burst with the force of questions that swirled inside me. Fear of what I didn't know made me anxious. I began to panic and feared that if I didn't ask Aunt Eva the questions, I might never get the answers. Mom never spoke of her father in California. I could never remember her mentioning an accident. *What kind of accident did he have? Why hadn't I met him before?* I didn't trust that Mom would answer my questions later, even if she could. So standing next to Aunt Eva, I fixed my gaze on my great-aunt, ignored Mom, and asked all the questions I didn't know to ask before that moment.

Aunt Eva patted the back of my hand to stem the tide of them and smiled to quiet Mom's protests. Then she began to tell us a story.

Eva explained that Mammon was the oldest of eight kids. He was born in the little town of Georgiana, Alabama, where both sides of his family had lived since slavery. They had become sharecroppers who found it harder and harder to stay ahead of the expenses for their growing family. When Mammon was about twelve, he and his father traveled to Pennsylvania to work in the coal mines, hard work that Mammon hated. They returned home for a short time but set out again looking for better jobs. Finally, in 1915, news that Henry Ford had just doubled the daily wage to five dollars to work on the Model T assembly line attracted Mammon, his brothers, his father, and uncles to Detroit.

While the other men worked on the assembly line, Mammon sought another way to make a living. He started a policy business, a kind of gambling operation. He traveled from one house to another, deep into the suburbs where he collected money that people bet on certain numbers. When their number hit, he returned to pay out the winnings. Mammon took the profits and bought vacant lots all over the Township and brought the rest of his siblings, his mother, and other relatives to Detroit.

"He was killed," Mom blurted suddenly. She looked stricken

and turned her head away from us as though on the verge of tears.

"How?" I asked as a long seam ripped inside me. The thought of Mom crying really scared me. I didn't want to see it, but I wanted to know what had happened.

"He was out collecting a policy a few streets over and a drunk man ran him down as he opened his car door," she said, her voice sounding small and flat as though she was a girl reliving that day. Sadness pinched her usually bright face. Speaking that one sentence seemed to have exhausted Mom.

"I was three when he died," she said another second later.

Three years old? I was eight and the thought of Dad being killed filled me with fear. Dad had come to school to defend me, we'd scrubbed the cherub when our house was attacked. *Who had gone to school when Mom had trouble? Who had defended Mom?* Then I thought about the picture of Little Janet on the steps and understood her hard, sad expression in a different way. It was taken not too long after Mammon's death.

The whir of the air conditioner made the only sound in the room for a minute. The pain of what we'd just shared overwhelmed all of us. I could feel Mom's anguish and saw for the first time the pain in her girlhood. I suspected that the loss explained why Mom didn't tell many stories. It was too hard. Aunt Eva looked at each of us and then drew the pictures back to her side of the table. Even though the story upset me, I was glad that Aunt Eva had told us about Mammon and showed his picture. I was relieved that Mom had explained his death to me. But for all my relief, I could tell that Aunt Eva looked worried, like all the sadness about Mammon might ruin our visit.

Once she'd slid some of the pictures back into the album, she broke the tension with a question.

"Do you girls know that we're sitting in a Hall house?" Eva asked. She knew we needed to change the subject.

"What's a Hall house?" I asked.

She explained that her mother, Ruby, came from the Hall family, a long line of bricklayers and carpenters. When they were slaves in Georgiana, they were famous for their skill. After slavery ended, they went to a place called the Tuskegee Institute for more vocational training. When they came north to work at Ford, they built houses for themselves and all of the Halls and Deans who followed.

She described the plan that all Hall houses follow. A basement beneath the house, then on the first floor they built a vestibule, kitchen, living room, dining room, bedroom, and half bathroom, and three bedrooms and a full bathroom upstairs. They built every Hall house from brick and sometimes created different exterior designs in them. The only difference was whether the door was located on the left or the right side of the house. I looked around the house all over again and marveled at the fact that my own relatives built it. I pondered what it must've been like to build a house from scratch and then keep it in the family for more than a half century.

Eva left the room and returned in another minute with a strange-looking contraption. It was covered in rust and dented. But Eva cradled it in her lap as if it was a treasure. The base was so bent that it wobbled. I'd never seen anything like it, except an old phonograph, but the handle was in the wrong place, on top of the metal chute rather than on the side. She explained that Ann Stamps, her other grandmother, kept this coffee grinder and passed it down to her mother Ma Ruby, and on to her. She turned the coffee grinder over and slipped out a piece of old paper from the corner of the base. Then she carefully unfolded the crumbling paper that explained that during slavery the women in our family passed down the coffee grinder from one generation to another.

"Their skills and this coffee grinder were the only things they took with them from slavery," Eva said. "They tried to leave all the rest of it behind."

I didn't know exactly what she meant by "the rest" but knew enough to know that it must have been terrible.

"You should have this now," Eva said as she placed the grinder on the table in front of Mom.

Mom looked stunned and closer to tears than ever. She stroked the grinder and sniffed.

We sat at the table for another hour or more, hearing stories, sorting through photographs, asking questions. Before we left, Mom asked Aunt Eva if she could get copies made of some of the oldest pictures we'd seen and promised to bring them back before we headed home to California. Aunt Eva agreed. We all embraced Aunt Eva again and said long good-byes at the door. I didn't want to leave. I could've stayed in that house all day, stood beside Eva, and heard her version of our family story. It was more complicated than Frenchie's pressed version; jumbled and painful but more clear. I felt happy that I learned so much more than I'd known before but remained confused about why Mom had so rarely discussed this place and these people. It made me curious about what else I still didn't know.

As we wound through the Township, Natalie and I devised a new game, spotting Hall houses. We raced to see which of us could spot one first and Mom declared the winner. The game also became a family history lesson because each time we spotted another house that my great-great-uncles had built, Mom described who lived there. As she offered details and shared funny stories, I could feel Mom's delight in our interest and pride.

The rest of the trip was filled with fun and adventure. Grandmother's basement became a source of added fascination after the trip into Frenchie's world. After we got Grandmother's permission, we examined every crevice in the mornings after breakfast. We met more relatives, heard more stories, and some things began to make better sense. We traveled to meet Grandmother's sister, Aunt Rose, on her dairy farm, and even visited Uncle Ray's vacation house in Canada. But nothing compared to our first day in the Township where I saw Mom in such a different way. I had seen her in ways I never had before: young and pained. But for as many questions as that day answered, scores of new questions about my mother took root in my mind.

For as long as I could remember, Mom had kept an old steamer trunk in the guest room of every house we'd lived in. I realized she had learned that from Aunt Eva. The trunk was from another era—worn brown wood and dry leather straps. The lock still worked, but the key was long lost. Inside Mom kept our family treasures—Natalie's meticulous baby album, imprints of our infant feet, and impressions of our little hands cast in clay. Mom tucked holiday cards into one another alongside old letters in their envelopes. She arranged fading photographs and slides by year as carefully as Frenchie did. Soccer ribbons and sashes full of merit badges folded into the corner. Whenever our names or faces appeared in the local paper, Mom put a clipping into the trunk. The trunk held every certificate Natalie and I had ever earned. No matter how small our part, Mom collected at least one program from each of our school plays or community theater performances. Under the chipped hinged lid rested evidence of all of our triumphs and all of our family's highest highs.

When we returned to California a few days later, Mom took the envelope full of pictures she'd had duplicated from Eva's stash to the specialty frame shop and spent hours trying to match pictures and frames. Natalie and I brought her one frame after another, trying to be helpful because we were all so excited about hanging the pictures. But Mom took her time and politely dismissed our suggestions. She wanted the frames to be perfect. She selected a few gold ones to hold her parents' wedding picture and the portrait of Mammon. She chose four weathered frames that looked as though they had been fashioned from wood ripped from the side of an old barn.

At home, I looked over Mom's shoulder as she placed the photos of her parents in the gold frames that complemented the pictures. The corners of Mom's eyes wrinkled every time she saw the image of her father. She ran her finger over the glass, even after she polished it. Looking at him seemed to hurt. I couldn't tell whether the pain was because she'd nearly forgotten what he was like because she was so young when he died, or if the memory of his death and his absence was so sharp for her. Mom put the pictures in the little library that she had just added on to the house. It was a beautiful room, formal and slightly cold, filled with porcelain figurines, a small antique desk, and old books. But we never sat in this room, so no one would see the pictures that often.

After she'd finished with her parents' pictures, Mom turned her attention to the four older photographs. I stared at pictures of my great-grandparents, Ruby Hall and Russell Dean as young people. I also studied the pictures of my great-great-grandparents—Mary Dean Ballard and Mack Hall. Mom had the framer cut two openings in the mat, one for the picture and the other for a buff piece of parchment that she had singed on the stove. On it she had written each person's name and the family lineage down to Natalie and me.

Mom removed an oil painting from the family room wall and hung the four pictures on the wall alongside the coffee grinder. Even though I didn't ask her, I guessed that Mom's pain explained why these older pictures belonged in the family room and the portraits of her parents remained sequestered in the library. The fact that Mom placed them in such a prominent position meant that I would pass them countless times every day. The pictures transformed the wall, the room, and even our entire house and made me feel less isolated. I was a daughter and a sister, but I had also become a great-granddaughter. For the first time, we had ancestors to watch over us, which made it seem as though I could feel the roots of our family tree. These were the first family pictures displayed in our house, and I was thrilled.

Mary Dean Ballard's picture from the late 1800s fascinated me most. The elderly woman sat at an angle, sunlight bathing her left side. This woman had a sober, forceful face that I couldn't help but study. Mary stared into the camera. She had pulled her center-parted gray or white hair behind her large ears, perhaps into a bun. She was old, but her flesh remained taut— hollow cheeks and a bony jaw. She did not smile and her thin lips were pursed enough to define her slight chin. Her forehead was relaxed, but her eyebrows arched to frame round spectacles. Her skin was the color of sugar cookie dough, yellow and very fair.

Bent from the elbows, her forearms rested on the arms of the chair. A spiky fur draped her shoulders and fell on either side of her chest. Ruffles decorated her collar and revealed a delicate neck free of wrinkles. The bold flower print on the dress was large and the repeat was uneven. The floor-length dress bunched and puckered in her lap, imprecisely arranged.

Eva had told us all that she knew about Mary: that Mary grew up as a slave—her father was a white man and her master, her mother a black woman and fellow slave. Like her mother before her, Mary Dean Ballard bore the children of white and black men. Aunt Eva also explained what she didn't know. Mary Dean Ballard refused to tell her children or grandchildren about her life in slavery. Like Ann Stamps, who'd left everything behind but the coffee grinder, Mary left her stories behind or simply kept them to herself. No matter how much anyone prodded, Mary always said the same thing, "You don't want to hear about those days."

I puzzled over this woman, who looked nothing like her son, my great-grandfather. Studying her picture as I passed it every day, I recognized something new in her expression. Mary Dean Ballard emptied her face of all emotion in the picture. If Mom had learned to drop the curtain of emotion from Frenchie, then Frenchie learned it from Mary Dean Ballard.

I often wished I could have met Mary and convinced her to tell me her story.

{ chapter five }

SLAVERY AND CIVIL RIGHTS

From the first day I met her in September 1979, my fifth-grade teacher, Mrs. McCormack, reminded me of a Disney fairy godmother. In the early weeks of school, I noticed how her eyes glimmered with wisdom and good humor. When she taught, her round face burst like the sun into a smile and shone with genuine interest in the ten-year-old mind. I loved everything about her. Mrs. McCormack laughed often. When she got firm, she still remained calm and easy. She was genteel and wore plaid wool skirts, tasseled loafers, broadcloth shirts that hung heavy with starch. Her wrist tinkled with gold bracelets, and she wore a monogram pin. She carried a basket instead of a purse. Best of all,

Mrs. McCormack loved history even more than I did. I hadn't known her long, but I had already decided that Mrs. McCormack was the best teacher I'd had at Lunada Bay School, maybe my favorite teacher of all time.

One autumn Monday morning as another ocean gust blew through the thin walls of our classroom trailer, room 17, we waited for our lesson to begin. I sat in the middle of the third row, just off dead center of the room. I slipped my spelling words into my Pee-Chee folder, took out my history book, and closed the creaky-hinged desk. We sat with our backs to the windows and away from the best view in the entire school—the rolling hills, jungle gym, and soccer fields of the playground. The chilly air made for numb fingers and breath you could see. My hands were still freezing and I shoved them between my thighs for a second and then rubbed them together. It was time for our history lesson. I couldn't wait to get started.

"Boys and girls," Mrs. McCormack began, "you will all participate in the Parade of American Heroes. Each of you will portray your favorite American. Read all you can, plan your costume, and then we will have a parade."

I gasped in anticipation and started planning. This was the best assignment ever—better than the first Thanksgiving diorama I'd made in third grade. It was even better than building a California mission out of sugar cubes I'd constructed last year. I vowed to have the best outfit in the parade, not a crazy getup like the one I'd used to mock Grandmother, embarrass myself, and hurt Dad. Even though it had been three years since my stunt, the memory of it still made me wince. No, I vowed, this wasn't going to be a stunt. This was really serious, and I knew I'd need a proper costume.

"George Washington," one boy said.

"I am going to be Abraham Lincoln," another countered. I was too excited to even get upset about how many choices these boys enjoyed.

"Betsy Ross," a girl said.

"I'm going to be Tracy Austin," said one of the popular girls who spent her afternoons at the tennis club. She whipped her long blond hair off her shoulders as she called out the name of the local tennis player who had just become the youngest woman to win the U.S. Open.

I heard another girl behind me let out a huge sigh of disappointment after the tennis club girl announced her choice. I had been at the school long enough to understand the pecking order. The less popular girl would defer to Miss Tennis Club in the same way that everyone else made way for the popular kids in the cafeteria.

I had already selected my hero, but I did not speak her name. After three years with these kids, I understood more about how I was different. I had come to understand that much more than my pecan skin set me apart. My history, my family's history, the history of people like me also made me different. Being so different was both good and bad. In this case, it was good because I knew that I wouldn't have to fight any other kids to march as my hero any more than I had to fight them on the playground. Those days were over.

I set my heart on Harriet Tubman.

From the first moment I learned Harriet Tubman's story, I loved her. She was born a slave. A master's blow led to a series of fainting spells. She feared sale, so she escaped from slavery, returning to free her family. When I learned that she worked as a conductor on the Underground Railroad and traveled by night to lead hundreds of other people to freedom, I stared into the California night and searched for the same North Star she used to guide her. In my mind, I walked alongside her as she spied on the Confederate Army during the Civil War. I loved all the names people used to celebrate her, especially Moses. She was brave and daring. My eyes lingered over every detail of Jacob Lawrence's series of Harriet Tubman paintings that showed the relentless spirit as well as the sorrow of enslaved people's lives. Harriet Tubman was my hero.

As I sat at my desk, I knew that marching in the parade as Harriet Tubman would also help me handle my unfinished business with slavery. The memory of another history lesson, one I'd learned late the previous year in fourth grade, steeled my resolve to make Harriet Tubman perfect. Sitting there, amid those whispering fifth graders making plans, my mind drifted back to the day when I learned the most painful history lesson of my life.

For most of fourth grade, we'd studied Columbus and Jamestown, the Pilgrims and Plymouth Rock, the American Revolution and the Constitutional Convention, the California missions, and the Gold Rush, all without a single reference to black people. Then, as we studied the Civil War, the black people showed up. I felt, for the first time, the vast and painful differences in the ways that black and white people talked about slavery.

Following my fourth-grade teacher's instructions, I'd opened my textbook to the appointed page without much thought. I stared at the rough and grainy black-and-white photograph that occupied the top half of the page. Dark people stood at the edge of a vast field bursting with fluffy cotton balls. Blank-faced women wore scarves on their heads, rough gingham blouses, and long, worn skirts. Burlap bags overflowed at the feet of men whose hours of labor had made tangles of muscle and sinew. Farther down the rows, faceless men and women stooped and hunched in various stages of picking—too busy, or maybe too afraid, to stand or look up. The textbook slaves looked helpless and muted.

I fell through the surface of the picture as I stared at it and felt myself drowning in the confusion of contrast. Until that moment, I had only learned about slavery from black people. Both times it had aired, I had watched *Roots*, the television mini-series based on Alex Haley's bestselling book. The enslaved people were the stars, the experience shown from their perspectives. In his artwork, Jacob Lawrence showed chained bodies, slavery's sorrow, and the terror of escape, alongside the brilliant colors that showed humanity beneath the bondage. Lawrence always showed slavery in the context of its transcendence.

I could barely hear the words my fourth-grade teacher spoke to try to explain the image. She'd barely made sense. What I did hear involved a lot of coughing and stammering between words. I guessed that she had never taught the subject of slavery in the presence of a black student.

That day, I had felt my classmates' eyes on me. Some girls stole glances; most of the boys gawked at me. It felt like they were trying to find the slave in me—waiting for the scarf to magically appear on my head as my desk suddenly overflowed with cotton.

The textbook picture also told me a version of my own family's story that my ancestors simply refused to tell. At home, we revered my formerly enslaved elders. We spoke of them by name,

Papa Jules Joseph on Dad's side, Mary Dean Ballard and Mack Hall on Mom's side. We treated these people as honored ancestors, which meant we also respected their wishes. Our family did not preserve photographs of people in the midst of their enslavement. We only kept photographs taken once they had become free. When Mary Dean Ballard left slavery, she took nothing from it. She took her stories to her grave and so my family had none. On the day I met the textbook slaves, I had no pictures or stories with which to refute this other version.

Even though I passed her fine portrait every day, Mary Dean Ballard could not and would not challenge what I saw on that textbook page. Her refusal to speak about her enslavement to anyone actually suggested a life as bad as the one I saw depicted and bound between the covers of the textbook. That day, I learned about how other people saw slavery and enslaved people. The slaves bore the weight and the shame of slavery, as though it were their fault. Everyone else got to relish the Old South as a place of big dresses and funny accents. They got Rhett and Scarlett while I got Mammy without the humor. That day, I felt the anguish and the awkwardness of slavery in a new way.

As we closed our books and headed out to recess, a couple of kids had gathered around me and peppered me with questions.

"Jennifer," one white-blond girl asked me, "were your parents slaves?"

"No" was all I said. I was trying to keep walking and prevent more kids from gathering. *Weren't you listening to the teacher?* I wanted to ask her. *Didn't you see* Roots? *Slavery ended before my parents were born.*

"How about your grandparents?" asked a short girl with warts on her hands. "Were they slaves?"

Kids overheard us and slowed their steps to listen.

"No." I was beginning to feel like a bug trapped in a jar. The questions pressed on my mind like dirty fingerprints and made me feel angry and alone.

"What about your great-grandparents?" asked another girl.

These kids were so sure that I had slaves in my family and that if they just asked enough questions they'd find them. How could they be so sure that I was the only person in the class who had a slave for a relative? Why didn't anyone bother to ask me if I had slave masters in my family? I could answer yes to that question and would have blown their minds. But the truth was that if they'd asked me, I couldn't have told them much about the slave owners. We never talked about them, mentioned their names, or paid them any respect. We certainly didn't display their pictures in our house.

"Were *any* of your relatives slaves?" the first girl asked in frustration.

The other girls seemed as impatient with me as this one. I wanted to go to the blacktop and play dodgeball and change the subject. I wasn't ashamed of the answer. I just didn't want these kids whispering about Jennifer's slave relatives all through lunch. I'd had enough questions.

"Yes," I finally conceded, "some of my ancestors had been slaves." I left the staring girls behind and headed for the playground. My answers felt feeble, but I didn't want to say any more to these girls. Besides, Mary Dean Ballard and Mack Hall were my ancestors, not just slaves. I wasn't there to entertain these kids with my family tree. What else could I say?

Since that day the previous year, I had been searching for a way to talk back to that textbook picture and not give it the last word.

I'd been longing to tell the other kids in my class another story that would say more than that picture and that paragraph. Harriet Tubman was my answer. Hers was the story that would allow me to explain that slaves did not just lay down in horror. The parade became my best chance to throw off the shame I had worn since that day and leave it behind forever. Harriet was my solution. She was my hero.

"I want to be Harriet Tubman in the parade," I said as Mom opened her car door. I stood barefoot in the driveway and spoke the words aloud for the first time all day. Even saying her name made me feel so proud, and I knew Mom would understand.

"What parade?" Mom asked, trying to keep pace with my thoughts.

"There's a Great American Heroes Parade at school," I said, "and I am going to be Harriet Tubman. We can go to the fabric store and get everything we need."

Over the years, I'd watched Mom sew everything from curtains to dresses, often without the benefit of a pattern. Best of all, Mom made our Halloween costumes from scratch every year. She'd asked what we'd want to be, take us to the fabric store to select everything right down to the notions, and then whip us costumes better than everyone else's. I'd sit beside Mom as she cut the fabric, and sometimes she'd even let me cut scraps to practice. I'd hold the pins and hand them to her one at a time. Then she'd remind me how to thread the machine and allow me to press the foot pedal while she guided the material. If we weren't in too much of a rush, I'd even get to sew a straight seam. Best of all, I'd awake one morning with my finished costume hanging on my door.

I'd already planned my Harriet Tubman costume and could clearly envision it. I'd need enough fabric for a long calico dress.

I couldn't use one of Mom's silk scarves with the flower prints or equestrian scenes. The scarf I'd use to cover my hair would have to match the apron, a cotton triangle that looked worn, maybe even frayed. Some buttons, maybe some ricrac, a zipper, and we'd have everything we'd need. I'd also need some black ankle boots and an overcoat, which would require a trip to the thrift store. I didn't want anyone to mistake me, or Harriet Tubman, for a textbook slave, so I thought about wearing a toy gun in a holster or a bandolier of bullets across my chest, Pancho Villa style. With Mom in my corner, I knew Harriet Tubman would be amazing.

But Mom remained quiet as she took her papers, books, and purse from the car. When she stood up, she simply said, "Let's think about this," without even really looking at me.

So I did, but I sensed her hesitation and began to worry.

The next day, Mrs. McCormack asked each of us to name our hero.

"I'll be Neil Armstrong," said a boy who loved space.

"Thomas Edison," another boy said.

"Harriet Tubman," I said in a near whisper when it was my turn. My faint voice surprised me, and my tongue caught on the words.

"I want to march as Harriet Tubman," I said again in a stronger voice, trying to borrow some courage.

No one said anything, and Mrs. McCormack just moved through the rows listening to the students name their heroes and helping those who hadn't picked a hero find one. Then she dismissed us for recess.

"Jennifer," Mrs. McCormack asked brightly as I raced through the door, "what about Rosa Parks?"

At that moment, I could not appreciate how fortunate I was to have a teacher who could compare the relative merits of Harriet Tubman versus Rosa Parks and form an opinion. So I sat and waited for the offense to continue.

"She was the woman in Montgomery, Alabama, who refused to give up her seat on the—" Mrs. McCormack said brightly.

"I know who she is," I interrupted as I folded my arms across my chest, trying to keep Harriet Tubman close to me.

"She was a pioneer in the civil rights movement," Mrs. McCormack continued. I knew it was true, but behind the words of praise for Rosa Parks, I heard the music of rejection for Harriet Tubman.

I would not look at Mrs. McCormack.

"Rosa Parks is okay, I guess," I said.

"Think about it," Mrs. McCormack suggested. Maybe she heard the reservation in my voice and decided not to push too hard.

By the end of the day, I had thought myself into a funk and felt too upset to take my regular route home. I steered my ten-speed bike down Paseo del Mar, the street closest to the ocean, and thought about Harriet Tubman. I hated it when grown-ups disguised commands as suggestions. The angrier I got, the faster I pedaled. Mom did it all the time, and Mrs. McCormack's suggestion tangled with Mom's reluctance and made me resent both of them. The strong wind in my face made me gasp for breath, but I pedaled harder. I shifted my bike gears and tried not to fight the wind. I needed to march as a freed slave. I had to show my classmates that there were slaves who'd broken out of bondage and seized their freedom. I wanted to let them know that my enslaved ancestors had survived. I would have to find another way. As I rode the rest of the way home, I planned out my strategy to convince Mom, and I also thought of an alternative in Frederick Douglass.

Halfway through my plate of baked chicken, broccoli, and buttered rice, as I sat with Mom and Natalie at the table, I raised the subject of Harriet Tubman. I tried to sound matter of fact and hoped that my thoughtful planning would help convince Mom. I ticked off the elements of the costume that I had designed in my head. I described the dress and the shoes, the overcoat and the scarf as Mom pushed long grains of rice around the edge of her plate. But as I talked about the head scarf, I got nervous. I spoke faster and faster and sputtered my plan about the gun in one messy run-on sentence. Everything sounded better in my head. Mom's face twisted at the mention of the holstered pistol. She stared at me blank-faced. I couldn't bear her rejection, so I changed direction.

"Or how about Frederick Douglass?" I asked. "I already have short hair." Since I'd begged Mom to cut my hair into an Afro last year shortly after meeting the textbook slaves, I thought I might as well use it as a selling point. I kept talking over Mom's silence as I carried my plate to the kitchen counter.

"I could wear my costume from *A Christmas Carol*," I said. I had played Ebenezer Scrooge in a local theater company production of the Charles Dickens classic. I mumbled my way out of the room and then ran upstairs to find the Scrooge costume.

I rustled through my drawers, opening and closing them, moving shirts and socks, trying to remember where the costume had gone after my final performance two years ago. I opened my closet and picked through the church clothes, skirts and dresses, that hung there. On a bent wire hanger deep in the closet, I found the entire costume. I kicked off my sneakers and took off my clothes. I slipped into the black pants deeply creased at the knee. They still fit in the waist, but they fell at my ankles. I ignored the yellow makeup ring on the shirt collar and began to button it. The sleeves of the shirt rose above my wrists. I pulled on the matching black morning coat, but it felt tight across my back and the arms were too short. I had forgotten how to arrange the ascot and set it aside. I looked like a scarecrow, and hurried past the hall mirror too afraid of what I'd see. I walked back downstairs and into the family room. I tried to remain hopeful, but I felt the wind of resistance again.

"I know it's short," I began before I entered the family room, "but can't you let out the hems?" I asked.

Mom stopped sweeping the floor and leaned on the broom as she stared at me for a moment. I was glad Natalie had gone to her room and closed the door, because I didn't want her to say anything about how tight the outfit looked on me. Mom walked over and folded up the cuff on my sleeve, inspecting it in silence.

"This isn't going to work," she said. I tried to maintain my hope, but I knew she was talking about more than the hems. Frederick Douglass was impossible, too. My eyes started to sting. I didn't dare protest or try to ask her any more questions because I didn't want to get punished for back talk.

I let my footsteps fall as heavily as I dared as I returned to my room. I tried to slam my door, but thankfully it caught on the carpet. I was trying to conjure my Jan Brady moment, but Jan Brady didn't have problems like this, even when she wore that dark, curly wig.

I flopped onto my bed and hugged my pillow. Why didn't anyone want me to be Tubman or Douglass? I had played all kinds of characters in local plays. Mom congratulated me when I played the fox in Pinocchio and roared with laughter during my performance. She applauded when I sang the Charlie Brown solo during our school chorus performance. She didn't mind when I played the stingy Victorian Englishman. What was the difference? But even as I lay there, I knew the answer. The trouble was I was trapped in polite suburban silence where so much pain hid. None of us, not Mom, Mrs. McCormack, or even I, wanted to admit the truth of the matter. I couldn't march in the parade as a slave, not even Harriet Tubman. I knew even then that my mom and my teacher were trying to protect me from the ugliness of slavery. The problem was that I had already seen it, and I couldn't get it out of my mind.

This was a burden too heavy for me to lift and bear by myself.

I took off the costume and changed back into my clothes.

I went back to the family room and flopped into the space beside Mom on the couch. I wanted to be close to her, but I couldn't look into her face. We both stared at the television.

"Mrs. McCormack suggested that I march as Rosa Parks," I muttered.

"Rosa Parks would be wonderful," Mom said, her voice flooding with relief as she wrapped her arm over my shoulder and pulled me close to her.

The week before the parade, it still hurt too much for me to get excited about Rosa Parks. I felt I had betrayed Harriet Tubman and myself, and I kept my distance from Mrs. McCormack, Rosa Parks, and the assignment. One afternoon, Mom handed me a worn grocery bag from Goodwill Industries. The stench of age and despair clung to the bag and its contents. I peered inside but couldn't bear to look at the clothes. I took the bag up to my room and put it in the corner.

Two days before the parade, I knew it was time to make peace with Rosa Parks. I began by looking over the pictures we had of her in our house.

Staring at Rosa Parks as she sat on the bus seated in front of a white man, I marveled at her calm. My eye took in all the texture—the folds in the skin of her neck and her perfectly tailored suit jacket. Her ripples of hair and coiled bun. Rosa Parks looked nothing like those textbook slaves as she gazed out the window. In many ways, she reminded me of Mary Dean Ballard. They shared the same impeccable posture, wore wire-framed glasses, and shared the same shade of skin. But in that moment, I also saw something particular in Rosa Parks—she pointed her refusal in a different direction from my great-great-grandmother. She didn't try to conceal the insult of discrimination. Mary Dean Ballard had refused her children to protect them from slavery. Rosa Parks refused the bus driver, the town of Montgomery, and Jim Crow himself when she wouldn't move to the back of the bus. Rosa Parks hadn't been a slave, but I could feel the way that segregation made her suffer. As I recognized the "regular woman" in Rosa Parks, I began to see the hero in her, too.

Even though Dad had lived through segregation and was a teenager during the yearlong bus boycott, he never mentioned that time. So I found it more confusing than slavery. It was hard for me to understand having to depend on the bus. I never rode the bus in Palos Verdes. My parents drove me everywhere, or I rode my bike. But even though I didn't ride the bus, the idea of having to sit in the back, just like drinking from "colored" water fountains or riding in different train cars, resonated with me.

It would mean that I wouldn't be able to sit with my friends or make friends. My closest brushes with segregation were the restrictive covenants in Palos Verdes Estates that forbade residents to sell their homes to black or Jewish families. No one in the town enforced the laws, but Mom told me that the codes remained on the books and had not been repealed.

I still missed Harriet Tubman, but I knew that she lay beyond my reach.

I also knew that, for all their differences, Rosa Parks and Harriet Tubman shared the same problem of obscurity in my white suburban world. Our textbooks told the story of segregation and boycotts in less than a paragraph. I doubted that many other kids would know any more about Rosa Parks than they did about Harriet Tubman, so I knew I'd have to explain who she was. As I looked into the bag, I wondered how to turn the heap of polyester into Rosa Parks. How would anyone know who I was besides a black lady on her way to church?

For the first time since Mom handed me the outfit she put together for me from Goodwill, I pulled the bag from the corner and tried on the clothes. A sea-foam green polyester skirt and matching jacket; a cream-colored blouse that buttoned in back; a pillbox hat with the netting; a gray wig; black patent leather shoes with a chunky, sensible heel became the elements of my redemption. Inside one of the shoes, I spied a pair of black cat's-eye glasses with rhinestones in each corner. It was far from the handmade costumes Mom usually crafted, and the store-bought old lady outfit made me feel a bit sad. But I understood the point of the outfit and tried to shake it off. Besides, the last time I pretended to be an old woman, I had felt so ashamed of myself. This time, I promised to make everyone proud.

From this Goodwill bag emerged an icon. I slipped the wig onto my head and smiled at myself in the corner mirror. I really looked strange standing there. I laid out the suit jacket and skirt on the side of my bed. Then I reached in and grabbed the blouse. I set the shoes on the floor. From my sock drawer, I pulled out a pair of white tights that I usually wore to church—a few stray balls of blue lint clung to the legs, but I didn't care. I balanced on one foot and pulled them over my feet and onto my legs. I buttoned the blouse and looped a big floppy bow at my neck. It hung down over the pleats that creased the front. I pulled on the skirt, zipped it at the back, and slipped into the midheel pumps that sported a large gold buckle. Finally, I unscrewed the hat pin and slid it into the pillbox hat and wig.

The sound of the thick heels on the hardwood hallway made everything seem more serious. I stared at myself in the floor-to-ceiling mirror. I had become an older woman and I couldn't help smiling at myself. As I walked down the stairs, with every step I felt closer and closer to Rosa Parks.

Through the glittering glasses frames, I stared at myself in the mirror. I had discovered Rosa Parks. I squared my shoulders as my shoes clacked on the steps and then on the hallway tiles. In the mirror at the bottom of the stairs, I could see myself and could feel Rosa Parks emerging in me. I stifled my smile and surged with pride as I marched into the family room.

Mom sat on the couch.

"Oh, Jen," Mom gasped and chuckled at the same time.

"I am," I began in my acting voice, "Mrs. Rosa Parks." Then I straightened my shoulders and marched in a tight circle in front of the television.

"All right," Mom cheered, holding up her fist.

Dad walked through the door and whistled. He was home early and I was thrilled to see him.

"Hello," he sang out as always.

I spun around on the heel of my old lady shoe to present my full outfit.

"Hi, Dad," I said in my acting voice, "I'm Rosa Parks." I shifted my stance and beamed.

"Doesn't Jen look wonderful?" Mom asked.

"She looks ready to march," Dad said.

"Can you drive me to school for the parade tomorrow?" I asked.

"Mrs. Parks," he said, "it would be my pleasure."

I turned to Mom. "You're coming to the parade, right?"

"I wouldn't miss it," she said. "I'll even bring the Polaroid camera."

I walked upstairs and knocked on Natalie's closed bedroom door. I stood in the threshold of her room and saw Natalie sitting at her desk staring intently at a math problem. She didn't look up, and I didn't want to interrupt her, so I stood there and listened to the Stevie Wonder song playing on her stereo. Natalie erased a bit of her work. I stood still, waiting for her reaction, surveying her perfectly made bed, her neatly arranged clothes— her room looked so different from mine.

Finally, she looked up at me and a broad smile spread over her face.

"Wow, Jen," she said, "you look terrific."

"Thanks," I said, relieved by her approval. "I just showed Mom and Dad."

I kept my arms at my side, trying to remember Mrs. Parks's composure.

"What should I do for tomorrow?" I asked Natalie, hoping for some pointers. Natalie was in middle school, nearly a teenager. I needed her approval and support.

"I don't know," Natalie said. "We didn't have this parade when I was a fifth grader. But you'll be great."

Her smile told me that she really believed in what I was doing, and I was grateful for that. I closed the door and said good night.

As I walked into my room, I thought about how excited everyone in the family was about Rosa Parks. I guess I hadn't expected them to make such a big deal about my outfit. But I was doing something no one in our family had done before, which, as the youngest, was a big deal for me. Tomorrow, I would tell the story of civil rights. I undressed and laid each piece of my outfit on the end of my bed. Then I took a bath and went to bed. As I drifted off to sleep, I reeled off my instructions to myself—stand up straight, don't smile or frown, be proud.

The gray morning light filled my room as I awoke the next morning. Parade Day, a day for heroes. I got out of the bed, went to the bathroom, brushed my teeth, and washed my face. I rolled on extra deodorant and sprayed and picked my hair even though I would wear a wig all day. Back in my room, I dressed in a flash.

Downstairs, I took off my suit jacket and folded it on the back of Dad's chair. I wolfed down my bowl of cereal, brought it to the sink, and looked at the clock. I had more than an hour to wait. I put my backpack closer to the garage door.

Dad emerged from his bedroom nearly dressed except for his shoes that he always left downstairs.

"You're all ready to go," he said.

"Yeah," I said.

I followed him into the hallway as he selected a pair of dress shoes. Slipping on a pair of older shoes, he walked into the garage where he kept all of his shoe-shine stuff. Dad maintained a small space beside his car where he kept all of his shoe gear in a wooden box—worn undershirts and washcloths; small, rounded brushes with wooden handles for the Kiwi cream polish; rectangular brushes with boar bristles for buffing; black, dark brown, and cordovan polish along with navy blue and a creamy polish that looked neutral on the leather. He also kept matching shades of dye in bottles that had cotton pads attached to the lid, as well as liquid wax to add a glossy sheen. In the corner of the box, he tucked tightly woven dress shoelaces in different lengths and shades to match each pair of his shoes. He visited an old cobbler in the city who replaced heels and soles before they wore down too far. Dad polished his shoes the same way he got his car washed every Friday and the same way that he prayed on his knees: routinely and unquestioningly.

He picked the perfect shade of cordovan brown shoe polish and dabbed an old undershirt into the paste, then slipped his hand in the shoe. He massaged the polish into the leather until all the scuffs disappeared and the leather had a dull patina.

Dad really cared for his shoes.

"You can tell a lot about a man by the way he cares for his shoes," he always said.

He set his shoes on a shelf to let the paste wax cure for a few minutes.

"Let me have your shoes," he said, pointing to my thrift store pumps.

I grabbed a pair of my own muddy sneakers from the steps and handed him the pumps. The inside of the sneakers felt damp.

"Did you ever sit in the back of a bus?" I began.

He held my shoe by the heel and rubbed away the scuffs with a clean corner of the rag. "Yes."

"What was it like?" I asked.

"I didn't like it, but that's just what we had to do," he said. "But Mrs. Parks changed all of that."

Dad handed my shoes back to me. They gleamed.

Then he picked up his own shoes and buffed each one into a high gloss in eight strokes. He used a long metal shoehorn to slip on each one and then leaned over to tie them.

"Let's get you to school," he said.

I ran in the house to gather my things.

Dad almost never took me to school, even on rainy days. So, as I loaded my stuff in the backseat and sat in the front with Dad, I could feel the importance of the day. We coasted along Palos Verdes Drive West, a street too busy for me to make part of my regular route. We both listened to the headlines on KNX 1070 AM radio, and Dad turned up the volume to hear the traffic report. My request put him in the thick of rush hour traffic to Los Angeles and he would crawl to his office. But Dad didn't seem to mind.

Dad pulled into the car pool line in front of the school and waited his turn to drop me off. I kissed him before I opened my door.

"Thanks, Dad," I said.

"You're welcome," he said. "Have a good day and enjoy the parade."

"I will," I said as I grabbed my backpack and lunch from the backseat.

As I walked down the stairs, I relished the awe of the little kids. As I got closer to the fifth-grade classrooms, the atmosphere changed. Regular school clothes gave way to elaborate costumes. First, I caught the tail of Davy Crockett's coonskin cap through the mist. He was all clad in brown buckskin. The morning fog lingered longest on the edge of the playground in front of our class-

Jennifer Baszile

rooms. As I walked up the hill past the classrooms, I passed Martha Washington and goggle-clad Amelia Earhart. The handball slapped against the wooden backboard as General Patton's canteen clinked when he ran for the ball. Abraham Lincoln's beard, hat, and topcoat sat in a pile while another boy played soccer.

"Who are you?" my friend Dana asked me. She was a tall, skinny girl who'd asked me about the slaves in my family the previous spring.

"Rosa Parks," I replied.

"Who's that?" she asked.

"A woman who would not give up her seat and move to the back of the bus," I said.

"Oh," my friend said. "Why would she have to move to the back of the bus?"

"Because she was black," I said in a firm voice, staring into her eyes "and that's where black people had to sit before Rosa Parks. That's where my dad had to sit."

Dana looked uneasy, maybe even a little embarrassed. She didn't ask me another question. She just backed away from me.

Standing there I finally understood justice in a new way, not the animated *Super Friends* variety. I also realized that there was more than one kind of courage. Rosa Parks was just as brave as Harriet Tubman. She just relied on herself and other people who walked and boycotted their way to their rights. Courage was her most powerful weapon, more important than a toy pistol or the string of bullets that had been so central to my fantasy.

When Mrs. McCormack opened the classroom door, I admired her full-length gingham dress with a white apron and a white bonnet hung around her neck. She looked like a pioneer woman. I didn't know she was going to dress up like the rest of us but was glad that she did. Standing in line, I released my grudge against my teacher. Mrs. McCormack had been right all along. Rosa Parks belonged in our parade. We all needed her there, a living breathing American hero still alive and living in Detroit. Mrs. McCormack became my favorite teacher all over again because she had seen that long before I could.

{ chapter six }

THE MAKEOVER

As I arrived on the Margate Intermediate School campus, in 1980, everything about life seemed much more complicated: six teachers instead of one, lockers instead of desks. Three elementary schools merged into Margate, and so along with seventh and eighth graders, my social world exploded. We were again the youngest at the school, and the eighth graders seemed so much more sophisticated than we were.

By the beginning of sixth grade, my body's adolescent freakout was in full and frightening swing. Hair in new places, the changing smell of my sweat, training bras—my body was changing fast and I could hardly keep up. I stood in its hot spotlight.

As soon as I got to Margate, I realized that adolescence and straight hair seemed to fit together better than adolescence and my three-inch Afro. The freedom from rain bonnets, umbrellas, and swimming caps no longer felt so great. I wanted to fuss over my hair, make a big deal about it like my white friends did. I wanted to join Mom and Natalie in their afternoon trips to the beauty salon when they got relaxers. Even though Natalie had gotten her first relaxer at eleven, Mom had learned from Natalie's experience that eleven was too early and already told me that I had to wait until I was fourteen. I began blowing out my hair as straight as I could with the hair dryer and then using Natalie's new electric curling iron. I looked like I had a head full of black cotton candy.

To top it off, I had just gotten braces. The roots of my teeth ached with the tension wires installed to straighten my bite. The metal bands cemented onto my teeth cut the inside of my cheeks, trapped food, and made my mouth stink. The rubber bands that held my jaw in alignment by day snapped without warning, and the headgear I wore at night made me drool all over my pillow. I didn't feel anywhere close to pretty.

My uncle Sonny's announcement that I was "the Other One" stuck in my mind like gum in the crack of my shoe. Pretty sat on a high shelf in my mind, beyond my reach. I didn't have a single clue about how to wear makeup and so just wore watermelon or green apple lip balm. Like half the girls in my grade, I doused myself in Bonne Bell perfume to cover my stink. I just wanted to look better than I did, to look okay, but even that seemed to mean a lot of work and effort.

The stakes of being pretty also skyrocketed. Girls were supposed to be pretty, not for its own sake but to impress boys and please their parents. Adolescence was not a process of gracefully budding womanhood; it was a period of relentless scrutiny and ceaseless correction. Most of the girls I knew, including me, had already begun wondering and worrying about our bodies, agonizing over how we looked to everyone but ourselves. We were all having our blossoming femininity staked, pruned, or pinched back in some way or another.

Even Natalie, the prettiest girl I knew, spent middle school wearing a brace to adjust her spine after the pediatrician diagnosed her scoliosis. The steel frame, foam pads, and Velcro closures stretched from beneath her chin to the tops of her thighs. Those had been hard years, but now Natalie was in high school with a boyfriend who called her Peaches, lots of friends, and a place on the drill team.

Luckily, my new friend Amy and I talked about the work of being pretty all of the time. She was a new girl who had just moved from the Midwest. She had a pale, splotchy Nordic complexion that burned easily in the California sun. She wore braces. She dressed her ruler-shaped body in super-slim jeans and clingy tops. A curly permanent added volume to her fine shoulder-length blond hair. Even though we seemed like opposites, we both longed to be pretty and feared that we weren't.

After school, we walked to her house and retreated to her room to flip through *Teen, Seventeen,* and *Glamour* searching for beauty secrets. Amy always found more to imitate than I did and stood in her bedroom mirror trying out new looks. I still searched the pages for ideas that might help me and studied the magazines like sacred texts. But pretty black girls appeared on the pages as infrequently as black people showed up in my textbooks, though I always felt glad when I saw them. Amy always made a big deal of the rare occasion when she found a black model on the page. I appreciated her help but never pointed out the differences between the models and me. When they did appear, black teenage models wore bone-straight hairstyles.

The stack of *Ebony* and *Jet* magazines Mom kept on our coffee table were more frustrating. The grown women featured on their pages had even longer hair, wore designer clothes, and stiletto heels. The bathing beauties in *Jet* posed in bikinis and filled them out in ways that I feared I never would. Mom didn't subscribe to *Essence*, but whenever Natalie brought one home, I never identified with those women either. Besides, they were women, not girls.

A few weeks into the school year, posters announced the first dance of the year. It was the first boy-girl dance that any of us had ever attended and it was all anyone talked about.

During class, kids passed even more notes than usual.

At lunch, I heard my friends talk about cute boys. Everyone laughed as we wondered loudly who might ask them to dance, which began a conversation about bases, especially about first and second base. They gossiped about how boys tried to slip their hands under shirts or on rear ends during the slow songs. I mostly listened and noticed that no one talked about the actual dancing part of the dance. Most of the talk centered around what to do when asked to dance.

I prayed that someone would ask me to dance but drew a blank as to who. The only black boy in my grade never spoke to me and avoided my eyes when we passed each other in the halls. None of the guys in my classes seemed the least bit interested in me. I was afraid that no one would ask me to dance and that I would have to stand on the sidelines hoping and waiting.

The upcoming dance made Amy's and my afternoon magazine studies even more intense and focused. We talked outfits
and strategy. But the more we talked, a growing sense of dread
filled me.

"I'm thinking about skipping the dance," I said.

"Oh no," Amy said. "Why?"

"Because," I said and let my voice trail off. I couldn't admit the
reason: that I wasn't sure anyone would want to dance with me.

"You've gotta go," Amy pleaded. "I can't go by myself. I'll look
like a dork."

"I just don't think—" I said. "I mean, you know its kind
of . . . well."

I couldn't get the words out. If I couldn't even explain this to
Amy, there was no way I could explain it to Mom, who always
insisted that I take advantage of opportunities to "practice my
social skills."

"We'll stick together all night," she said. "I promise."

I still couldn't say anything.

"I know," Amy said. "Let's go to Buffum's department store
and get makeovers, like real ones."

Amy already wore makeup: black mascara and eyeliner that
gave her raccoon eyes, powder blue shadow, frosty pink lip gloss.
Sometimes she covered her zits with foundation and concealer,
but both made her skin look too yellow. All her efforts made her
face look fake.

A makeover sounded like a great idea. A genuine department
store professional seemed like just the expert to help me. The
drugstore makeup, tightly wrapped in plastic, would be no help
at all. You couldn't sample or try it on. No one was there to show
you how to wear it and make it work. A professional might be

able to salvage what was beginning to feel like a lost cause. Professional makeup tips would definitely make me look my prettiest and boost my chances of dancing.

"Okay," I said.

First, I had to convince Mom.

That afternoon, I walked into Mom's room.

"This Saturday, can Amy and I go to the mall?" I asked Mom. "Her mother can drive us," I added, sprinkling on the additional sweetener.

"What for?" Mom asked. She didn't like us to "hang around" anywhere, especially the mall. She thought it a waste of time, and as much as she hated wasting time, she hated the thought of wasting money even more.

"Well," I said, "the dance is coming up and we just wanted to look around." I didn't mention the makeover. I had never really tried to wear makeup and neither did Natalie, so Mom never had to make a rule about it. But I had heard Mom talk about "fast girls" lots of times. Fast girls were the girls who tried to attract the wrong kind of attention from boys, the girls who wore heels, the girls who wore lots of makeup. But forget being "fast." I was just trying to get up to speed.

"I guess that would be okay," she said.

"Thanks," I said as I smiled to myself. I couldn't wait to dazzle Mom with my great new look. I could see her reaction in my mind. I'd get out of the car and walk up to her. She'd smile when she saw the new Jennifer and tell me how pretty I looked and then take me back to the store to buy all of the stuff. She would be happy and I would finally feel good about myself. I called Amy with the great news and felt excited about the dance for the first time. I couldn't wait for Saturday.

On Saturday morning, I spent extra time picking my outfit for the makeover. I wanted to look mature and serious. I buttoned the pink canvas cover on my wooden-handled purse. Inside I put my Velcro wallet and lip gloss. Even though I never used it, I stuck a plastic brush inside the purse to take up space. A few quarters and dimes clanked in the lonely interior, which still looked empty and shriveled. Mom dropped me at Amy's house and then her mom took us up to the Peninsula Shopping Centre. We were both so excited but stayed calm and kept our plan quiet as we rode up to the mall.

We opened the tinted glass doors and walked into the cool and crisp store. The closing doors muffled the rushing applause of the fountain outside and focused our attention on the instrumental version of the Carpenters' hit "Close to You." The store had just opened and salespeople counted change at the registers. The store was like a shrine: polished glass display cases, gleaming mirrors, and marble floors so glossy I could almost see my reflection. Racks of costume jewelry twinkled as hats and purses hung at precisely spaced intervals. Everything was perfect.

I knew this store well and had been coming here for special outfits and sales for as long as we lived in Palos Verdes. I always had the same sensation—an ideal version of life. But we always had gone to the girls' section for clothes and new pairs of patent leather buckle shoes. I had passed through the cosmetics department on my way into or out of the store, but I had never stopped or paid much attention.

Amy hiked her purse higher on her shoulder and walked over to the cosmetics department. I did my best to imitate her but got more timid and nervous with each step.

The saleslady, dressed in all burgundy with huge shoulder pads in her blazer, rested her folded elbow on her hip and clutched a frosted atomizer of perfume. There was only one word to describe her: glamorous. She stood beside the aisle poised to offer samples. She watched the door with expectation, anxious to make her first sale of the day. But without many customers, she kept looking at herself in the mirror. She wiped lipstick from the rim of her mouth. A lone woman carrying her purchase walked through the early-morning silence of the store, striding toward the rest of her day. We fell in behind this woman, but we could not keep up with her quick clicking steps. The saleswoman planted herself in the lone shopper's path and chimed the name of the perfume and the free gift that accompanied it. The shopper passed without a word and the saleslady checked her makeup again.

By the time she turned around, Amy and I had approached her.

"I'd like a makeover, please," Amy said. The woman first looked beyond my friend to the empty store, and then to the atomizer she would have to cradle like a baby if she said no. Then she regarded Amy for a long moment.

"We're getting ready for the school dance," Amy continued. I marveled at her ease.

"Really?" the saleslady said. She put the atomizer on the counter. "Sure, have a seat."

"Tell me what you use on your skin," the saleslady said.

"Right now I'm having a major breakout," Amy said as she lifted her bangs to reveal her forehead full of pimples. "I use the soap, toner, and lotion from your line," Amy continued. "My mom got me started last year."

Amy was way ahead of me in the skin care department, even though the products weren't really working all that well.

"Great," said the saleslady. "Good skin care is essential, especially at your age." She held Amy's face between her hands and studied it.

"We're just going to make you look more natural," the saleslady said. She pulled a high metal stool with white leather cushions in front of the counter. "Sit down."

The lady disappeared behind the counter as Amy climbed onto the chair. The stool's cushions squeaked as Amy made herself comfortable. She placed her purse on the back of the chair and folded her hands in her lap.

When the saleslady reappeared, she carried a handful of cotton balls, wedges, and swabs. As she came back from around the counter wearing a pair of huge tortoiseshell glasses, carrying these tools, I wondered about her definition of "natural." The saleslady saturated a cotton ball with makeup remover and swept it over Amy's eyes. The department store lights made Amy's face look hard and blotchy as the saleslady removed all traces of Amy's drugstore makeup. With all of her makeup off, Amy looked twelve again, but her skin was really mottled and red.

I marveled at the pristine palettes. Row after row of eye shadows shimmered in faint shades. Pinks—baby-hued, coral, and salmon. Blues—powder, teal, and peacock. With so many choices, beauty seemed inevitable. But all of the shades were chalky and pale, a seemingly endless variety within a very narrow band. The saleslady rubbed the swabs into the shallow pots of color and dabbed the excess on a tissue. The woman had so many choices and she searched for the shade that was just right.

My friend grinned at me in excitement and I grinned back, thrilled that we were in the hands of a professional.

The saleslady said very little as she rubbed a concealer stick on Amy's pimples. In an instant the yellow center of Amy's pimples and their red edges both disappeared. Next the saleslady poured liquid foundation on a wedge and then spread it on Amy's face. It matched her skin perfectly. She picked up a sponge applicator and studied Amy's green eyes before selecting a shade of pale green for her eyelids. My friend smiled as instructed and the woman put a blushing pink on the apples of her cheeks, but then she sucked in her cheeks and the woman put a slightly darker shade in their hollows, which made my friend appear less gopherlike. The saleslady dabbed the lip brush into an apricot lipstick and spread it to the very edge of Amy's mouth to make her thin lips appear bigger.

As the saleslady swirled the fluffiest brush into a container of loose powder, she brushed it all over Amy's face and neck.

"Don't leave an obvious line at your jaw." Finally, she replaced the black mascara Amy wore with brown mascara, and the saleslady stepped back to appraise her work.

"What do you think?" she asked as she handed my friend the mirror.

"I love it," Amy said as she grinned. She raked her bangs into place and turned to inspect her profile.

The saleslady had delivered the natural look she'd promised and the post-department-store Amy looked much better than the Amy who'd first walked in. Her skin looked perfectly even, her eyes seemed more open, and her lips looked plump. Her cheeks blushed with vigor. She was a prettier and more polished version of herself.

"Wow," Amy said as she turned her head from side to side in the mirror. "Thank you."

"You really look great," I said.

Amy's transformation filled me with envy. It seemed like we stood on opposite sides of an invisible line. It seemed like Amy had become a pretty girl, and I had been left behind. It didn't matter to me that it was an illusion and that Amy was still the same girl underneath. She looked so much better than she did before and much better than I did. I felt left out. Amy jumped off the stool but still peered into the mirror, amazed by the results.

"May I have a makeover too, please?" I asked. I was so anxious to begin my transformation that I interrupted even before my friend had decided what to buy. I needed to see the better, prettier Jennifer who just might exist a few brushstrokes away. I couldn't see her but hoped that the saleslady could; I needed her to hurry up and work her magic on me so that I could join Amy in the pretty world.

The saleslady raised her eyebrows in surprise and hesitated an instant. "Of course," she said. "Have a seat."

I was too hopeful to wonder much about the woman's hesitation. I jumped into the seat and tucked my purse into my lap. I looked around the store and noticed that a few more customers had trickled in. Amy couldn't resist her reflection, and her pleasure seemed to deepen with each glance.

I clenched my knees together and waited to meet pretty Jennifer. The saleslady placed a fresh supply of cotton balls, foam wedges, and swabs on the counter. Then she stepped closer to me and held my chin with her bent index finger. I smelled the minty clean of her breath and the spicy floral perfume. In that moment, I knew I'd made the right decision, placing my trust in a trained professional with genuine skill. I stared into her eyes as she surveyed my skin.

"You have clogged pores on your nose," she said in dismay.

"Really?" I tried to act surprised by the little oil craters that had erupted on my nose in the last three months. The beauty magazines all described combat with blackheads, no one talked about whiteheads and how to treat them.

"You really should consider a toner to control the oil," she said. She pulled a bottle from the skin care display, unscrewed the cap, and shook toner onto two cotton balls. My nose filled with the scents of menthol and witch hazel. For an instant, every pore on my face blazed and then cooled down.

"There are three steps of basic skin care," she said as she took up two more cotton balls and swept my whole face again, "cleanse, tone, and moisturize." As she said this, I felt like I was in beauty special education. I cringed at the brown patches on the cotton balls. I felt clueless. At home, I lathered the soap in my hands and slathered it on my face just like the white girls did in the magazines. After she finished degreasing my face, the saleslady stepped back and stared at me again.

"I am going to give you an evening look," she said before she spun around and disappeared behind the counter.

Amy and I exchanged excited glances. *An evening look was just what I needed for the dance,* I thought to myself. I didn't want a natural look. I was the Other One, after all.

The woman knit her penciled eyebrows together in concentration as she considered her first move. She creased a powder puff over her index finger and reached to the darkest shade in the palette. I glanced down and watched the circular motion she used to press the puff into the pot. It was a deep orange, the color of a tanned white person. The pinky orange stain on the puff reminded me of the flesh-colored Crayola crayon, but I did not complain. I reminded myself how different the colors looked in the display than on my friend's face. The lady shook the excess off the puff onto a tissue, then raised the puff to my face.

"Close your eyes," she said.

I obeyed and felt the fibers of the puff dance across my skin. I inhaled the faint whiff of lilac. She dabbed the puff into the powder again and pressed it into the creases around my nose back to the hairline; the puff brushed my Afro. She raised my chin and worked back to my ears. With each step I felt myself drifting from natural to glamorous, and thrilled with excitement.

"Okay," she said. "Now let's do your eyes."

I closed my eyes and felt the heel of her hand resting gently on my cheekbone. She started in the outer edge of my eye and used long vertical strokes working from my lashes to my eyebrows. I could feel the firm pressure of the strokes on my eyeball. *Remember this pattern. Remember these techniques,* I said to myself, confident that I would want to re-create this magic at home. She stopped for a minute and then repeated the same strokes in the center of my eye. I moved my legs to the side so that she could get into the corner of my eye. I smelled the perfume of her lotion and felt the heat of her palm on my face. I never knew that so much attention was supposed to be devoted to eyelids. Dramatic eyes must hold the key to an evening look. I tried to keep my eyes closed and my head still.

When she finished the first lid, I glanced over at the pile of swabs. The colors seemed stark but pale. I would never have picked them myself. *But that was the point,* I told myself, *to get some professional help.* I closed my eyes as she performed the same process on the other lid. I was dying to see how I looked.

The saleslady wiped her index finger on a tissue and dipped

it into a pot of creamy blush. She dotted her finger along my cheekbone and then smoothed out the color.

"What's this one called?" I asked.

"Desert Rose," she said, studying the effect. Desert Rose. I tried to memorize the name of the blush. I didn't have enough money in my wallet to buy all of this stuff and the soap and toner I so clearly needed. I needed to remember the names so that I could bring Mom back and get everything I needed before the dance.

"Now for your lips," the lady said.

She used a fuchsia pencil to trace a line in the middle of my mouth and then brushed on a matching shade of lipstick. The lipstick smelled stale, as if it had been open and on display a long time.

The final touch was mascara, jet black for me. The saleslady pumped the wand into the tube and asked me not to blink. Then she pulled my eyes open to reach the base of my stubby lashes.

"Don't blink," she said. The ribbed metal shaft twinkled in the store lights. She gave my upper and lower lashes a thick coating of the mascara, and when I blinked my lashes clumped as if they had been taped together.

"There," she announced. "All finished." She stood back for a better view and she handed me a mirror.

I looked at Amy before I raised the mirror to my face. Amy was not smiling. Maybe she was jealous.

Kabuki Jennifer blinked at me in amazement. The middle of my face was completely ashy and chalky. My eyelids screamed with the peacock blue, kelly green, and cotton candy pink shades arranged like fanned playing cards. It looked like she had drawn my cheekbones with a felt-tip marker. My stubby lashes clumped together and folded in from the weight of all the goopy mascara. The baby hairs around my face had become dusty, and the rim of my chin revealed the true color of my skin. I was mismatched and uneven. I looked more ready for Halloween or the circus than the school dance. The pouting minimouth she'd made for me quivered in despair. I blinked back the tears that I could feel gathering in my eyes. I didn't want to cry or hurt the woman's feelings. She had really tried.

"Thanks," I said weakly. I jumped to the floor and studied the marble tiles afraid that if I didn't I might cry.

"I really tried to give you an evening look," she said. "You know, mysterious and dramatic."

"I know," I said. "Thanks." I wanted to leave. Pretty was beyond my reach. We all knew that she had failed miserably, but no one wanted to admit it.

"I'll take the shadows, powder, blush, and lipstick," Amy said.

"Coming right up," the woman said as she disappeared behind the counter to ring up Amy's makeup.

Amy and I looked away from each other. What could she say? What could I do?

As Amy counted her money, the saleslady looked at me.

"Anything for you?" she asked brightly.

"May I have the soap, please?" I asked.

"Would you like the toner, too?" she asked. "It could really help."

"No, thanks," I said. "Just the soap."

She pulled a box of soap off of the shelf behind her.

I paid without looking at the saleswoman again.

The lady handed the folded bags to both of us.

"Enjoy, girls," the lady said. "Have fun at the dance." She resumed her position at the edge of the counter.

"I need to go to the bathroom," I announced.

"It really doesn't look that bad," Amy said.

I knew she was lying, and that only made everything worse. I hurried down the staircase and bolted through the men's department, nearly running by the time I reached the ladies' room in the corner of the store.

I threw my weight against the heavy door to open it. I stood in the plate glass mirror of the ladies' lounge. I lost the fight against my tears, and as they streaked down my face, they caught the mascara, turning it into little black rivers that cut through the powder.

I felt completely stupid. I should have known better. Mom couldn't even buy makeup in Palos Verdes. She had to go to a larger mall, a thirty-minute drive from our house to a poorly lit corner of the May Company cosmetics and fragrance department to find the single line of products stocked for black women— Flori Roberts. Mom always endured a long wait for a saleslady to come from another, busier counter. Then the saleslady never knew anything about the actual product line and couldn't answer any of Mom's questions.

I walked back to the sinks. I ripped a stack of paper towels from the dispenser and turned on the water. I lathered my hands with soap. I wet the towels and rubbed all over my face. I did it about three times until I was sure all of the makeup was gone. Then I rinsed. The minimouth the saleslady drew on my mouth resisted the rubbing and so I just stood there and rubbed harder until it disappeared. Then I dried my face with more paper towels and ignored the tight feeling of my skin. We left the store through an exit on the lower level.

Amy wore her new natural look for the next week and all of our friends marveled at the improvement. It seemed that we were growing apart with each day that passed. The dance was all anyone talked about, and anticipation exhausted and distracted nearly everyone. Dread of the dance washed over me in waves, and by Thursday, I just couldn't wait for it to be over. Even though the Friday afternoon dance was meant to take the pressure off students, it did not seem to be working.

When the last bell clanged on Friday, kids surged into the quadrangle. Everyone was so hyped with adrenaline. Playful shoving matches erupted between boys that looked like something out of *Wild Kingdom*. Girls exaggerated all of their gestures, and a torrent of flipping hair rippled like a stadium wave.

Girls rushed to the bathroom to primp. A long line stretched behind Amy and me. A few girls nervously peed in one of the two stalls, but most girls stood three deep as we all jockeyed for space in the plate glass mirror. Amy, like the more sophisticated girls, pulled out her new stash of makeup, wiped the creased shadow from her lids, applied more, and glossed her lips. Girls bent over to brush their hair upside down and nearly snapped their necks as they tried to flip it. The serious girls even sprayed their bangs with aerosol hairspray and then passed it around to all who wanted it. Amy took a few sprays and shook her head.

My face glistened with sweat and oil. I unwound some brown paper towels from the dispenser and ran them under the water. As I wiped the shine off, I felt the rough fibers on my face. I tried to sweep the stray strands of paper off of my face but the more I wiped, the more of the towel got left behind. I was plain-faced and helpless. I fished my pink plastic pick from the front pocket of my backpack and fluffed my Afro. The tight coils of my hair resisted the comb and some snapped off. The pick on my hair made a dull ripping sound that echoed in the bathroom. As I tried to pat the three inches of my Afro into a stovepipe style that was flattened on the sides, I doubted the choice to go natural. The dance seemed like a long, silky, flowing hair event. I swept my sparkled lip gloss across my mouth and smelled bubblegum. As I looked in the mirror at myself, I knew that this was the best that I could do, but it did not seem like nearly enough.

Amy had worn tight jeans to school that day. She unbuttoned her oxford blouse to reveal a tube top, untucked the blouse from her pants, and tied it at her waist to show her midriff. I flipped up the collar of my pink polo shirt and folded it under at the neck. I smoothed the seat of my white denim skirt, but that was about all I could do. I checked my legs for ash—patches of skin made gray from dryness—and noticed that I needed an extra bit of lotion. The white plastic hoops I borrowed from Natalie clanked and clattered as I got ready. I inspected the pair of white ballet flats I'd chosen to round out the look.

Amy and I met up with two other girls, Lillian and Justine. We were like two sets of best friends who hung out at lunch than we were four, equally close friends. Lillian, another recent transplant, had gotten close with Justine, a girl who had just returned from a year in London. As we walked over to the cafeteria, I recognized another difference between my friends and me. For all of the talk about the dance, the subject of actual dancing never arose. It seemed like we talked about everything else—makeup, outfits, cute boys, romance—but never dancing. It seemed strange that for all I knew about Amy, we never practiced dance moves together. In fact, I'd never seen her dance.

I knew that *I* could dance. Every Saturday morning, for as

long as I could remember, Natalie and I didn't watch *Soul Train,* we *rode* the soul train. As soon as Dick Clark signed off *American Bandstand,* we darted upstairs, selected our cutest outfits, and slid into position before the television screen as the animated funk train chugged into view. The smokestack billowed in time to the theme song as women's voices whispered, "Let's get it oooooon, it's time to get down." Over and over, they repeated the refrain, their voices growing stronger until Natalie and I spun in circles and clapped in time to the music. We worked with contestants on the scramble board, we practiced our coolest moves in the line dance, we did it all. We didn't even need to step into the studio. Natalie and I brought the studio to our family room.

But the kids milling around me whispering, shouting, and laughing like crickets weren't *Soul Train* dancers. The music that blasted from behind the closed cafeteria doors told me that we were not riding the soul train. I was in the world of Air Supply and Pink Floyd. I could feel the bass of the music from a few hundred feet away, but no one else seemed to pay much attention to it. I switched my legs together at the beat, warming up, but it seemed like I was the only one. The kids didn't know how to pay attention to the music. It was just background noise to them, something that they heard but did not feel with their bodies. Most of these kids had thought about everything but the music until that moment, and the pulsing beat seemed to make most kids anxious with the revelation that they would actually have to dance in a few moments.

Everyone was starting to get restless as we waited outside. Just then, a group of the fast kids appeared on the edge of the crowd. They had snuck off to the cross-country field to try to get drunk. The boys licked their lips over and over and seemed to lose control of the spit in their mouths. The girls looked like they had been laughing in their sleep. They were the only ones who seemed in any way relaxed.

A few smiling eighth graders from student council threw open the cafeteria doors and collected the tickets as they smirked at our naïve excitement. Inside, a handful of teachers and PTA moms tried to stay out of the way. The DJ had arranged his table on the stage, and mounted box speakers towered over the room and filled it with the sound of rock 'n' roll. The DJ was just a local high school techie who ran with the audio-visual crowd and had a large record collection. He had more enthusiasm than skill and spun records rather than mixed them as his single turntable didn't allow him to blend records into one another. The cafeteria looked like a dark cavern, and kids didn't know how to fill the space even as the glittering disco ball cast the floor and the wall with a rainbow of light. Clusters of boys and girls stood around the perimeter of the room unsure of what to do.

Amy and I stuck close to the other girls. I tossed my head back just like they did, but my Afro did not move. Fake laughing and bang tossing gave way to us all singing the lyrics of the songs we knew. But everyone was beginning to feel stupid standing and waiting. It was taking a very long time for anyone to get the hang of the actual dancing.

Then finally some of the boys who had boozed up to drop their inhibitions grabbed the girls they had taken into the field and began to dance. At the first chorus of Blondie's "Call Me," two couples took the suggestion and everybody else watched. Even though the boys had the courage to get out onto the floor, it was clear that they did not know how to dance. A popular boy just jerked his shoulders in vague proximity to the beat. His friend hopped from one foot to the other and kept his eyes on the floor. Mr. Jumpy got nervous and signaled to his friend who whispered to another girl, and then they joined the other kids on the floor. I couldn't believe how little attention these kids paid to the music. They heard it, but they didn't feel it the way that I did.

By the second verse, encouraged by the bobbing in the middle of the floor, other boys started asking girls to dance. The music was too loud to hear anyone's words, but the longer I stood with Amy and my friends, the more we tried to shout over the music. Kids fell into the mix as the center of the room began filling with bodies and boys found their courage and started asking girls to dance. By the beginning of the next song, the mass of dancers rippled farther outward.

Two boys walked toward my clump of girls. My whole body tensed with a deeper kind of anticipation than I felt when we waited to get picked for teams.

I stood with Amy and watched as the boys asked the other two girls to dance. They looked relieved not to be the last ones onto the floor and gladly accepted. Amy and I stood beside each other and tried not to get discouraged. *We'll be next,* I thought, *two guys will come over and ask Amy and me to dance.* We laughed and sang lyrics to pass the time, trying to look as if neither of us had a care in the world.

At the beginning of the next song, a dark-haired boy with pimples walked toward us and my heart started beating faster and faster. I knew his name was Don and had seen him around, but he hadn't gone to my elementary school and I knew almost nothing else about him. Don wore tight Lee jeans and a matching jacket, while most of the boys at the school wore Levi's. He'd worn black ankle boots instead of sneakers. *Be cool, be calm, act natural,* I told myself. Here it was, my moment, our moment. My whole body tensed in anticipation. I smoothed imaginary wrinkles from my skirt. The closer he walked, the more nervous I became. *Pick me, be cool. Pick me, be cool,* I silently pleaded. Don passed me and I watched his profile.

"Wanna dance?" he asked Amy.

"Sure," she said as she grinned.

As he led her to the floor, Amy glanced over her shoulder at me, lost in her own delight. Don and Amy were perfectly matched and made a cute couple. But they struggled with the beat. Their mechanical bodies and jerky moves looked strange. They danced with stiff legs and rigid arms. Watching them, I realized that their parents hadn't taught them to dance the way Dad had taught Natalie and me when we were really small.

As I watched Amy and Don, I folded my arms and stood alone on the edge of the crowd. There were no other girls I knew well standing anywhere close to me and I felt stupid again. As happy as I was for Amy, the pang of my own rejection pricked me. Her plans and my own, although so much the same, were turning out to be very different. I tugged at my shirt collar and fumbled with my earrings as if they were strands of long, straight hair.

The song ended, and Lillian and Justine came over to where I stood. Their faces were flushed with the exertion of dancing and the thrill of being asked. They huddled together and whispered but didn't say anything to me. They just fluffed their bangs with combing motions of their fingers and smiled. They had broken the ice and been initiated into the moment of adolescence. They seemed more relaxed. I could tell that they felt sorry for me and didn't want to make me feel worse. I was grateful for their silence.

I stood alone and apart from all that.

Then the music changed and a slow song came on. Don stared at the floor for a moment and then looked at Amy. I watched Amy and Don on the floor—they didn't move away but instead he held her on the floor rooted in conversation. They were one of the few couples who remained. He didn't fumble; instead brought his hands straight to her waist. Even though they stood about a foot apart, Amy looked slightly surprised as she put her hands on his shoulders straight out in front of her. She looked dreamy, as if the slow dancing were too good to be true. She beamed and her braces caught the light of the disco ball. They rocked back and forth like a seesaw. The dance floor was not at all crowded as Amy, Don, and now maybe six other couples danced through the song. The slow dancing seemed like a relief to the boys who knew even less about dancing than most of the girls. But Amy and Don were different from some of the other kids. With every chorus, Amy and Don drew their bodies closer to each other. It was like a scene out of an after-school special.

Everything about the dance seemed to cut Amy's way. She was so lucky. Her makeup had done the trick and more.

I hadn't even danced one song, not even a fast one. I felt discouraged and conspicuous and invisible all at the same time. I wanted to leave and go home. If I hadn't promised to wait for Amy, I would have left. But I had, so I stuck around.

Don and Amy fell into the next dance. She broke into a pointy-toed move and swung her arms in front of her. Halfway through the song Lillian and Justine suggested we go outside for a drink and some air in the outdoor lunch area. I gladly went with them.

When we came back inside, Amy and Don kept dancing and the smile on Amy's face just continued to spread.

I had run out of things to do to occupy myself and was feeling even worse about the whole thing. Standing there on the edge of the floor, I watched in amazement at all of the bad dancing going on. I decided that if my looks wouldn't attract a boy, at least my dancing might. I needed to dance, just to one fast song so that the dance wouldn't feel like a total bust.

I grasped for anything to salvage what was becoming a horrible experience. I thought of Mom always urging me to make my own fun. I thought about how, the previous afternoon as I confided my dread, Mom had told me to be brave and ask a boy to dance.

"You want to dance," she'd said, "not get a boyfriend."

Standing on the edge of that floor, I took comfort in Mom's instructions and tried to ignore the fact that Amy might be getting both a dance and a boyfriend. I wasn't Amy, I reminded myself. I'd settle for a dance.

I was taking a risk and I knew it. I scanned the crowd and saw a clump of boys who I knew from Lunada Bay. I walked over to them, screwed up my courage, and asked the boy who had been Abe Lincoln in last year's parade to dance with me. He was quiet and lanky. He had been standing around almost all of the dance like me.

"Do you want to dance?" I shouted over the music.

"What?" he asked, playing deaf.

"Do you wanna dance?" I yelled again.

"No, thanks," he said.

He stood with two other boys. The faster the experience was sinking, the less I cared about being rejected. The rejection felt about as bad as I thought it would, but since it had already happened, I stopped dreading it. *If I was going to strike out, I might as well go down trying,* I thought. So I just turned to his friend who stood silently by him.

"Do you wanna dance?" I asked.

He just shook his head no and looked down.

The third boy stood with them was slope-shouldered and shorter than me. I knew him only vaguely from third-period math class, but we weren't friends.

"What about you?" I asked in his direction, positive that he would reject me too.

"Okay," he said.

I felt more relieved than thrilled. I led him a bit away from his friends and to the edge of the crowd of seizing bodies and began to move to the music. For the first time all night, I felt good. I tried to forget the boy in front of me who struggled to find the beat and just began to dance, to enjoy myself for the sake of dancing. I knew I looked good dancing and could feel a few of the girls watching me. There I was, barefaced but really having a good time. Meanwhile, the boy seemed so unsure of what to do with his body that he broke into a jumping jack halfway through the song. I tried not to laugh. White boys really were clueless about dancing. The song ended.

When Van Halen's "Jump" came on, I took another chance.

"Wanna dance another one?" I asked the boy.

"Okay" he said.

This time, I switched into my *American Bandstand* moves. I didn't wiggle my hips as much as the *Soul Train* kids, but my feet knew what to do. My moves were fluid and easy.

I guess my dancing made my partner bold and he whipped out his air guitar. It didn't look like a move he had practiced in his bedroom or at home. First he strummed it like a novice, but with each beat he got more into it. I smiled for the first time all night. I lost myself in the music and tried not to worry about what would happen when the song ended.

{ chapter seven }

I DON'T THINK OF YOU AS BLACK

I CAUGHT MY FIRST glimpse of the gleaming white cruise ship as the airport shuttle bus pulled to the edge of the Miami Harbor. The Cunard *Fair Winds* was a confection of happiness, a gigantic cloud of pleasure, a dream. Even the ship's name sounded exotic. I knew that the best seven days of the summer lay ahead of me. Until that moment, the summer of 1982 had been loaded with enrichment programs—math labs, marine biology, tennis clinic, swimming lessons. All of my friends had spent their summers at the beach. I knew this because I passed them each morning at the bus stop where they sat in folding chairs and spun their boogie boards like tops. But not me. I had a mother who had a vendetta against "idle time." Whenever I asked to spend a day at the beach, Mom reminded me that I didn't need to work on my tan.

The summer had been especially intense because Mom had quit her teaching job the previous spring and life at home had been strange ever since then. She played housewife for a while, waking up early, coming downstairs in her quilted robe with full makeup, and offering to make us a hot breakfast. When no one accepted her offer, Mom took up some new hobbies. She became a charity maven who organized silent auctions for a downtown hospital. When she wasn't doing that, she met her friends for lunch, played tennis with other women, and shopped for tennis outfits. But she was even more involved in supervising my activities than before and made me tense by the middle of the summer.

I'd never taken a cruise before, but Natalie and I had been dreaming about taking one as long as we'd been watching *The Love Boat*. As we stepped onto the dock, music rang in my ears. "*Love, exciting and new . . .*" I wasn't looking for love, just lots of fun. Every Saturday night, I planted myself in the corner of the couch to watch *The Love Boat*. I knew every chord change and every inflection in the theme song. Julie McCoy, Captain Stubing, Gopher, and Isaac the bartender weren't just characters or crew members, they were my own personal ambassadors of fun and good times, my pals who had filled me with expectation. Mom didn't watch the show, but she planned all of our vacations and must have thought a cruise sounded like a new adventure. I squinted in the ship's glare and felt *The Love Boat* coming to life. My mind danced with images from the show—lazy poolside days, fruity drinks, and giddy frolicking; glitzy nights of elegant dinners and funky dancing. I couldn't get aboard fast enough.

If adults could discover passion and romance in an hour, imagine what I could do aboard the *Fair Winds* in *seven days*! I was hooked.

A roving photographer snapped photos beside the ship, and we assumed our poses and smiled. I cheesed, angling my body toward Natalie while Dad rested his forearm on my shoulder. Mom stood beside Natalie, widened her eyes, and shook her hair as she grinned. One, two, three, smile. We were quite a sight. We were the happy Baszile family, ready to cruise. We had taken a picture worthy of even Aunt Frenchie's album. Mom could send it as soon as we returned. The fun had already begun.

I followed Dad up the gangplank, Natalie walked behind me, and Mom brought up the rear. We stood in a crush of passengers anxious to leave, but I stopped and peered down into the mucky harbor water. Hulking ropes kept the ship tethered to the dock. Crew members wore gleaming white uniforms, welcomed us aboard in cheerful voices, and smiled as they urged us to keep the line moving.

Polished brass and rich red velvet decorated the main lobby where surging strangers bumped and jostled me. Retired men wore loud shirts with white pants and shoes, standing beside stiff-haired old women. Hundreds of families just like us, only white, milled around. I noticed it but didn't give the matter much thought because this was the norm at home. I was more focused on the fact that this crowd of total strangers and their loud laughter didn't bother me. I usually hated the way that crowds made me feel—small and vulnerable. But I was too excited to get annoyed and couldn't help but grin. I stood near a potted palm with Dad and Natalie marveling at the people as Mom stood in line to get our room assignment. A three-toned chime rang out before a woman repeated the same announcements over the public address. Her English was crisp and clipped, far too perfect to belong to an American. As the crowd swelled, I finally began seeing other black people sprinkled around the edge of the lobby like the conspicuous raisins in an ambrosia salad. Mom jostled her way back to us carrying three room keys and an armful of brochures.

We waited in another crowd of people who stood before the elevators for one that would take us to our cabin in the bowels of the boat. As we stood there, people stole glances at Dad and tried to figure out if he was famous or if they had seen him somewhere before. This happened on vacations and in fancy restaurants all the time, I wasn't sure why. I guessed that when white people saw a black man somewhere they didn't expect, they just assumed he must be famous for something. Dad didn't seem to mind the attention and always made it into a game.

Finally, a middle-aged white man who kept looking at Dad said, "Do I know you?"

"You might," Dad said with a sly grin. This was the answer he always gave—vague enough to keep them guessing without him having to lie.

And they struck up a conversation that other people quickly joined while we waited to continue the adventure.

Finally, the elevator came and we plunged below the main deck, passing floor after floor as the doors swept open, let other passengers out, and closed. It occurred to me that any famous person would probably have a room on the top of the ship. Dad nodded and smiled as his fans left us alone in the elevator. We finally got out onto the lowest floor. We walked down a long interior corridor bathed in fluorescent light. I felt the vibration of the churning gears and humming motors through the walls and under my feet. These were the least expensive cabins in the gut of the ship. We were as close to steerage and the waterline as passengers were allowed to stay. Still, I felt happy.

Dad unlocked the cabin door. The room was just wide enough for us all to stand shoulder to shoulder. A double bed occupied the far left, next to it sat a single night stand. Murphy-style bunk beds were tucked inside the opposite wall that meant that when we opened them, we would have maybe two feet of floor space left in the room between the beds. A closet and dresser were built into the wall beside the bathroom that was behind the cabin door. When the luggage arrived, we would have to cram it into the closet. There was no doubt about it: our room was cramped.

"This is all we need," Dad said. "A decent bed and a clean bathroom."

"That's right," Mom said. "We're not here to sleep, we're here to have *fun.*"

Their assurances were unnecessary. Natalie and I had not said a single word. We were too excited and knew our parents' logic too well to complain. *A room with a porthole or a balcony was a waste,* their lavish praise implied. *Who wants to sit inside staring through a window when you could be out on the deck?* I heard the same things on nearly every vacation. As much as I understood their argument, I also knew what it hid. Dad talked often about hating poverty. Mom said less about her experiences of lean times during her girlhood, but I knew that their experiences as kids made them careful with money. I knew that we weren't poor but saw how hard my parents worked for what we had. I just assumed that we could afford to have Mom quit her teaching job, but we could still not afford to waste money. Mom and Dad never discussed what they couldn't afford and would have been insulted if I had raised the subject. They always justified their choices in terms of good sense.

While Dad used the bathroom, Natalie and I unlatched the beds and pulled them from the wall. I didn't even care when she claimed the bottom bunk for herself. I was pumped.

Mom dug a piece of cinnamon gum from the bottom of her purse and popped it between her teeth. She sat cross-legged on the edge of the double bed with all the activity brochures fanned out beside her. She called out vital information: our early dinner seating and table assignment. Then she described the black-tie captain's dinner, midnight buffet, magic acts and punctuated them with little gasps and chortles of delight.

"Oh, girls," Mom began. Then she read the description of the arcade, then ping-pong, the limbo contest, the casino, and the lounge acts.

"Oh," she said in a swoon of pleasure. "There's a disco just for kids."

I had never been in a real disco for kids, just in the Margate school cafeteria with Rick Springfield and a glittering ball. This trip was getting better by the moment.

I half listened as I focused on my more immediate fantasy—the bon voyage. It was my favorite *Love Boat* moment, and I wanted to reenact it. Jack Jones crooned the last verse of the theme song, *"Welcome aboard, it's looooove"* as strings surged in the background of my mind.

I really wanted to get back to the main deck.

As Dad settled onto the edge of the bed, his face looked more relaxed than I had seen it in a long time. Sagging aluminum prices, thinner sales margins, and payroll pressures had worn him down in the weeks before we left. I had really worried about him. But here we were, about to set sail, and Dad had finally begun to set his worries aside. I was glad that he couldn't even call to check in at the office. He would have to just focus on us.

"Are you girls ready for some fun?" he asked.

"Oh yeah," Natalie and I both said.

Mom went into the bathroom and emerged a few seconds later, wearing lipstick, a fresh coat of powder, and a full smile. For the first time in months her smile looked genuine.

Natalie took time to gloss her lips and arrange her sunglasses on the top of her head. She had brushed all of her long hair straight back and looked ready to cruise.

When it was finally my turn, I raced into the bathroom, peed, then washed my hands. I checked to make sure I didn't have any dents in my Afro and lifted the collar on my polo shirt. I needed my first *Love Boat* moment to go just right.

Just before we left, Mom removed two keys from the envelope in her purse and handed one each to Natalie and me. I couldn't believe my luck; this was the first vacation when I'd been entrusted with my very own key—usually Natalie kept a key for both of us. My own key and deck after deck of adventure? I didn't have to ask permission or explain my comings and goings. I could rest, change outfits, and explore whenever I wanted. As I felt the cool brass key in my palm, the possibilities for shipboard fun exploded. I was certain good times lay just ahead. These would be the greatest seven days of my life.

Natalie and I walked down the corridor talking over each other about the whole cruise. Mom and Dad held hands and ambled behind us. Natalie and I kept turning around trying to hurry them with our glances, but they ignored us. Clearly, they didn't get the importance of the bon voyage. While we rode the elevator, Natalie and I just grinned and laughed for no reason.

By the time we reached the main deck, it was clear that nearly everyone aboard watched *The Love Boat*. The deck was crowded with people jockeying for places right beside the railing. People were packed three deep in some places. The dock was nearly empty, but it didn't seem to matter to anyone. It was as though everyone needed to be on the deck as the ship left port.

Natalie and I squeezed our way onto the railing in time for the captain to blare the horn. We both threw our right arms up into the air and gave our best beauty queen waves—fingers together, hands slightly cupped. As the *Fair Winds* left the dock and took to the open water, the wind grew stronger and blew through Natalie's hair. My hair didn't move, but I shook my head anyway. Even though the sun was about to set, I put on my sunglasses and watched the horizon in wonder. My adventure had begun—this was going to be just great.

The third day of the cruise, I woke up to the familiar sound of Dad's snoring. Roused from a heavy sleep very hungry, I lay in the dark unsure of the time but anxious to begin another day of fun. Lying in the darkness, I planned my whole day. I would go to breakfast and then go to the gift shop to buy a fresh supply of candy—chocolate, fruity chews, bubblegum that I could enjoy as I sat by the pool or just watched the ocean. I guessed that Mom and Dad would sleep late, so I jumped to the floor as quietly as I could and went into the bathroom. Then I took out a pair of clean shorts and a shirt. I pulled on my sandals. I didn't even brush my teeth. I picked my hair out to make it look presentable. I would slip on my bathing suit and grab my towel when I returned. Lotion and sheen conditioner could wait until I got back to the cabin after breakfast. I whispered Natalie awake and convinced her to get dressed and go with me to breakfast.

Ten minutes later, we picked the table where we had sat for dinner, greeted the waiter, and ordered. We chattered about the plans for the day. We'd spent the first two days poolside swimming and reading until dinner, and it had been great, but my back and shoulders felt itchy and sunburnt. When I changed for dinner, the shocking contrast created by the tan lines of my suit told me that I had overdone it in the sun. Maybe we'd visit the game room. Maybe we'd take another swim. There were so many choices for fun, so many chances to make the trip as good as I knew it could be.

After breakfast, we walked up to the gift shop and loaded up on a day's supply of candy. The day looked bright. We talked our way down the hall as I unwrapped a caramel and popped it in my mouth.

Outside the cabin door I heard the familiar sound of my parents' voices, but they sounded strained and fiery. When I put my key in the lock, the room fell silent. The cabin blazed with light, but no one said a word. Dad stood in the corner of the cabin between the closet and the bathroom wearing his pajamas: boxers and an undershirt. The sour expression in his eyes pulled down the corners of his mouth. He looked just like that when those people attacked our house. Mom stood barefoot and perfectly still in the bathroom as steam swirled around her. Her pink foam curlers framed her face like a halo. She leaned over the sink and waved the mascara wand through her lashes over and over again. Something had sucked all of their cheery relaxation and good nature out of the cabin.

I clasped my candy bag. Its rustling seemed so loud. I looked back and forth from Mom to Dad. Natalie and I waited and remained standing with our backs to the cabin door. Neither of us said a word. *What was wrong?*

"Sit down, girls," Dad said. "Your mother and I want to talk to the two of you."

Natalie and I arranged ourselves on her lower bunk and glanced at each other. Mom snapped off the bathroom light, as if she had heard her cue, and sat on the corner of her bed. Dad stood behind her as if posed for a portrait.

"We've been watching the two of you since we got on this ship, and we don't like what we see," Dad said.

On board the ship? I thought. *What had I done that they didn't like?* I flipped through my actions like the pages of a catalog and tried to find the offense before he named it. I drew a blank, and that made me even more nervous. Usually I had trouble telepathy and knew exactly what I was about to get in trouble for.

Each day, from the time I shimmied out of my pajamas and into my bathing suit until we met Mom and Dad for dinner, I'd been at the pool. In the late morning when it was relatively empty, I played games by myself and with Natalie. I was not too old or too cool to touch the bottom of the pool with my hands, twist myself into a ball, and really play in the water. I floated on my back for a while, basking in the thrill of leisure and pure fun. I took a break, slathered coconut oil all over my body, put on my Ray-Ban sunglasses, and read, *Are You There God? It's Me, Margaret* until Natalie and I ate a late lunch of grilled burgers in our lounge chairs.

Having run a nit comb over my actions, I was still drawing a blank. I had never even uttered the words Mom hated most, "I'm bored." Natalie and I just looked at the floor.

Whenever we got spanked as younger kids, my parents always demanded to know why we did whatever it was that had gotten us into trouble. "I don't know" was an answer that stoked Dad's rage and earned us extra strokes. So we always answered, "Because I wanted to." It became the default that seemed to justify the spanking. Owning our disobedience and confessing to our willful and intentional misbehavior never spared us the beating, but it did seem to make it go faster and put everyone in their proper place—me the crouching willful kid, and Mom and Dad the parents spanking their daughter for her own good. Here Natalie and I sat on the edge of the bed not knowing and getting more and more frightened by the second. I knew that this was the time for a quick admission of guilt, but I had nothing. This was not good.

Dad couldn't stand still another moment and began to pace the floor between the bathroom and the wall furiously. It was a short trip. One. Two. Three. Four. Back. One. Two. Three. Four. Back. He became more agitated with each step. Trouble was backing up like a broken latrine.

"Natalie," Dad barked her name like a drill sergeant. He jabbed his index finger at her from across the room.

She jerked her head up, her eyes wide with concern. "You've spent a mighty lot of time talking to that boy Jacques," he said.

Jacques was a bronze-skinned boy who parted his dark brown hair on the side who had watched Natalie in the pool. He kept swimming near her but didn't say anything for a long time. I could tell that he wanted to talk to her and whispered to Natalie that he had been staring. He looked about her age and was nice enough. Finally after about an hour, Natalie finally turned in his direction and introduced herself to him. A broad smile covered his face, and they seemed to talk easily from that moment. He was an only child traveling with his parents. He was from Louisiana. Natalie introduced me, too, but it was obvious that Jacques was interested in Natalie. After a while, they sat on the side of the pool and kept talking while I played in the water. Then the next time I looked up, they had dried off. Natalie put on her cover-up, and they were walking around the ship. She came back a while later beaming and talking about how much fun they'd had playing shuffleboard. Sure, she and Jacques talked at the pool and a couple of times on the deck, but I had been around. It seemed like no big deal to me; no different from home where Natalie talked to white guys all the time. Clearly, I was wrong. I looked at Mom, who sat like a sphinx waiting for us to think our way to her position. She followed the train of Dad's thoughts perfectly and shook her head in agreement as the curlers jiggled from side to side.

"That just doesn't make any kind of sense," Dad said. One. Two. Three. Four. Back. He kept pacing. I couldn't tell whether his steps wound him up or kept him calm.

"Just what do you think you are doing?" he said. He opened his arms and spread the palms of his hand in pleading. He sounded close to tears, but fury filled Dad's face. He didn't wait for her to answer. He broke off his marching and stepped into the patch of the floor between the beds and between Mom and us. He towered over both of us, and all I could see were his large muscular hands at his sides and the veins in his forearms. We sat in his shadow and dared not look at him.

"He's nice," Natalie said. She'd tensed her throat muscles just like I had and could only whisper.

"Nice?" Dad yelled. His voice rose into its upper register and the word sounded like profanity.

"He's from Lafayette, Louisiana," Dad said, almost ready to explode. "He's a white Southerner." He sliced through the air with his hand. "He'll never take you seriously, Natalie." He was yelling now, his voice breaking with rage. "He's never going to date you." He turned around, took a few steps backward and leaned on the dresser to catch his breath. One. Two. Three. Four. Back. Dad's rage was suffocating. I could barely follow the conversation.

Natalie did not utter another word.

Then Dad did what he always did before he spanked us with a belt: he laughed. Menace replaced the delight that usually infused his humor. It was a wild, back-of-the-throat laughter that pulled the corners of his mouth back to his ears and made him lick his bottom lip. He laughed to summon his anger to the right hand in which he held the belt before he brought it down on my bottom.

He stepped back into the middle of the floor. Mom only blinked as she watched the flow of his rage.

"I am telling you right now." He stood in place, but his body was shaking. He sat down on the bed beside Mom and leaned far into our faces and pointed his finger at us again.

"I am not raising you two for some white man." He narrowed his eyes to slits and glared from Natalie to me and then back again. Then he jumped up and resumed his pacing.

Even though Dad's hopscotch logic made no sense, I felt implicated. *Boy to man, swimming to sex, Natalie to me. We had covered so much space*, I thought. I had barely spoken to anyone on the ship, and yet I knew I was caught in the same accusation like a turtle in a shrimp net. So many things were tangled. In all of my fear and confusion, I had no room to feel angry at being swept up in Dad's accusation. To protest and point out that I hadn't flirted with a white boy would have meant abandoning Natalie, and I knew she couldn't bear the weight of my parents' outrage alone. We would be better off sticking together, I decided.

Mom sat on the edge of their bed nodding in tight-lipped agreement with Dad. She shared the fury that he channeled. She looked disgusted.

"We have been watching you girls since we got on this boat," Dad said again. "We have noticed something. There are all of these black kids on the ship, black kids around your age, and you two don't know the first thing about them."

"That's right," Mom said.

Black kids? I thought. *What was he talking about?* I had noticed black kids at the pool. I had been swimming around them. I had noticed them as our families ate lunch beside theirs on the patio. I had seen them across the dining room at dinner. But Mom and Dad didn't tell me that it was my job to introduce myself to them.

"You know the white boy," Dad spat, "but what about the black kids? Huh?" Mom folded her arms as Dad paced.

"Have you introduced yourselves to them?" Dad asked.

Was I supposed to? I thought.

"Do you know their names?" He was back over us again, yelling. Natalie and I cowered together, touching at the shoulder. Both our bodies were rigid with fear. Natalie and I looked at each other hoping to find a name between the two of us. Dad was so enraged, anything might set him off: looking up, keeping my eyes glued to the carpet, telling the truth, making up a name.

"No," Natalie and I whispered in unison.

I kept my eyes on the floor.

"I mean," Dad sputtered, "this shit has gotta stop." He balled his right hand into a fist and slammed it in his left palm with every syllable. "Right now." He wagged his head no, over and over again.

Why hadn't they told us all this earlier before it made them so angry? Why did they wait?

Dad panted and I could hear each exhale. His nostrils flared like a quarter horse near the end of a race. He sucked in air to steady himself. His shoulders fell with each breath. Finally, Mom spoke up. She glared from Natalie to me and back again. She looked insulted, as though we had betrayed her.

"Your father's absolutely right," Mom said into the silence. She enunciated each syllable in a frosty tone filled with contempt.

"You two have an assignment," Mom said. "You two have to introduce yourselves to every black kid on this boat. Learn their names and find out where they are from."

Natalie and I stared in amazement. Then I looked at Dad; the sourness had spread through his whole body, but at least he had stopped pacing.

"That's right," he said through thin lips knotted tight with anger.

"Today," Mom continued. "You have to learn all of their names today." The room grew smaller with each word.

"But . . . but," I tried to protest, but no other words would come into my mind or out of my mouth. Part of me wanted to deny that this ambush was real. But I knew that they were serious, deadly serious.

"I mean, okay," Natalie began, "we'll meet the kids. We'll do it. But today?" It was more of a plea than a question.

They raised their chins high in their air and brought them down in unison.

"You have until dinner," Mom said.

Oh my god, I screamed inside my head.

I sat beside Natalie frozen in disbelief. My mind raced. *Meet all the kids by the end of the day? How many were there? Where would we find them? What would we say? How could we be sure we hadn't missed one?* I panicked and my stomach heaved as I tasted the sweet berry flavor of the fruit chew I had swallowed as it mingled with the French toast, bacon, and milk from earlier. I gulped and my throat burned with breakfast and bile. But I closed the back of my throat against the mix. I did not have any time to be sick.

Mom and Dad just stared back at us, not backing off a single inch.

"You may as well get started," Dad said. He stood up, and I flinched. He walked over to the dresser, snatched his toiletry bag, and carried it into the bathroom. I heard the snap of the dental floss on the cutter and Dad began to floss his teeth. Our eyes followed him.

Then Mom stood over us. She knotted her lips and spoke through a straw-sized hole between them. "Now give me your keys," Mom ordered, holding out her hand.

"What?" I said.

"Your cabin keys," Mom said. "Give them to me."

"What do you mean?" Natalie said, confused.

"We're locked out," I said in a deadened voice.

"That's right," Mom said.

We didn't spend a lot of time in the cabin anyway—it was just a cheap, cramped room—but it was our shipboard home. Having our keys confiscated felt like a punishment. Being evicted from the cabin really felt dangerous and scary because it seemed like it might be the first step to being evicted from our family.

"You're not going to make me dislike you." Mom always said that at home whenever we got into her danger zone. If she uttered those words, I knew to shape up, quickly. I had lived in fear of her dislike my whole life and worked to avoid it even more than I tried to avoid a spanking. She always made it seem as though her favor depended on my actions. But every time Mom said those words, I always felt like I had freak power—the power to make Mom dislike me with my poor choices or bad decisions. If I made the wrong choice, who could possibly blame her for disliking me? For the first time in my life, Mom's face told me, I had crossed that invisible line. I felt Mom's dislike. She didn't just dislike my actions and my choices. Mom disliked me.

She snatched my key first and then Natalie's. The sound of metal on metal made the only sound in the room besides the twang of dental floss between Dad's teeth. Mom held those keys in her hand as though we had dropped them in the toilet before giving them to her.

"Get up," she hissed, her face frozen with disdain.

We rose from the bed, Siamese twins attached at the shoulder. I forgot my bag of candy. Natalie thought faster than I did and grabbed her book off the nightstand. My mind had already switched to autopilot and all I could do was copy her. I grabbed *Are You There God? It's Me, Margaret* from the foot of my bunk. I was finally old enough to read Judy Blume in the open, and if I was going to be outside all day, at least I could learn some new things about adolescent life.

Our books, usually our reliable shields against idle minds,

Mom's worst enemy, melted Mom's frostiness and in a minute her face blazed with outrage.

"Oh no, you don't!" she said, fuming as she yanked Natalie's book from her hands.

"Don't you dare," Mom snarled at me. Mom stared up into my eyes and I could smell her face powder. It was her turn to fume.

"Go," Mom barked.

Natalie and I turned to the door and walked like members of a chain gang.

Dad stuck his head out of the bathroom. He wore a full beard of shaving cream and held his razor in midair, pointing it like a finger in the direction of our faces. "Don't come back until you have completed your assignment." He turned his back to us and stared into the mirror.

We stepped over the threshold. We turned around to look at Mom. Our eyes filled with shock and pleading.

Mom stood with her hand on her hip, her head cocked to the side so that her curlers brushed her shoulder. She glanced at the keys in her hand and then held us in her gaze and slipped the keys into her Bermuda shorts pocket.

Just say something, she dared us with her eyes.

We said nothing.

She slammed the door in our faces.

There we stood locked out, on the wrong side of our parents. My throat blazed with acid as a bit of bacon jumped onto my tongue. I heard the deadbolt slide into place, and my knees locked right along with it. My parents' acceptance of me hung in the balance. I could not fail at this test.

I skipped past all of the questions in my mind and simply asked, "What are we going to do?"

I put my face so close to Natalie's our noses nearly touched. I opened my eyes so wide with fear that some of the sleeping crust in the corners cracked. I didn't even blink.

"Find those kids," she said as the surge of panic strained her voice.

Natalie turned her back to the cabin door. Then she started running full out, arms pumping. She was three cabins down the hallway before I realized where she was headed. When Natalie realized I was frozen at the door, she yelled at me.

"Jen, *come on!*"

I took off after her. Our hunt had begun. My heels dug deep into the soles of my sandals. I tried to cover as much carpet as I could with each stride. I had to catch Natalie. We had to stay together. We flattened a housekeeper in a pastel uniform against the wall and did not even look back to see whether our speed made her drop the armfuls of towels she carried.

At the end of the corridor, Natalie leaned over from the waist and rested her hands on her knees as she reached the hallway where we had to step over the raised threshold. Then she ran even faster down another short hallway. She threw open the heavy door and bypassed the elevator. We could not wait.

I thought of all the times back in Palos Verdes when I came home insulted that my friends said, "Jennifer, I don't think of you as black" or "You're not really black." *What do you know about being black?* I would always think to myself.

"Don't let anybody define who you are," Dad and Mom used to say whenever I told them about what my friends said. I knew that I was black, felt good about it, and never questioned it.

I thought of our Saturday talks perched at the end of the bed the morning after a school dance. I would tell them how I peeled reluctant white boys off the cafeteria walls like stickers and convinced them to dance with me on the edge of the dance floor.

"Jennifer," Dad would say, "you're a beautiful black girl." Whenever he said that, I felt hopeful. The black in that compliment was always really important.

"Who would want to be white anyway?" Mom always asked.

"Just be yourself" they used to tell me. "Be yourself and you will be fine." I relied on my parents' affirmation of my blackness. Dad's faith in my beauty had been my anchor. Their validation of my blackness was all that I had and until then, I took it for granted. I didn't fear losing just their approval, I feared losing their love. Sprinting down that hallway made me realize how much blackness and love were bound up for me.

But their advice to "just be myself" had failed me. Being myself had become the problem. It was not enough. Acting the way I did in Palos Verdes, acting normal seemed like the problem.

In that cabin, my parents flipped the script. It was not a twelve-year-old white girl saying "I don't think of you as black," it was both of my middle-aged parents berating me for not being black enough. They were not merely saying, "We don't *think* of you as black." They were saying, "We *know* that you are *not* black enough." "Blacken up." Our assignment was to learn some names. But the point of the assignment was to prove to our parents that we were really black.

Natalie climbed the stairs three at a time and was already on the next landing. She kept running; I could hear her breathing.

I made my way up the steps two at a time but slipped halfway up and fell forward face-first. I broke my fall with the heels of my hands and landed as though in mid-push-up. I raised myself to stand, looking at my meaty palms that were now red and dented with the imprint of the stair. I grabbed the railing. My shins ached, and my left one felt bruised. I leaned over and raised my leg to the next step so that I could check for blood. I hadn't broken the skin, but my legs were now scraped up and even more ashy. My spit had grown foamy with exertion, and I sucked my cheeks between my teeth to bring it to my tongue. Then I licked my entire hand from fingertip to palm and wiped my legs. It was all I could do to remove the ash and calm the sting.

I winced from the pain in my legs but still ran up one flight of stairs and then another until I lost count. My shins ached and then my legs got numb. I didn't stop.

Natalie had already thrown open the glass door that led outside to the lowest deck. The heavy damp air calmed some of my goose bumps and the sound of the ship cutting through the sea filled my ears. As I walked through the doors, Natalie stood whipping her head from left to right and then back again, searching for some sign of the kids. She turned back to the right, toward the main pool.

Most passengers were sleeping off good times—hangovers and stuffed bellies—while we jogged from deck to deck and passed bartenders, housekeepers, and towel boys.

We worked like bloodhounds trying to pick up a scent. We covered every inch of the ship in the same pattern each time: top deck to the pool and bar, lobby, dining room, casino, the gift shop, and the arcade.

Finally, a concerned purser stopped us on one of our countless rounds. We had passed him a few times already. He stood there in his gleaming white polyester uniform wearing his first and best morning smile.

"May I help you ladies?" he asked in his crisp English.

Natalie and I just stared at him, dazed by our panic. *What could we say?* It wasn't as though we'd lost a ring or misplaced our camera. The truth was too absurd. "Yes, please, we are looking for any black kid on the ship. It doesn't matter which one. Our parents have locked us out until we find all of them."

"No, thanks," we said and slowed our pace a bit to seem less frantic and conspicuous.

We camped in the lobby for a while hoping to catch one, but we did not see them. Then we lingered by the pool until it got crowded. Natalie ignored Jacques. The rest of the black kids were enjoying a normal vacation and got to sleep as late as they wanted. Not us. Our fantasy vacation had become a black boot camp.

Around lunchtime, we spotted our parents enjoying lunch with a black couple from New Jersey. Their faces free of the morning's fury, they seemed like regular people. We turned on our heels and walked in the other direction. We didn't dare see them without finding the kids.

Above the grinding sound of the arcade driving game and the dull clicking of the pinball machine, I heard loud peals of laughter and playful taunting as we walked down the hallway to the arcade.

I caught a whiff of myself. I had been running all morning. The adrenaline, fear, and the heat made my sweat ripe and musty. My armpits felt sticky. Shut out of the cabin, no key, with a life-or-death assignment, I knew I would smell all day, and it would just get worse. I spit on my index finger and excavated the sleeping crust from the corners of my eyes. I cupped my hand over my nose and blew hard to check my breath like they did in the mint commercials. Even though I hadn't heaved, my mouth smelled just like vomit.

I heard the muffled sound of video game music above the din of laughter. Through the glass doors I saw black teenagers goofing around and having a good time. The noise grew even louder as I opened the door. The clatter of the pinball machine and the cracking of billiard balls filled the room. The kids looked at us as we entered the room.

"Hi," Natalie and I said.

"Hey," several of them said.

"I'm Natalie."

"And I'm Jennifer," I said quickly. "We're from California."

We hung around the arcade all afternoon, engaging those kids, trying to be lively. The time didn't pass quickly; entertaining those kids was as exhausting as running the decks and pacing the halls. But we had to do whatever it took to make those kids like us. Mom and Dad's tirade had made it clear that simply learning their names might not be enough. We had to make these kids our friends.

We stayed with those kids until they excused themselves to meet their parents. Natalie and I lingered in the aracde, dreading facing Mom and Dad. We rehearsed all the information we'd gathered like witnesses about to take the stand. We filled in details that the other had forgotten. Natalie and I made quite a team. Back in California, we generally got along without too many problems. But our assignment had shown us both how much loyalty we shared. We felt as close to each other as we felt distant from Mom and Dad.

It was nearly dinnertime when we left the arcade, and we were still wore our casual clothes. We couldn't avoid Dad any longer. We couldn't afford to have our parents blast us for walking into the dining room looking sloppy. We had to change, which meant we had to face them. We were in enough trouble already.

Thirty minutes before our dinner seating, about six, Natalie and I knocked on the cabin door tentatively. We knew our parental inquisitors awaited us on the other side of the door. It was not a matter of success or failure, but something much bigger than that. We'd obeyed orders and learned the names and identifying pieces of information about every black kid on the ship old enough to talk. But I didn't trust that it would be enough for Mom and Dad. They might not be satisfied. They might claim that they wanted five details rather than four. Dread engulfed me as I stood beside Natalie.

Mom opened the door with a hard expression in her eyes. She stood there with her hand on the door for a moment as if deciding whether to let us in. I sagged under the weight of her scrutiny. Her cold eyes shifted back and forth between Natalie and me like a pendulum. Natalie and I had continued rehearsing facts and information the entire walk back to the cabin, but standing on the threshold, I feared we'd come back too soon. The information we'd gathered would determine the tone of the rest of the cruise, and the rest of our lives.

We offered subdued greetings to Mom and Dad, who glared at us in silence. We changed into our dinner outfits and only a tape line in the room could have made the fracture in our family more clear. Mom and Dad didn't utter a word the whole time we were in the cabin. I didn't have a good way to break the ice, so I just grabbed my sweater and followed the rest of the family to the dining room.

Our usual waiter and busboy greeted us and pulled out our chairs.

"Well," Dad demanded once we'd been seated, "what did the two of you do today?"

Natalie and I spoke in one steady stream that neither Mom nor Dad interrupted. Our presentation was jittery and mildly frantic. Natalie and I stumbled over each other sometimes, rushing to add details that the other had forgotten. In all, we'd met ten kids that day.

Natalie and I interrupted our soliloquies just long enough to give the waiter our dinner order, then plunged back into the description. Dad laced his fingers together and a smile spread across his face. The more details we added, the more he grinned. Mom loosened her clenched jaw and watched Dad, waiting for him to speak. The clanking of salad plates reminded me that I sat in a dining room rather than a courtroom, but I still couldn't help feeling on trial. Dad wiped his mouth and cleared his throat.

"Okay," Dad said, "you two really hustled today."

Through our entrees and the cheese course, they lectured us about the value of knowing black kids. Their strange logic seemed perfectly clear to them. But as I sat there and listened, I realized what they weren't saying—that our inattention to the handful of black kids on the ship was partly their fault. If we'd stayed in Carson, we'd know plenty of black kids. In fact, we'd know mostly black kids. But Mom and Dad had brought us to Palos Verdes. They'd selected the community and insisted that we "bloom where we'd been planted." We'd done what they'd asked when we'd moved to Palos Verdes, and we'd done it again all day as we scrambled up and down the decks. They also never asked us whether we even liked the black kids we'd met. On this subject, our opinion didn't matter.

By the time the waiters paraded a procession of flaming baked Alaskas through the darkened dining room, it was clear we'd passed the test. I unclenched nearly everything for the first time all day. But I also knew that the vacation had changed. I had to monitor my own behavior, make sure that I didn't cross this invisible line again. Natalie and I excused ourselves to go back to the room and change. Part of what we explained as proof of our commitment was an invitation that the kids we'd met had extended to us. Mom and Dad congratulated us on our acceptance. We were about to meet the black kids for a night of dancing in the disco. Mom had told us where we'd find our confiscated keys, and on the surface, everything seemed restored, back to normal. But I knew how much had changed.

{ chapter eight }

NO LYE

AFTER MY SIXTH-GRADE MAKEOVER debacle, I completely withdrew from the realm of mainstream beauty. The days of intense beauty tutorials had ended as Amy and I spent less time together. She and Don got serious after the dance, and we drifted apart. I didn't read teen beauty magazines alone. Versions of *Glamour* and *Seventeen* targeted to the challenges of black teenage girls didn't exist. I knew better than to expect a white girl, even a really nice one, to understand. I stayed away from department store beauty counters and avoided the makeup aisles in the pharmacy. I'd learned my lesson. So I kept to myself.

During seventh grade, I drifted alone in the alternate universe of beauty isolation. Aside from *Soul Train*, I didn't have a whole lot of good pop culture models to imitate. On top of that, I wore braces, and no one looked cute with braces. So I decided to go into beauty hibernation and maintain a basic hygiene regimen until I was prepared to take the next step and get serious.

By 1983, the spring of eighth grade, when I took my first tentative steps outside my appearance cave, I didn't like what I saw. Straight teeth, corny clothes, and bad hair—I was a walking fashion disaster. I knew it was time to break out. High school was right around the corner. Before I could step foot onto the campus of Palos Verdes High School, I knew that I had to get my act together, which meant taking the biggest step of all: my first permanent hair relaxer. There was no getting around this. My hair simply had to be as straight as it could be. It was a huge and necessary step. My hair was the real key, the most important facet of my transformation.

For me, a relaxer meant *glamour* and serious beauty. Even though *Essence, Ebony,* and *Jet* didn't speak to teenagers, they made black women's beauty standards completely clear: long, straight hair. Sure, every now and then a cover featured a woman with an Afro, or an intricate pattern of cornrows, but even to most black people I knew, those styles seemed exotic. Very few black women had naturally straight hair, but in the early '80s, everyone I knew still considered long, straight hair, courtesy of a relaxer, the gold standard.

I'd wanted a relaxer for nearly two years, begged and pleaded for one, but Mom always turned me down. She said I wasn't ready for the responsibility of rolling my hair in curlers and wearing a silk scarf to bed every night. Relaxed hair was even more delicate and finicky than pressed hair, she always said. I also suspected that the extra expense of touch-ups and trims added to Mom's reluctance, but I never pinned her down about it.

No hair salon on the Peninsula served black women, so they had to travel a fair distance to find a stylist. Since I couldn't drive yet, a relaxer meant Mom had to drop me off and pick me up from my appointments. Expense, extra responsibility, and a commute to the salon were the three strikes that had kept a relaxer out of my reach. I had been begging, but Mom wouldn't budge. I needed something to help my cause. Ironically, the announcement of the first Black Heritage Association pool party finally changed Mom's mind.

After we'd returned from the floating Inquisition, Mom and Dad talked with other black parents who lived in neighboring towns about the trouble of raising black kids on the Peninsula. All of these adults moved their families to Palos Verdes for the same reason: the schools. But none of the parents grew up in a place like this. These doctors and surgeons, lawyers, dentists, aerospace engineers, school principals, and veterinarians grew up in all-black neighborhoods in the segregated industrial Midwest, the rural South, in Nigeria, or in the West Indies, and most of them graduated from historically black colleges and universities where they had been part of thriving fraternities and sororities. They worried that their kids didn't see themselves as black kids in a way that they could recognize. So less than a year after the cruise, Mom, Dad, and other concerned black parents founded the Black Heritage Association. They claimed that the BHA was a group established to give us a richer sense of black culture and black pride. But deep down, I think the parents were more worried that we wouldn't date other black kids unless they intervened. In reality, they should have called it the Black Hormone Association.

After a shaky start, the BHA had become a teenage social set for black kids on the Peninsula. Originally, it seemed sort of fun meeting these kids. There were more kinds of blackness on display than I had ever seen assembled in one place. Even though most of us tried to play it fairly cool in the beginning, we were pretty glad to get together. Still, the meetings and the scene that developed around them created a new kind of competitive forum.

In the bright glare of the BHA social orbit, I began to feel as though I was falling *way* behind. None of the excuses I used to explain my detachment at school held up around the BHA kids. For all of the ways that we were different, they were my peers.

This was how the BHA broke down.

The BAPs, Black American Princesses, were city girls and recent transplants who knew what they were missing. They almost never came to the meetings. When they did show up, they stuck together and ignored most of us. They were the girls who rushed down the Harbor Freeway on the weekends to meet their Baldwin Hills or Ladera girlfriends. They knew all the latest dances, not by watching *Soul Train* but by going to house parties. They acted detached, like they knew that another world existed outside Palos Verdes and their time spent here was merely a temporary interruption of their future lives. Their fathers were doctors and they intended to marry doctors.

BAPs also had a common look. Gucci or Louis Vuitton bags hung permanently in the crooks of their elbows. They wore lots of black eyeliner and hot pink lip gloss. They bought their designer clothes from Westwood or the Beverly Center mall. Their hair was long, past their shoulders, relaxed, and curled.

The Black Valley Girls lacked the BAPs' cool reserve. Palos

Verdes had become the center of their lives, and they were the peppiest and bubbliest girls of the bunch and said "like," "totally," and "as if" all the time. They had relaxers, but because they spent so much time in Palos Verdes, maintenance had become a problem. Their hair was short and broken at the ends. They tried to hide their new growth by curling the hair on the crown of their heads, perching a pair of sunglasses on the tops of their heads like a headband, and giving themselves some bangs. They couldn't stop talking about *Flashdance* and cut the necks out of their sweatshirts to look like Jennifer Beals. These girls were really loud and talked about cheerleading tryouts. I noticed that the shorter their hair, the bigger their persona.

Three girls, "the Kittens," as I always thought of them, shared the same café au lait skin and light brown hair that brushed their shoulders. They were cool but not certified BAPs. They always sat close together like kittens tucked in a basket. They opened their sleepy eyes wide in surprise whenever spoken to, purred their words, and covered their mouths as they giggled, which was every five seconds. But most of all, these girls lapped up the attention of BHA guys like warm milk. Unlike the BAPs, who thought themselves too cool, these girls knew that guys stared at them and stuck out their chests in response.

The BHA meetings also helped me see the strange things that suburban adolescence brought out in black kids. I'd known one girl, LaVena, since we were little girls. We were the same age and grade but never attended the same schools. Our mothers chatted in the supermarket and we played together at holiday parties. The last time I saw her before BHA started, she and I seemed more alike than different. But a very different girl showed up at the BHA meetings, a pretend around the way girl, who cocked her hip as she stood, rolled on the edges of her feet to sweep her hips from side to side. LaVena constantly pursed her lips and ground gum between her molars before she popped tiny bubbles and blew bigger ones on the tip of her tongue. She couldn't stop talking about the latest music on KGFJ radio, the station that played what people eventually called "urban music." She tried to talk like the kids who called to give shout-outs on the radio, but there weren't any radio shout-out types in PV. As much as she tried to act and sound as though she lived in South Central or the Long Beach housing projects rather than in a modern bungalow, it was only an illusion. LaVena didn't have a driver's license and would have to take at least five buses to get to these neighborhoods. Besides, her parents worked opposite shifts and probably wouldn't take her there.

The boys were as varied as the girls and broke down into groups according to the sports. The basketball players, tall, muscular guys, fared the best. The black kids universally admired their hoop skills, which also meant that they could travel into Los Angeles and fit into a category that those kids recognized. The basketball players also were local celebrities and campus stars, admired by white jocks and surfer guys who slapped their hands hoping some of their cool might rub off. White cheerleaders and popular girls also swarmed around them.

There were the tennis guys who came to the meeting straight from the club wearing their tennis whites and Rod Lavers, the collars of their Lacoste shirts flipped up. They were genteel and aloof. They showed up at parties wearing argyle sweaters and vests and loafers without socks. They cultivated a preppy cool that translated from the private tennis clubs to the school courts, where they were celebrated and envied. They spoke in a nearly lockjawed manner but could switch on a dime and jive with the basketball players. These guys knew all of the latest R&B but also kept up with the English punk groups and ska bands.

The scrawny guys with the squeaky voices, who didn't play any sport and looked as terrified as I felt, suffered the worst. With nerdy clothes, corny sneakers, and pimply faces, they lingered on the fringes of two worlds. It looked as though some of these guys still let their mothers cut their hair, which, coupled with their skinny bodies, meant that the BHA girls ignored them and the athletes avoided them.

But all of the boys shared one thing in common: their taste in girls. The boys honed in on the girls with the longest, straightest hair. Light skin and a nice rack didn't hurt either, but the moving hair seemed to cast a spell on these guys.

I was sure that no one else at the meetings had ever been locked out of a cabin on their vacation for not being black enough. But the sour expressions on these kids' faces told me that they'd endured their own uneasy moments with parents.

My BHA participation calmed down Mom and Dad in some ways, but I knew that I was a single misstep from a cruise repeat, and I never wanted to get labeled a black heretic. After the meetings, I did my best to hang around and mingle. The cruise had taught me that I didn't want Mom and Dad to doubt my commitment to knowing black kids, so I talked to the girls. But it was clear that at the BHA meetings, just like at school, I was a kid without a group. I slipped through the cracks of the BHA social scene. I didn't really fit into any of the cliques that had formed. Sure, I was friendly with everyone and people seemed to like me fine, but from week to week, I wasn't thriving. My faltering struggles on the BHA social scene became a stronger force than my own desire and compelled Mom to do something that she had refused to do for the last two years: it convinced her to let me get a relaxer.

Mom insisted that I stop washing my hair a week before she even called Teddy's Hair Place to book my appointment. I had to prove to her that I had the discipline to keep my hands out of my hair. I stood so close to Mom when she called for the appointment that I could hear every word of the conversation.

"Just make sure she doesn't scratch," Teddy said.

"Oh, I'll make sure of that," Mom said.

Discipline and rules: the pillars of the relationship between a black girl and her hair. I thought that the whole point of the relaxer was to have hair that moved freely, that bounced and shook in the breeze. Natalie and Mom explained that a virgin relaxer required a significant buildup of oil, dandruff, and dirt to act as a barrier against the lye and other chemicals that would straighten my hair. Any breach of the barrier, by scratching, combing, or other disturbance, would make me very sorry on relaxer day. I thought I understood what they said and tried to take their warnings to heart, but a small part of me wondered if they exaggerated. I had never been to the salon with Mom or Natalie when they got their touch-ups—the process always took hours.

As soon as Mom ended the call, I ran to the bathroom mirror and stood there pulling my hair straight, trying to imagine its length after the relaxer. The "before" Jennifer, the Other One, faded. The "after" Jennifer emerged in my mind's eye, and I smiled at the thought of my straight, bouncy hair. I was excited by the thought of my transformation. There was so much riding on it. A relaxer would finally make me look like a *Soul Train* dancer. The girls always seemed so glamorous to me; my only models of sophisticated teenagers and young adults looked like them. They were together, knew the latest dance steps. Granted, some of the *Soul Train* crowd seemed a bit odd, but most of them seemed hip in just the way that I hoped I could be one day. The barefaced girl with the Afro was mere weeks from a total transformation into an attractive teenager, a high school girl, ready to embrace life.

At home, I flipped through the old *Ebony* magazines stacked on the coffee table looking for styles for my newly relaxed hair. Aside from cars and food, women's hair products were the most popular ads, so I had plenty of choices. All of the relaxed hair looked the same, bone straight and glistening with hair sheen. I found my dream style worn by a model in a home relaxer kit advertisement. Layers of large curls covered the top of her head, then tapered to her ears. Vertical curls faced one another, and her hair skimmed her shoulders. She wore a pink V-neck sweater the color of cotton candy. She had about the same complexion that I did. I ripped the page from the magazine and trimmed the edges. I knew from *Seventeen* that girls "in the know" brought pictures to their stylists.

At school, I didn't even bother to tell my white girlfriends about my upcoming transformation. They wouldn't understand. How could they? The only permanents these girls knew of were the ones designed to *add* curls and texture to their hair. Explaining my kind of relaxer to them would be about as easy as trying to describe color to the blind. Impossible.

I did tell my friends, Stacy and Faye, two of the other black girls in my grade. Neither girl attended the BHA meetings. They'd both been on punishment for a long time after trying to sneak a car out of Faye's parents' garage and crashing it into a wall of the house. I'd hung out with them since the beginning of the year. I was closer to Stacy. We talked about my appointment a lot. Stacy and Faye got it. They both had Jheri curls—another kind of chemical treatment that transformed the tight natural coils into dripping ringlets that dangled and bounced. The big trick with a Jheri curl was to apply just the right amount of activator, the greasy, meaty-smelling spray that they put on their hair every day. They had to pump enough to keep the fragile curls glistening and moisturized, but not enough to drip and stain their clothes. PE class made this a nearly impossible challenge.

I breezed through the first week, high on anticipation. I combed my hair carefully, making sure not to scratch my scalp. When Mom saw me so much as raise my hand above my forehead, she reminded me not to touch my hair. The second week, as the sweat and oil built up, the internal hair police were on constant patrol against any scalp disturbance. The third week proved the worst. My hair looked terrible—an uneven tangle of naps interspersed with curls. I felt and smelled the buildup on my scalp and prayed that no one else could. Tiny brownish-gray flecks and specks dotted my hairline. They rose from my scalp like tiny balloons and divulged the presence of hair scum. I brushed them away whenever I saw them, but I feared grazing my scalp. Besides, it proved a losing battle. By the day of my appointment, I had become a twitching fool, trying to pin my hands to my sides, fantasizing about water on my scalp.

That day, I rushed home from school and Mom drove me the thirty-five minutes to the strip mall in the city of Torrance that housed Teddy's Hair Place. At every other traffic light, I checked inside my purse for the folded "after" picture I planned to show

Teddy. I was too fixated on the picture to realize that Teddy had been doing Mom's and Natalie's hair for years and I had never met him and knew nothing about his salon. Mom and Natalie never talked about the place where their appointments stretched over hours. Mom never referred to the man who put his fingers in her hair every six weeks. She simply pulled into the parking lot and kept the motor running as she handed me the check and told me she'd return in three hours.

When I arrived at Teddy's salon for my four o'clock appointment, I was a little disappointed. I had expected a mystical temple of beauty, a black version of beauty parlors I'd seen in the movies, bustling with female stylists fussing over their clients, women laughing under hair dryers as manicurists buffed their fingernails. Teddy's place was quiet except for the smooth jazz playing in the background. I saw a spark plug of a man, forty-ish, paunchy, and soft through the middle, who stood behind a black vinyl styling chair. The thick black waves of his hair rose and flowed down to his shirt collar. I couldn't tell whether he straightened or just expertly cut his hair. Teddy wore a hulking turquoise cuff bracelet on his wrist and a chunky silver ring on his pinky. If you didn't know, you might think Teddy was gay. That was the trick about Teddy—he didn't seem conventionally masculine, but he understood women in a way that only a man could.

A middle-aged black woman sat there and watched Teddy remove the last roller from her hair. She closed her eyes as Teddy raked his hands through her large curls and let her head fall back. He picked the ends of her curls with his long fingers and rounded nails that were slightly longer than I expected to see on a man. After Teddy finished styling her hair, he sprayed a cloud of oil sheen. The woman shook her head, eyes closed, and then opened them dreamily and smiled as Teddy made some final adjustments. After Teddy removed the black smock, the lady wrote him a check and made her next appointment. Finally, she slipped cash into his hand. She held his palm for a second longer than required to deposit the money, which made me think there was more between them than just the woman's hair.

Teddy turned to me, all business, the woman charmer disappeared. He sat me in his chair, raising me higher by pumping a lever at the base. He studied me for a minute. I didn't feel even halfway cute under the fluorescent lights and Teddy's sharp eye. He brushed his fingers over my hair, touching and picking through it without much appreciation. After a long exhale, Teddy cinched a thin towel around my neck and draped me with a rubber smock that covered my torso, arms, and the chair I was sitting in. I could see only the tips of my sandals. Teddy sighed. I wondered but didn't have the courage to ask why. Though I suspected that Teddy liked flirting and giving touch-ups to grown women more than he cared to put a relaxer on an adolescent girl's virgin hair.

I looked at myself in the mirror and didn't feel that I measured up, despite wearing my favorite outfit for the experience— a denim skirt and a green shirt. I wanted to match the new and improved me, but in front of Teddy and the mirror, I was beginning to lose my nerve. I tried to remind myself that this was my "before" moment, Jennifer before the transformation. I promised myself that everything would be better once my hair had been straightened and styled.

Teddy snapped a pair of latex gloves onto his hands. Then he put a tub of petroleum jelly on the counter and scooped out a full index finger's worth. He slathered it all around the edge of my hairline. The Vaseline border was an inch wide, cold, and heavy. He spread it behind my ears and greased the lobes of my ears and all around my neck. He hummed along with the radio.

Teddy walked to the back of the shop and reappeared wearing a vinyl apron and carrying another tub, this one white with red letters. He put it on the counter. Reaching into the tall cylinder of blue liquid that also sat on the counter, Teddy took a thin comb with plastic teeth and a thin metal tine on the other end.

"Have you been scratching?" Teddy asked with raised eyebrows.

"No," I said.

"Good," he said. "Then this shouldn't be so bad."

As soon as he unscrewed the tub and ripped back the foil, it smelled like something straight out of chemistry class—acrid and metallic. It overpowered everything.

Why did Mom, Natalie, and now Teddy fixate on the scratching? How bad could it be? I wondered. At that moment, it dawned on me that I didn't actually know very much about how this relaxer was supposed to work. I'd seen plenty of before and after pictures of natural versus relaxed hair, but not even *Essence* or *Ebony* offered articles that described the actual process. Almost every black female over the age of twelve I knew wore her hair this way, but no one talked about how the magic actually happened.

Teddy separated my hair into sections that he had to clip in place with steel hairpins and laid a thick coat of relaxer on the roots of my hair. At first, all I felt was the weight of the cream, which was heavier than mayonnaise but lighter than elementary school paste. It felt cold and I wondered about all the scratching fuss. Teddy worked steadily from the roots and coated every strand. My hair straightened under the pressure of a comb that glided more easily than I could ever remember. I looked totally ridiculous—a forehead full of petroleum jelly and a head full of Crisco.

"How are you doing?" he asked as he screwed the top back on the tub.

"Fine," I said. My hair straightened by the second. I was too excited to take my eyes off my head. I knew I was going to look just great.

I heard water running at the back of the shop, the snap of gloves coming off. Teddy reappeared with an egg timer in his hand.

"We're going to try to keep this on for thirty minutes," he said. "We'll see how long you last." Teddy wound the timer and the clicking began. *Try? What was Teddy worried about?* I didn't know but felt sure I could last the entire time.

After setting the timer, Teddy went about other salon business; he studied his appointment book, opened and then closed the register. He put a few combs into the blue liquid on the countertop and wiped down the counter. He tossed an empty foam cup in the trash. I hadn't noticed a water fountain in the front of the shop. Then he reached into a small fridge beside his station. He took out a big jug of wine, Almaden Chablis, Dad's brand. After pouring a cup, he almost fell into one of the chairs beneath a hair dryer and stretched his legs in front of him. Cup in hand, he reclined, closing his eyes, and lost himself in the music.

For the first five minutes, I thought about the picture in my pocket. If Teddy could just make my hair look like the model, I knew that a new and better Jennifer and a thriving social life would emerge. I imagined myself at the next Black Heritage meeting, my hair as straight and well styled as any other girl's there.

A faint tingle mingled with the familiar cool feeling on my head as Al Jarreau crooned "We're in This Love Together." I loved the song and sang the words under my breath. "And like berries on the vine, it gets sweeter all the time," he sang as a sax solo began. The relaxer was ending my little girl beauty—ribbons and hot combs, medieval curling irons and the kitchen beauty parlor. I bid a final farewell to the world of Stay Sof Fro conditioning spray, Wild Root hair lotion, and struggles with Afro picks. This ended middle school and my cotton-candy-headed phase.

When the song was over, the timer said I was halfway finished. But the seconds began to creep and a warmer sensation started to tickle my scalp. I tried to distract myself by thinking of the rising heat as the beginning of serious, professional beauty. Natalie had explained that after this relaxer, I'd be initiated. Once the hair had been relaxed, it didn't frizz again, and I'd only have to get the new growth touched up every two months or so. In between, I'd be just like the rest of the girls in Black Heritage. I'd have straight hair, too, and in that way, a little more in common with my white friends than ever before. With each second, I stepped one inch closer to the world of brushes and bobby pins, silk sleeping scarves and rollers. I stared into the mirror and vowed to roll up my hair every night, even before Mom reminded me. My braces were also about to come off soon, and then I'd just have to wear my retainer at night. I was about to emerge from my cocoon into the realm of high school and dates, hand-holding and kissing.

Teddy was off in the throes of the George Benson tune on the radio and his wine.

The warmth I'd felt on my scalp was now replaced with a fiery roasting kind of heat that made me understand all the worries about scratching. The chemicals had eaten through the thick layer of oil, dandruff, and dirt that had built up and made full scalp contact. The nature of this heat felt different from the steam scorches created by a hot comb on a damp scalp. I clutched the armrests and locked my jaw. Years of pressing had taught me well, and I tried to distract myself, to endure the discomfort with as little complaint as I could manage. But the heat had its hooks in me.

My scalp suddenly felt covered in mosquito bites, burning and rising with pain. One after another the stinging patches erupted, in the baby hairs over my right temple, the place that I snuck scratches most often. One by one, other bites reminded me of other breaches of the dirt barrier until finally my head tingled with every clandestine scratch. Even the oldest, most minor disturbance roared to life. A lesson learned. Swift punishment delivered. *Next time*, I vowed, *I will not scratch anything*. Even though Teddy would apply the chemicals only to the new growth at my roots, I didn't ever want to experience this kind of pain again.

Four minutes left, but I couldn't be sure because my eyes had filled with tears of alarm and pain. A blazing, blistering sensation overtook me. I wondered how long until the chemicals would penetrate my scalp, corrode my skull, and liquefy my brain. But I couldn't ponder the question too long because a splitting sensation at the crown of my head began. It felt as though the chemicals had broken open my scalp and made it weep actual tears.

"Um, Mr. Lyde," I whispered. "Excuse me, Mr. Teddy."

I didn't know exactly what to call him and felt something shutting down inside me. I had to convey my panic before the cream penetrated my brain. I had never felt anything like this; it was worse than the worst burn I'd ever gotten. But as I squirmed in the chair, I realized I could not escape the blazing heat that grew more intense with each second. Sure, it was hot under the plastic smock, but this was panic sweat. Beads formed above my lip because the Vaseline barrier smothered my forehead.

Teddy rose from his seat and sauntered over to me in no particular hurry.

"It's getting too hot," I said.

"That means it's working," he said. "Just sit tight."

"No, sir," I said, straining to be polite. "I don't think that I can."

Teddy pressed his lips into a straight line and walked away. The scorching heat convinced me that nothing could make this worse or slow the timer any more. Teddy reappeared and again he wore gloves to protect his hands from the chemicals that had been left on my scalp nearly thirty minutes. He reached into the blue liquid for another thin comb and walked back to the sink to rinse.

Why isn't this man running to douse this fire on my head? Can't he see the tears in my eyes?

"There's just one more thing before we take you back to the bowl," Teddy said as he looked at my tear-stained face in the mirror.

One more thing?

He took the back of the comb and laid my hair flat on my scalp. My hair yielded, all its curly resistance gone. Before the relaxer, my hair stood up to water, or any kind of moisture, and became even more springy. It "talked back" to combs and had broken teeth of many a cheap pick, thwarted more than one brush. But the chemicals he'd combed through every pasty strand changed all that. Satisfied, Teddy set the comb down on the relaxer lid that faced up on the counter. Then he massaged my head with the palm of his gloved hands. I felt Teddy's hand slip in the vicinity of the most intense splitting sensation. My scalp wept some kind of fluid, and I just prayed that it wasn't blood. This felt worse than rubbing alcohol on a fresh cut; in fact, it felt like salt pressed into the most terrible gash ever, except maybe worse.

Hold on. I searched my mind for the payoff for all of this pain: my return to school, the next BHA meeting, a boyfriend, a great high school career. *Hold on,* I chanted as I sat on the verge of a blackout, dizzy and raw with excruciating pain. *Why didn't Natalie tell me that it was going to be this bad?* The timer dinged.

"Okay," Teddy said, "you can head for the bowl."

My legs felt shaky and unsteady. I wanted to bolt but could only manage a stagger. I sat down in front of a black shampoo bowl and Teddy guided me back onto the neck rest. Then he released a lever that kicked my legs in front of me. He turned on the water, but it didn't feel at all cool or relieving. If I hadn't been so overwhelmed by my burning skin that I was sure was about to blister, I would have realized how much better this was than getting my hair washed in the kitchen sink. The water felt like a fire hose as it blasted out of the sprayer and peeled skin from my scalp—one more torture.

"This will all be over in a minute," Teddy said. "I'm about to neutralize you." The first words of comfort he had spoken. Teddy explained that the neutralizer would stop the chemical action of the lye relaxer. Without it, he explained, the lye would continue to work, burn my scalp, and make my hair fall out. As far as I was concerned, the only thing left *was* my hair falling out.

Teddy removed an opaque brown jar from the cabinet above the shampoo bowl. The smell of rotten eggs pushed me to the brink of gagging when he unscrewed the top. He took out a plastic measuring cup and filled it with warm water, then shook some of the powder from the jar. I swore I heard a fizzing sound when Teddy poured the solution on my head. A dull ache replaced the burning sensation. Fizz. Stink. I unclenched my muscles. He rinsed my hair, and it actually squeaked. Everything—curl, dirt, oil—had been stripped from my hair and scalp. There was nothing left.

Teddy squirted some fruity smelling shampoo from the dispenser into his hand. He worked up a lather cloud for no real reason other than to cover the egg smell. He washed and rubbed and then scratched my scalp with his nails. It felt like rubbing a cut before it healed. Teddy rinsed my head and then spread conditioner all over. My hair felt amazingly light. As he rinsed, the water ran over my hair, and I pictured myself breaking the surface of the water able to slick my hair back, rather than having it all seize up into a tangle of stubborn coils and curls.

When I sat up a new sensation replaced the pain and the panic: excitement. I couldn't wait any longer. I grazed my fingers over my head and lifted a clump of limp, straight hair. So this was what beauty felt like. I wanted to answer the big questions of the day. How much length had the straightening added to my hair? How much hair would I be able to shake? Newly baptized, the thrill of conversion surged through me.

It took a single towel to dry my hair this time, no more infinite ringlets to trap water. I couldn't wait to go swimming—whip my hair around and wring it dry between my fists like my white friends did.

Back in the styling chair, seated before the mirror, I stared at my reflection, lost in a fantasy pool party dream as Teddy combed my hair straight. When he did, I felt a little wet hair on the back of my neck and prayed it would touch my collar. The only thing better than relaxed hair was *long* relaxed hair. The glistening metal handles looped around Teddy's thumb and index finger stirred me from my dream. Scissors. Teddy explained that I had some damaged ends and needed a trim to even everything out. *A trim? Cutting or losing hair was not part of the deal.* The relaxer was all about length, not loss. *Besides,* I thought, *I hadn't even shown him the picture yet or had my style consultation.* I felt out of control, worse than at home because I could not argue with a professional.

The snipping began, and my panic rose with it. He took less than a half inch off the top, which felt like too much. Then he cut even more off my sides. With each snip, I felt my chance at cute fall away. Teddy had stopped swooning to the music but hummed his way through the cut. He guided my chin to my chest and began cutting the back, where he cut most drastically. I couldn't see the mirror but watched in horror as my hair slid down the smock and into my lap. When I looked at myself in the mirror, I was further from the model in the picture. I wanted to cry.

"Don't worry," Teddy said as patted my shoulder. "It will be fine."

But I wasn't at all convinced, and Teddy must have registered my doubt. In the next minute he spun me around in the chair, away from the mirror so that I could no longer see what was happening.

Teddy opened a drawer and brought out a box of tissue paper, smaller than the ones used in bakeries but just as noisy, a spray bottle filled with a cloudy solution, and a tray of hair rollers in three different sizes. When I asked Teddy why he was setting my hair rather than blowing it dry, he explained that the chemicals had taxed my hair enough for the day. For the next thirty minutes, Teddy parted, sprayed, and rolled my hair—the biggest, electric blue curlers at the top, midsized green ones for the sides of my hair, and small pink ones, not much larger than the barrel of a pen, for the back. He bobby-pinned each roller into place until my head looked like a rainbow.

As I sat beneath the domed dryer, I felt suspended between the thrill of my relaxed hair and the disappointment of my trim. My relaxer hadn't been what I expected. Sure, I'd gotten the straight hair that everyone in BHA prized, but pain had been the price. Nothing about the process had made me feel attractive—a head full of burning paste, smelly neutralizer, an excruciating shampoo and condition, and all I felt was relief that the blistering undertaking was over. But the "trim" had hurt more than all of the burning. The BHA meetings had shown me that long hair was the single standard of attractiveness, and all the trimming had made it impossible for me to achieve that anytime soon.

When the dryer clicked off, Teddy removed all of the rollers, pins, and papers to reveal a crown of stiff curls. Nothing flowed. He picked each curl with his fingers, then with a wide-toothed comb. A bit more fluffing, and a cloud of oil sheen spray later, and Teddy pronounced my style complete. I had more volume than length, and my hair didn't move, but it did look different, and better than when I'd walked into the salon. Teddy whisked off my smock and handed me a mirror while he rotated the chair so that I could get a full view of the back. The style grew on me by the minute. I looked pretty good and I felt different.

Mom walked through the doors just as I rose out of the chair. She greeted Teddy and then turned all her attention to me. She cooed and fussed over the style.

"Now, you've really got your look coming together, Jen," she said. "You look really cute." I really needed Mom's approval and was grateful for it. I was looking better. Not model or magazine perfect, but better. I was happy for that.

We paid Teddy, thanked him, and promised to call for another appointment in six weeks. All the way home, I checked myself in the side mirror and in the one on the visor. Okay, I thought, I look good, better. I could go to school, and then the BHA party and mingle.

The BHA pool party marked my relaxed hair debut. Perfectly curled and still glistening with the oil sheen Teddy had sprayed, I couldn't wait for the other kids to get a load of my new look. Full bouncy curls covered the top of my head. Teddy had trimmed the sides slightly shorter so that my hair tapered at my ears and around my neck. I didn't look exactly like the pink-sweater-clad model whose soft curls covered her neck, but Teddy's tapered fingers and long nails had worked their magic and brought me pretty close. I was close enough.

I couldn't have chosen a more complicated venue for my first appearance. The BHA pool party was unlike any other I had ever attended.

The pool in the pool party was beside the point. It was part of the backdrop and the pretense of the gathering.

What did I like best about pools? No sand, no crunch—just warm, clean water.

I was a pool expert. We'd had a pool since we moved onto Chelsea Road. After a day of swimming at the high school pool and at other friends' houses, I'd swim in the afternoons at home. On the weekends, I'd plunge into the water right after breakfast and float away past the prune stage, until my entire body was waterlogged and soggy. But I loved it all the same. I had spent countless hours in the pool in our own backyard. I practiced diving off the board, flips, cannonballs with the broadest splash pattern. I counted how many seconds I could hold my breath under water.

In Palos Verdes, pool parties had been a way of life, and I knew the flow of the party by heart. White kids and water went hand in hand. Water made white girls' hair even silkier; it flowed behind them in the water, lithe. The most a white girl had to do was rinse the chlorine out of her suit.

Black girls and water? A far more twisted dynamic. A black girl around the swimming pool meant a rubber swimming cap. If you were lucky, you avoided the chinstrap but never the cap itself. All that water just made a tangled mess of braids and ponytails. Natural hair drank water, and with it the chlorine and pool chemicals that could dry the hair and make it brittle. With all that rubber suctioned to your head, there was absolutely no way to look cute.

Pool water and relaxed hair were even more incompatible. It was a double whammy. Relaxed hair, weakened by the lye and chemical straighteners, could barely tolerate all of the chlorine. If not rinsed immediately, the sun would cook the chlorine into the hair and make it even more fragile and liable to breakage. Breakage would lead to haircuts and even shorter hair. Girls with relaxed hair actually needed the rubber swimming cap even more than girls with natural hair, but by relaxer time, the need to look cute trumped the need to protect the hair. If anyone ever managed a careful rinse, relaxed hair still needed to be blown dry and styled. Wet, relaxed hair rarely looked cute, especially if it remained short. The solution? Stay out of the water. So, as a relaxer newbie, I had already decided to stay out of the pool.

This wasn't just a garden-variety pool party because it was a BHA party. This pool party had little to do with actual swimming and even less to do with water. These kids acted like we didn't all swim, didn't know how to swim. The problem? Too much relaxed hair made everyone around the pool tense and the other girls were too preoccupied with keeping dry to comment on my hair.

Did that stop any of the girls from wearing bathing suits? Absolutely not. Bathing suits and the display of skin were the whole point. No one sat by the pool in shorts or pants—it wasn't done. So that afternoon all the BHA girls—BAPs, Valley Girls and Kittens— all wore their cutest bathing suits and even some tanning oil or lotion to cover the ashy spots, and we sat in lounge chairs beside the pool. The striped, or polka dot, two-pieces were fairly standard. The daring girls wore string bikinis with ties at the hip and scant triangles of cloth to cover the least amount of chest possible. Me? I wore a royal blue one-piece. A few brave girls dangled their feet in the pool until a splash of water came too close to their precious hair and they retreated. Most of the rest of us didn't dare even to approach the pool because we feared prankster boys might push or throw someone in the water and leave her looking like a wet cat.

The first hour of the party was pure torture.

By the late afternoon, the emphasis of the gathering shifted from the pool to the party. A driving synthesized drumbeat pounded the speakers as an androgynous voice started singing, "I just can't believe all the things people say, controversy." I had never heard anything like it. The music was funky like regular R&B but also had a futuristic dimension that I loved. Fascinated, I asked my friend the name of the artist. "Prince," she said. I knew I had to own the entire album. It was hypnotic. I loved it. Slowly, kids focused more on the music and less on the water, and everything relaxed.

Even the coolest kids couldn't restrain themselves by the beginning of the second song, "Sexuality," and a spontaneous dance party broke out. The BAPs, the jocks, the Kittens—everyone was moving in one way or another. Prince's shrieking sent us all over the edge. Our collective excitement was overwhelming and pushed everyone beyond their comfort zones.

I was captivated and my hair felt perfect, perfect to bob my head in time to the music and lay down some of my coolest moves. I was nowhere near the best dancer in BHA, but my *Soul Train*ing proved very helpful here. In the BHA crowd, the minimum threshold for good dancing was much higher than in the Margate cafeteria. This was the payoff for all of bad dance experiences and the pain of my relaxer.

{ chapter nine }

THE SETUP

EVERY YEAR, IT HAPPENED. Two young lovers, desperate for privacy, parked to admire the moon and the clear view of the Pacific. The moon's glow, reflected off the rippling water one block from my house, was so seductive, so enchanting. It was the realm of steamy windows and racing hearts. Maybe he got the idea to drive over the curb and through the scrub weeds that grew in the open field for a better view and more privacy. Without guardrails or lights to guide him, the driver misjudged the distance. The car pitched over the edge of the cliff, crashing end over end five hundred feet down a wall of bedrock. But in the dark isolation, no one heard the crash or their cries. A trail runner chasing the horizon was usually the one to spy the tire tracks or tangled brush and alert the police. I can't recall a night rescue.

Pictures in the *Palos Verdes Peninsula News* varied but always contained the same elements—a wide shot of the mangled car being hoisted back up the cliff by its rear fender, distant enough to obscure the dead body pinned behind the wheel. Other times, the picture captured white sheet–draped remains of the girl who'd crashed through the windshield or landed on the rocks. It was always the same story of passion, danger, and the perils of young love.

I teetered on my own cliff, the high school social world. I wasn't part of the in crowd, even though enough people knew me to get me elected to the student council. I was visible, black, and easy to notice. Besides, Natalie was the homecoming queen, the first black one in school history, and she reigned my freshman year, which helped and hurt. Being "Nad's" little sister kept me off the social fringe and I got invited to a fair number of parties. But people never pressured me to drink or offered me drugs, at least partly because Natalie hadn't done those things either. I had other reasons to avoid alcohol: I knew it wouldn't make me more popular. High school was proving treacherous enough without me stumbling around stupid and slurring my words. I knew that there were no guardrails for me socially. Why use alcohol to make high school any messier? It was confusing enough. To understand what was happening, I needed to be sober.

Neither a relaxer nor regular BHA meeting attendance had drawn any more attention to me from BHA guys. Sure, I knew them better and managed to be friendly with most of them. My social universe had expanded, and now I chatted with the few black kids I saw in the halls at school. I went out with the group after BHA events and even took trips to Westwood and walked the streets around UCLA every few months or so. I was great at hanging out in groups, but none of those guys asked me out on a date. I was stuck.

I had plenty of white guy friends, marching band guys, football players, student council officers, kids I knew from class. The guys I knew from school puzzled me in a different way than the BHA guys did. I talked to my school friends through lunch, they called me nearly every afternoon and we enjoyed long, engaging conversations. I felt flustered in their presence, but the discussion of the next step never emerged. Sometimes, these guys asked me "what if" questions: "What if you went on a date with a white guy?"

I'd reverse the hypothetical question: "What if you asked a black girl on a date?" Their answer never changed: "My parents would kill me." The answer not only foreclosed dates and romance but also made me sad and angry because I suspected that they were hiding their own fear and embarrassment behind their parents' disapproval. Almost none of the guys asked what my parents would say, maybe because dating white guys wasn't taboo in their minds. So I rarely had to repeat Dad's assertion that he wasn't raising me for a white man. Until the conversation with my white guy friends brought me face to face with the limits of integration, I entertained myself with a succession of phone buddies drifting in ambiguity.

By December of tenth grade, 1985, the drift ceased being any fun at all. My friend Mark had ruined it for me. He played drums in the marching band and I was on the tall flags squad. We talked on the phone, at football games, and somehow managed to maneuver into each other's path almost every day. I felt an attraction but knew to play it cool. He even invited me to a movie and came to my door wearing hip clothes and the faint scent of cologne. Mom acted friendly when she greeted him and made conversation until I had finished getting dressed. Since I'd told her about Mark's invitation, she'd been excited and encouraged me to go out with whomever asked. I couldn't tell whether she began dissenting from Dad's strict line on not dating white guys because she was worried I'd never get a date or because she had rethought her position since the cruise. I suspected it was the former. Still, the night Mark came to my door, I thought that my drifting days were over. He picked me up in his ragtop classic MG, burgundy with a black interior. I floated through the movie, wondering what else the night might bring. Then it was home, back on the doorstep without a kiss. The next week, Mark's best friend Don explained how Mark had considered inviting me to his father's company holiday party and my heart thrilled, until he finished the sentence, "Just to see what would happen and how everyone would react."

There it was. This guy, who I at least considered a friend, had created a space in which I was a novelty, cherished like a sideshow freak for my shock value. I thought Mark had seen me as a person, appreciated my humor. With his little holiday party plot—that he never even had the courage to try—he had shown me that we weren't really even friends, not in any way that I understood friendship. He had also shown me that he was not prepared to make me a main attraction in his life. He was too afraid to really take me out in public as anything more than a friend. We weren't just a couple of kids interested in each other. I had fallen right into the trap that Dad had pointed out to Natalie with Jacques on the cruise years before. I couldn't feel too badly, though.

Just a few years earlier, despite Dad's warnings, even Natalie had been trapped when the white quarterback took her to the movies, called her, but then ignored her and asked a white girl to the winter formal. The difference between Natalie back then and me now was that, despite her anguish over the quarterback, Natalie had been popular. She had attended every school formal. Then she had gotten a steady boyfriend, a black guy, another member of BHA, a basketball star. Natalie enjoyed a social life that attracted newspaper coverage, which meant another article for the family album. After the quarterback, Natalie decided to date black guys exclusively.

My future prospects looked dim. Suk was the first person I ever met who intended to have an arranged marriage. I envied my friend from Punjab who didn't date at all. Her parents would arrange her marriage at the appropriate time, she explained, and select a suitable man. She seemed to stand apart from the absurdity of young love. She confessed pressure to look attractive, to keep her weight down, but the goal it served seemed so much more important—marriage. She appeared comforted by the clarity.

After Mark, I had plenty of white guys as friends, but I never again let myself, or them, confuse the situation. What remained of my social life became an exercise in deflection. I talked on the phone but always kept things light and remote. When I felt their conflict among enjoying my company, wanting more of it, and their fear of ridicule, I pulled back. I anticipated the "my parents would kill me" confession and steered them, and me, through it easily. I didn't even flinch as I reassured them and didn't ask what of their own fears they stashed inside their parents' disapproval. I avoided conversations about prejudice and bigotry. I kept quiet, smiled, and withheld my sadness, then told myself that it felt easier that way. I became a "really cool friend" and when their attraction to me subsided, I listened to their stories about attractions to other girls. I even encouraged their pursuits. Worse than having low expectations, I trained myself to have no expectations at all.

I restrained myself in the domain of friendship and platonic interaction. After the Friday afternoon football games I went out with some of my friends from marching band and tall flags, girls and guys. We watched a movie at someone's house or caught *The Rocky Horror Picture Show* and shared a plate of fries at Bob's Big Boy. The group thing felt like a safe and inconspicuous alternative that kept the edge off of my loneliness through most of the fall. I could mix in with the crowd even if I didn't blend.

Still, it was better than being home on Friday night. A quiet Friday night at home wasn't a possibility, though I would have preferred it and fantasized about curling up with a blanket and staring at the television. The most relaxing day of the week was the most tense one in our house: Mom hated Friday nights.

A sullen teenage daughter sitting on the couch was the last thing that Mom needed on a Friday night. My presence there would just remind Mom of Dad's absence. He had a thriving social life that none of us shared and that we barely discussed. Nearly every Friday night Dad was "in the streets," the term he'd used since I was a little girl to describe his evenings out in Los Angeles, though I had no idea where. The way that Dad said it when I asked where he'd been told me that I was entitled to just one answer and no more questions. He never invited Mom out into the streets with him. He came home late, slick and sleepy-eyed, tie loose, collar open, smelling like a bar. We never met any of Dad's street "friends." He never invited them to the house.

On the occasional Friday night that Dad did spend with us, long ago when I was in elementary school, Dad promised to go and live with his "other family." I could never tell exactly how he meant the statement—as a joke or a threat. Sometimes I felt bold and demanded he name his other children and give the location of the house. I never laughed, or even smiled, at the joke. Mom and Natalie wouldn't chime in when Dad asked what we would all do if he went to live with them. Mom never pretended to have other children or another husband. She never frightened me with threats that she would abandon us. Other times, on our way home from an evening that had been less than perfect, I'd worry that that my misbehavior was driving Dad away. Then, I would just stare out of the window and wonder when the other family would come and take our places. I was never sure whether Dad actually had another family or what he did when he was "out in the streets." So I just prepared myself for the possibility that they might show up. Since high school, Dad was out every single Friday night and had even stopped joking about his "other family."

I don't know what Mom said to Dad about his Friday outings. They never told me, and she refused to discuss it at all. Since Mom had stopped working, Dad stayed in the streets even more often.

The more I grew up, the worse it became. Natalie was gone, and I wasn't a little girl who needed a story before bed.

Mom channeled her powerlessness to bring Dad home into a campaign to get me out of the house on Friday nights. So Mom made my stalled dating life her other distraction.

First, Mom locked on to my appearance. She never called me the Other One but in her own way told me I was "a diamond in the rough." High school was big for Mom, too, and she announced that it was time to "get my look together." Since my makeover disaster, I had given up on getting "a look." Whenever I complained about the pointlessness of all the primping, she chided me for not paying more attention to my appearance. Since my braces came off, Mom pestered me to smile to show the teeth she'd spent "all that money for." She nagged when I knit my brow the same way I'd done since I was a baby. She worried that my face would freeze that way. She shopped without me and brought home bags of miniskirts and shirts in matching pastel shades. On those days, the family room became a runway on which I was forced to strut and preen while Mom critiqued each outfit and returned those she didn't like. She really was Aunt Frenchie's niece. Never mind how my life felt, Mom was interested in how I looked.

But clothes could do only so much.

Mom's other big complaint with me was my attitude. She claimed I was "too picky" when it came to guys. She berated me for not wanting to "shop off the rack," which to her meant I needed practice, no matter the quality of the guy. I needed to date.

The BHA meetings clued me in to other black kids' struggles with the strain and the confusion. The luckiest kids paired off within the BHA clique and saw each other all the time. Others withdrew to the city. A few boys pursued white girls whose parents refused to allow them through the front door and snuck through the window instead. They met their dates down the street, at the dance or the movies.

But all the expectation, fear, and isolation just broke some kids. Like Robert, the boy who had asked me on my first date, they cracked. Our mothers arranged the date after they bonded over their troubled kids. Mom came home with the date arranged in principle. I couldn't remember Robert and so didn't resist. In fact, I was kind of optimistic. This time, a date might really go somewhere. So when he called, even though I had to strain to hear the words he spoke in a whisper, I agreed to the date. Mom kept harping on how nice a boy he was and how much we had in common that I neglected to ask what he looked like.

The black Hobbit who stood at my door answered that question in full. He was maybe five feet tall, shorter than Mom. He slouched and was so nervous he shook. His yellow V-neck sweater and blue pleated pants made him look prepared more for a seat in the front pew than a first date to the movies. He kept his head down, looking at his hands or maybe at his surprisingly large feet. If his mother's station wagon hadn't been idling in my driveway, I would have sworn he stepped right off the page of a Tolkien novel. When he finally looked up into my face, I saw that he had large eyes and a pie face covered with pimples.

Standing there, looking at this unhappy stump of a boy, I wondered what Mom thought that I had in common with him. What did she imagine we shared?

The night slid downhill from the door. No matter how many questions I asked to engage him in conversation, he only muttered one-word answers. At first I thought him nervous, but he never relaxed. He creased his mouth into a line and stole furtive glances at me. Even during the movie when we sat together in the dark, I could sense the tension. Finally, I realized this boy was more than shy; he was the most vacant person I'd ever met. When I thanked his mother for the ride and closed my front door, I knew there would be no second date. What had just transpired barely qualified as a first. There was no point.

I got a huge shock the next time I saw Robert. A semigoth punk rocker had replaced the black Hobbit. Flock of Seagulls hair stood where his close Afro had been. He'd slicked the sides of his hair back and then flattened the top and combed it forward to give it an angular kind of look. Gel had hardened everything, and it had become stiff. He'd shaped a huge forelock of hair into a point that he draped over one eye. He still held his head down and looked up over his lowered brow and the hair dagger. The black eyeliner that now rimmed his eyes lent a menacing edge to his formerly fearful expression. He dressed all in black: a leather jacket covered in chrome zippers, a shirt with an asymmetrical collar. He tucked his balloon pants inside pointy black boots with a slight heel and wide cuffs folded down. Chains hung from his waist and on the ankle of his right boot.

Dad was the only one who consistently told me, I'd "never have trouble attracting guys." Whenever he said "guys," the "black" was always assumed. In the dating world, white guys didn't exist for Dad. As much as I liked the affirmation, I found the statement confusing. So much of the compliment seemed wrapped up in the way I looked to guys. I didn't have "skinny legs," the worst blight a woman could possess. But I could also see the space between "no trouble" and "great romance." "No trouble" sounded like a minimum standard. And while Dad's Friday night forays into "the streets" had created a kind of barbed filter through which I screened his praise, "no trouble" was better than "the Other One," and I was grateful for it.

Keeping guys would be my challenge, according to Dad. My expectations were simply far too high, unreasonable. These high standards, he claimed, made me "harsh" and made me "too rigid." He told me that I needed to be softer so as not to scare guys away. Dad and Mom developed a name for this fatal flaw: "big engine." The big engine—surging power but no control—the big engine could blow and overwhelm at any moment.

I felt totally discouraged by Christmas. Pictures of Ethiopian children with distended bellies and flies in their eyes flashed all over the television as English and American pop stars asked, "Do They Know It's Christmas?" The song was everywhere and I couldn't help but learn the lyrics. The somber tone of the song's first verses matched my mood. I couldn't wait for Natalie to get home from Berkeley so I'd have company and a rescue from my gloominess. We had become even closer since she'd started college. She understood me perfectly when I confided my troubles and made me feel better when I shared my strike-outs.

Natalie's own dating life seemed to reach a new height when she began dating an older guy, Mitch Robbins, who seemed to adore her. He lived in his own apartment and knew he was headed for law school after graduation. His broad pecs and meaty biceps strained his shirts. He drove a BMW. He nuzzled and planted kisses on her cheek all the time without making it seem goofy. He wrapped his hands around Natalie's waist in a way that screamed passion. He had the most confident touch I had ever seen. Even Natalie's most serious high school boyfriend never acted this manly and confident.

Dad regarded Mitch with suspicion, gazed at him, flinty and watchful. His reluctant conversation with Mitch made it clear that he had his eye on the guy. Dad made it clear that Mitch had done nothing to earn his respect. Comfort in our house was not a privilege Dad extended to Mitch. Dad preferred Mitch on his toes, reaching, where Dad could see space between him and the ground. But Dad also knew that he had little room to complain. Natalie had attracted an ambitious black man on his way to a secure professional life. Dad insisted that Natalie observe the high school house rules: no guys past the living room, doors open. We all knew that Natalie slept over at Mitch's apartment, but no one even considered him spending the night at our house, even in the guest room. The only thing more absurd was the notion of Natalie sleeping at Mitch's. Home from college introduced a strain into their interactions that didn't exist at Cal— saying good night.

When Mitch came to our house the day after Christmas, he brought Natalie an etched gold bangle bracelet that she adored: serious jewelry from a serious guy in a serious relationship. Natalie couldn't stop shaking her wrist and smiling. She seemed to have it all.

The gift and their interactions didn't make me jealous. I felt really happy that Natalie's boyfriend so clearly adored her. She was pretty and lovely; of course, he should adore her. No. Natalie's good fortune just made me sad for myself in a way that I hated. I wondered if anyone would ever express that kind of longing for me. Would I ever inspire a gold bangle? Would a guy ever look so content wrapping himself around me? I drew a complete blank.

The next day, after Mitch brought Natalie back from the movies, he brought me a present. We sat in the family room watching the tail end of the late movie. Nearly over, the movie was beside the point as Natalie and Mitch snuggled on the couch. They didn't want to say good night. Casually, Mitch suggested that his younger brother, David, and I go out on a date sometime soon. I looked up from the television and gave Mitch my full attention. A brother? A date? It sounded interesting. Mitch explained that like me, his younger brother, David, was smart, really funny—just my type. He was a year and a grade older. All I had to do was give Mitch permission to have his brother call me after the New Year.

Mitch offered me hope, rather than pity, which I really needed. I pictured a slightly younger version of the suave college man sitting before me and couldn't help but smile. Mitch seemed to have good enough taste to choose Natalie. A date with a city guy? *Ignition.* This might be it.

As soon as Mitch left, I asked Natalie a million questions, but she couldn't answer a single one of them. She'd never met David before. In fact, New Year's Eve would be the first night she met Mitch's parents.

Natalie and Mitch returned to Berkeley without Natalie getting a chance to meet David. Still, I felt hopeful and waited for my phone to ring. A week after the start of classes, Natalie called to tell me to expect a call from David. I heard Mitch in the background asking Natalie about my reaction. *Liftoff.*

I pictured a city prince charming, riding into my life to rescue me from the awkwardness of my PV existence. I imagined movies and dinners near my house, late nights at the under-eighteen dance clubs I heard about on the radio. Sure, nightly telephone calls, hand-holding, and making out would be great, too. But it was the social life I craved. Bringing David to a football game, I'd show him off to my friends. I envisioned dazzling formal pictures where we smiled arm in arm, the picture of love and possibility. My first prospect of a real boyfriend suddenly seemed so real.

Five minutes later, I answered the phone on the second ring and tried to sound calm. The voice on the other end sounded a little nervous, but throaty and pretty deep for a high school guy. Natalie and Mitch paved the way for the conversation, which flowed easily. David kept saying "that's cool," after I answered his questions, but it was far better than the silent brooding I had gotten with Robert. David liked to read and to dance and wondered if we might go out sometime. I gave him my calmest "sure" as I agreed to the upcoming Friday night, even though inside I had freaked out completely. *Friday* night? What a bonus.

As if it couldn't get any better, David said that he didn't yet have his license and then casually explained that his parents had agreed to give him the family limousine and driver to take us out wherever we wanted to go. *A limo? A chauffeur?* I couldn't believe how amazing this night was becoming. So long, Robert and the back of his mom's station wagon. Hello, luxury and pure style. *Finally,* I thought, *a real date.* David suggested a movie, which I thought was a fine idea. He agreed to pick me up at seven and go to Del Amo mall to see the show.

At school, my Friday night friends weighed a trip to the movies or dinner out, but I stayed quiet and explained that I had a date and so it didn't matter to me. My girlfriends wanted details, but I just kept talking about a city guy, an older guy, and watched the shock on their faces. To white kids, even more than the BHA members, life ended at the edge of the hill. Maybe they toured the beach cities, but they looked down on those kids because they were not as wealthy. But the city and black city kids were totally different matters, matters of mystery and excitement. When we played Banning High School for football, the nearest all-black school in our league, the school arranged extra security in case some PV football players talked too much trash and couldn't finish what they'd started. The BHA kids all made a big deal of strutting over to the Banning side to buy concessions and show that we were cool, even if we didn't know anyone. Their halftime show consisted of cheerleaders and a band that played Michael Jackson hits, while our band played Gershwin's *Rhapsody in Blue.*

So a date with a city guy took me from the fringe of the PV dating scene to the center of envy and admiration. I offered only the juiciest, vaguest details about David, the ones I knew would most intrigue my friends—the older city guy, the family driver, and the limo.

I dressed meticulously for the date. I stretched preparations over a few hours. First, I gave myself a Noxzema facial and kept the white paste on my face until the menthol vapors made me dizzy. When it came time to pick an outfit, I laid out three different bottoms: a pink skirt, a pair of new Guess jeans, and a pair of mint green cords. I wore my white sweater with the deep V-neck. I planned to sling a thick, white belt over one hip, Madonna-style. After a long shower, I let all of the steam out of the bathroom, filed my nails, soaked them in dish liquid—just like Madge suggested on the commercials—and then polished them a coppery orange. I let my nails dry and walked through a perfume mist to scent my body. After I'd dressed, I sprayed Aqua Net hair spray on my drooping style and then used a curling iron set on high to add new curls. The combination of heat and hair spray made my hair stiff and made me feel sure that my do would last through the evening. A coating of blush, blue eyeliner, mascara, and reddish-brown lipstick, and I was ready to meet David. I had twenty minutes left before he was due to arrive, but neither sitting nor standing felt right. I didn't want to pace the living room because he could see my reflection through the glass doors that faced the street. *Be cool.*

Ding dong. Mom answered the doorbell and welcomed David inside. He sounded good, low voice just like I remembered, polite to Mom. Mom called out to me, and I tried to wait a few seconds before I started down the stairs and met *my* city guy. As my feet hit the tile, I felt crashing energy in the center of my body that made me catch my breath.

When I looked into David's face, mine fell. Fingerprints, smudges, and thick glasses concealed his squinty, dilated eyes. He flashed a gummy smile and his baby teeth looked dingy. His corn kernel head looked strange atop his gangly body. The skinny black tie and white dress shirt gapped wildly at his needle-thin neck. He swam in the checked sport coat whose sleeves he had rolled up to look cool but didn't. The pants and the shoes didn't matter; his upper half told me all I needed to know. The meatless young man standing before me looked nothing like his macho brother, Mitch. He held out his hand, and I noticed long, dirty nails on his bony fingers. Strike three.

I hitched up my lips, sure to show my teeth, opened my eyes wide, and tried to be warm as we greeted each other. Dating was turning out to be far worse than the most horrible Margate dance. All the labels heaped on me, and the ones I heaped on myself, surged to the front of my mind and replaced my anger with anxiety. I was the Other One, the struggling younger sister, the diamond in the rough. Rough diamonds couldn't be choosy. *Take what you get. Maybe this was the best I could do,* I thought. So I chanted Mom's instructions like a mantra—smile, make small talk, practice my "come-on." My job for the evening was to get David interested in me, wanting more of my company, yearning to call me back. Besides, maybe David was kindred diamond in the rough and we could polish each other.

Mom stood beaming as I excused myself and retrieved my purse, her saccharine voice echoing in the entryway. Upstairs, I looked in the bathroom mirror one more time. I wanted to close the door and cry, change out of these clothes, and stay home, even on a Friday night. But I knew that I couldn't. David had been driven all the way from the city, Natalie and Mitch wanted an update tomorrow morning, and Mom wouldn't hear of me turning down a date. I knew what she expected me to do. I dabbed the tears about to overrun my mascara, sniffed the thick-

223

ness down my throat, and stared into the mirror. Bright eyes? Check. Full smile? Check. I walked downstairs in full charm mode, ready to dazzle David.

The limousine idled at the curb. At least a limo, even if it was slightly old, felt more exciting than riding in a wood-paneled station wagon. A tall man opened the door with black-gloved hands. Even on this cool night, a slick of oil covered the driver's pocked face. He smirked as I said hello and slid into the back-seat. I didn't know whether to wear my seat belt and waited and watched to see what David would do. David didn't reach for the belt but straddled the middle seat and the one beside the door. As he placed his hand on his knee, I noticed his arm trembled. David and I talked continuously about music, school, movies, and books, anything not to fill the vast space with silence. David never mentioned Mitch, and I never mentioned Natalie.

By the time *White Nights,* starring Gregory Hines and Mikhail Baryshnikov, started, I'd relaxed and felt as though I'd made a friend. David was easy to talk to and actually made some pretty funny observations. I didn't feel any sort of chemistry, and the thought of romance had vanished for me, but at least I thought I could enjoy all the ballet and tap dancing and then go home without feeling too badly. I watched the screen and tried to remain absorbed in the dancing but noticed David out of the corner of my eye. The changing light in his glasses told me that he kept turning his head to look at me every few minutes or so. I stared at the screen and avoided him. A few minutes later I felt hot breath in my ear and David asked if I was enjoying the movie. I nodded yes but looked straight ahead. It seemed as likely that he was checking in as he might be making a move to kiss me, and I knew I didn't want to kiss him. I'd caught a sweet yet musty smell from

David's direction whose source I couldn't pin down until that moment. It came from his mouth—stubby teeth and a funky scent didn't add up to a kiss for me. When I kept staring at the screen, David finally gave up trying to look into my eyes. Halfway through the movie, David stretched and rested his arm on the back of my seat. A few moments later, his hot palm rested on my shoulder. I felt his twitching arm against my neck and tried not to get annoyed. But I had to weigh the insult of asking him to remove his arm against my annoyance. I should have been more courageous. We hadn't agreed to ice cream or anything else after the movie, partly because neither of us had mentioned it, partly because we didn't know each other, and partly because David had a long ride back home. We took the long way to the parking lot and chatted about the movie; neither of us loved it.

I had no idea how the driver had passed the time, but he somehow seemed even more like a weasel, shifty-eyed and smirking as he opened the door. I slid across the seat to the far side of the car and David took the middle seat this time. The backseat fit three maybe four people, so I didn't feel crowded even though I noticed the move. *This will all be over soon,* I told myself. We drove up Pacific Coast Highway talking about the movie plot more than it deserved. We had just crossed into Palos Verdes Estates, and the absence of streetlights made the moon faint out of the tinted windows. David put his arm on the back of the seat but caught sight of his sweaty armpit and put it back down.

"Do you want a cigarette?" he asked me.

"No," I said, surprised. I knew kids who smoked pot, but no one I knew smoked cigarettes.

"Mind if I do? They're clove," David said.

"Sure, I mean, no, I don't mind," I said.

He reached into his coat pocket and fumbled for the pack, then opened it. He perched a slender, brown cigarette on his lips and struck a match. His need for an ashtray forced him back to the opposite side of the car. He puckered his lips as if he were sucking a bottle and drew hard on the cigarette. It wasn't a good look, but the smoke seemed to steady him with a buzz. He rolled down the window all the way and a burst of cold air filled the car. He puffed smoke out the window and drew heavily again.

"You look cold," he said as he patted the seat beside him. "Do you want to come closer?"

I felt no attraction to this guy but didn't know how to say no. He seemed pretty harmless. He'd come all the way from the city, he was Natalie's boyfriend's brother, and if I didn't have to make a scene, I wouldn't. I scooted into the middle seat, my body stiff with cold and concern. David put his arm around me in a single, smoother motion this time, and I held the hand that dangled too close to my chest for me to relax.

The thought of Monday's lunch with the girls pressed on my mind as pointedly as David's spindly arm resting on my neck. I'd witnessed the Monday afternoon grill session too many times to fool myself into thinking I could escape without details. These girls were like hyenas on the savannah tearing through skin and cracking bones between their jaws to get to the marrow of any date—the details. I knew what they wanted to know. I had heard the questions often enough to recite them from memory. I hadn't helped my case at all. I had tantalized them with juicy tidbits for as long as I'd known about the date. For once, I wanted to be envied and admired, instead of just a spectator sipping Diet Coke and eating chocolate chip cookies as some other girl blushed her way through her description of a weekend date. My friends had been so intrigued. I had created such mystery. I'd stoked their curiosity and relished their envy. The truth was that the date was a total bust. So much so that I knew that I wouldn't accept another date with him or invite him to a formal. At least if I let David kiss me, then I'd have something to tell, a success to report. Besides, I needed to get my first "real" kiss over with.

David unclasped my hand and nudged my chin toward him. I plugged my nose from the inside because the cloves made me queasy. Then he planted his mouth on mine. I felt a stubby tongue pressing between my lightly parted teeth and tried to open my mouth a bit wider. David had no clue what he was doing. We slapped tongues for a few moments before I pulled back and closed my mouth. David kept his eyes closed and then opened them as a smile flooded his face. My mouth tasted newly stale.

The kiss settled what had been loose in David all night, but little of it seemed to do with me. He seemed to kiss me for the same reason I let him kiss me—to check it off the list. He lit another clove cigarette and exhaled like the leading man in a movie. But I felt like anything but a leading lady. I had not kissed him back at all passionately. I merely tried to keep up as he probed my mouth like a dentist in training. I didn't want to encourage further contact. David's arm remained draped over me, and I kept my body rigid, on alert for a grope or a graze.

What was so wrong with me that I couldn't even get one decent date? Forget the fairy tale, I just wanted to appear in something other than the horror reel opposite someone other than Flock of Hobbit or Gumby. *What was I doing to drain all of the magic out of my social life? Where was the magic? Where was the whimsy?*

What was I doing to attract these guys and these kinds of evenings?
The kiss just made me sad.

Five minutes stood between my front door and me. I began
unwinding my good night before we entered the kick the can
square at the top of my block. I just kept chattering, even as David
spoke. I wanted to exit the car without having to invite him back
inside or commit to a call or another date. The limo pulled to the
curb, and I didn't wait for the driver to open my door. Ceremony
meant time, time meant more words, more words meant another
possible kiss. I opened the driver's side door myself and swung
my legs out as I assured David he needn't walk me inside.

"Good night," I called with finality. "Thanks again." I slammed
the door and was moving faster than David could speak. He just
rolled down his window and watched me walk up the driveway.

Light bathed the living room and the staircase. Mom had
turned on every outdoor fixture in the driveway and courtyard.
She never turned on all these lights for Dad; they were for David
and me. The house looked perfect. Mom hadn't missed a single
thing. The lights beside the front door remained out, the perfect setting for a good night kiss. But the thought of going out
and coming home before Dad somehow made the evening even
worse. And I didn't need to feel any worse.

In one way, I dreaded the call I had promised to give Natalie
after the date. We'd been so excited, so optimistic. I had committed to give her all the details, but I would have to report defeat
rather than victory of any kind. There was just no pretending.
Even worse, I'd have to keep the anger out of my voice because
I knew Mitch would be listening and wondering.

More than a rough night with one guy, walking inside the
house, I felt as though the night had told me about my whole

life and my future prospects as long as I remained trapped in this place. But the blazing lights also told me that David didn't matter, he was a "good enough" placeholder. That was the difference between Mom's fantasies and mine. She was willing to "make do." I wasn't. I offered few details as Mom interrogated me about the evening. She wanted to know whether I had been nice to David. She didn't ask my opinion of him. She was in full convincing mode. She complimented David lavishly—nice boy, good conversation, really smart. Mom just ignored the smears, the smudges, and the creep factor. They didn't exist for her, and if I mentioned them, I'd get another speech about high expectations. I didn't bother to challenge her because I didn't know how to counter her analysis and deep down feared she was right. I dragged myself up the stairs.

Standing in the bathroom mirror as I doused a cotton ball with baby oil to remove my makeup, I felt monstrous and beyond all help. The way I looked made the disaster even worse. I couldn't on the surface of myself see what made me so ghastly. I'd done everything Mom said. I'd memorized all the tips and tricks.

If I had to mine rough diamonds, I'd rather not mine at all.

Somewhere near the core of myself, in spite of what Dad and Mom said about my high expectations, I knew in that moment that I wasn't asking for a lot. I just wanted a decent guy to like me and for me to like him. *Was a stuffed bear or a rose on Valentine's Day too much to ask? Was a dreamy slow dance an absurdity? Was a passionate kiss unrealistic?* Even if it didn't last, I longed for one good, joyful moment. But I refused to date David just to prove that I wasn't too choosy.

I had given the date the very best I had to offer. I had remembered all of the lessons, instructions, and urgings. I had practiced my skills all night. But as I went to bed, it dawned on me that there was no point to practice for more nights like this one. Trying ached too much.

Lying in bed that night, I opened the hood of my heart, unscrewed the bolts that held my big engine in place, attached the hooks to the hoist, and rested my big engine on blocks. I closed the garage door and turned out the lights on love.

{ chapter ten }

KENTUCKY FRIED ME

June 1985: crisis. It was the end of my sophomore year, and for the first time in my life, the twelve weeks of summer beckoned that I had absolutely no idea how to fill. In my life and in our family, a summer without a plan was unheard of. I had spent most of my previous summers enrolled in one kind of enrichment program or another—tennis, science, or theater camp; summer school; soccer day camp; an Eastern prep school program. I always had some way to occupy my time. The previous July, Mom and Dad had blown a wad of cash sending me back to South Hadley, Massachusetts, to the Summer Math Program at Mount Holyoke College. It had been a complicated experience, but my math grade had improved. Since then, though, the aluminum industry had become too tough for any of us to contemplate back-to-back educational junkets on top of Natalie's college tuition.

Work was central to the way that my parents were raised and the way that they raised us. From very young ages, everyone in their families had jobs, usually more than one. Children didn't just perform their chores; they *always* made money. As kids, Mom and her sisters worked alongside their mother cutting and dyeing paper flowers for Mother's Day, then they'd fan out through the Township selling them and bring the money home. They made and sold Easter corsages. When Grandmother returned home from a shift at the hospital or the factory, she made custom hats or suits for church ladies, and the girls, including Mom, helped her. In middle school, Mom worked the register at her neighborhood corner store. In the years since she'd quit her teaching position, she'd volunteered with joblike intensity.

Dad had begun working even younger than Mom, and it had never been optional. After school and on weekends, he served as a houseboy and then worked in the rice fields. He kept a few pennies to buy something to eat but gave most of his earnings to his mother to help make ends meet. By high school graduation, Dad had held a series of jobs—driving and parking cars, cleaning white folks' houses, and even waiting tables as his uncle catered their fancy dinner parties. More than a matter of economic necessity, for my parents working had become a way of life.

As long as I could remember, my parents had always told me the same thing: my education was my first and most important job. I was expected to work at it, full time. Except for occasional weekend babysitting, Mom and Dad had outlawed jobs during the school year. I simply wasn't allowed to work for school clothes money or to buy a slick car. Their no-work rule was a point of economic pride as much as it was a part of Mom and Dad's achievement agenda for us. They provided what we needed not what we wanted, which was an improvement over their childhoods.

As the summer of '85 approached, my friends puzzled over my frenzy, and despite speaking English and explaining my situation over and over again, they didn't understand the pressure I faced. During the summer, thanks to reruns of *Gidget* and *The Monkees*, lots of PV kids dedicated themselves to living the vintage California summer fantasy. The Beach Boys music became a detailed handbook, and kids blasted the songs as soon as they dropped the tops of their convertibles. No one could grow up in Palos Verdes without knowing most of their greatest hits by heart, not even me. At fifteen and sixteen most kids I knew were busy living the dream: lazy beach days, surfin' safaris (even if they didn't surf), and "fun, fun, fun." David Lee Roth had just topped the charts with his remake of "California Girls," which gave the early weeks of summer a strange sound as I listened to the radio and wrung my hands over the twelve weeks ahead of me. So most of the options that my friends entertained just didn't apply to me.

Hanging out? Forget it. Those were two words I rarely uttered. Whenever Mom and Dad heard them, they always unleashed the same tirade. Who had time to hang out? Life was too serious to waste time. They always *seemed* busy and rarely sat down for very long in my presence. I asked for permission to go out with the caution of a bomb squad technician. I provided minute-by-minute itineraries. The tight surveillance on me was especially curious because I had never done anything to merit such intense distrust. I hadn't pulled half the teenage stunts I heard about at school, not even the run-of-the-mill stuff: sneaking out, sneaking guys into my room, borrowing a car without permission, joyriding with alcohol, or smoking pot. I was toeing the parental line and never gave them any reason to worry. The only thing worse than hanging out was doing nothing. "Nothing" wasn't an option, so I didn't dare consider the idea or even use the word.

Cruising? Sure, if a 1976 Chevy Nova, whose brown paint was rubbed down to the base coat, did the trick for you. I'd inherited the car in May, after I passed my driving test with flying colors. But with my license came limits: no freeway or city driving. I didn't mind too much because it was hard to make myself look or feel cool in that car. It had a dented fender where Natalie had jumped a curb and rammed a mailbox during an early driving lesson. Dad took it to Tijuana, Mexico, for reupholstery but hadn't fixed the fender. It was a whale of a car, complete with rust barnacles. Dad called the Nova a "perfectly good car," which meant it screamed safety, reliability, and practicality. That car and I had too much in common. Cruising was simply a variation on the themes of hanging out and doing nothing.

Sleeping in? If adults with full-time jobs and side gigs didn't linger in the bed past eight in the morning, my parents reasoned, then no sixteen-year-old could either. Weekends were days for overtime and work at a second job. My ten o'clock weekend curfew precluded late nights. No late nights meant no need for late mornings. Besides, Mom and Dad offered one solution for teen fatigue: early bedtime.

So, at sixteen, for the first time in my life, the summer presented my first real opportunity for a job. In some ways, it was perfect. Even Mom warmed to the idea. I would get out of the house and be productive. With the exception of sex, Mom loved anything that involved getting "experience," and my first non-babysitting job would surely provide plenty of it. Dad would approve of me earning my own money, developing my work ethic, learning discipline, and keeping my hands off his money clip. Who could argue?

Even though I had overcome the objections at home, a few obstacles stood in my way. I had no experience, no skills, and virtually no confidence. That fact ruled out the handful of retail jobs that every job-hunting kid on the Peninsula wanted in the mall. Competition was stiff, and struggling adults kept a tight grip on the best-paying gigs. Some kids who opted out of the beach fantasy worked at an aquatic theme park called Marineland, but there were more applicants than jobs there, too. Few other retail businesses existed, and fast-food franchises were prohibited in Palos Verdes Estates. There were only a handful of restaurants, and my favorite was a Mexican restaurant, but it had a full-time professional waitstaff. The beach bunnies attending community college worked as hostesses at the local seafood restaurant and at the new Italian bistro. Being a hostess required two things that I lacked: cool clothes and a perky attitude. Even if I could land such a job, I just couldn't picture myself saying "Welcome to the Admiral Risty" a million times a night with any credibility.

How did a kid with no skills and no experience catch a break?

Family connections usually made up for inexperience in Palos Verdes. Some kids worked as paid interns in the huge aerospace corporations where their parents were executives. Others worked with relatives. Family friends provided another route to answering phones, filing, and fetching coffee in air-conditioned com-

235

fort. Nepotism nearly always guaranteed that regular employees handled the kids with a very light touch.

The handful of kids I knew whose parents emigrated from the Middle East or Asia worked in family firms without pay or complaint. Whether retailers, import-exporters, or restaurant owners, pitching in was a way of life. The summer assistance was an extension of the weekend help they offered during the school year. These kids had grown up in the business, had played there as little kids, and they knew the employees. They understood the businesses as extensions of their families.

Baszile Metals Service, our family business, had existed for nine years, but I knew, even without asking, that I wouldn't work there. When he'd started the business, Dad used to talk about it as a family venture, something that Natalie and I would inherit one day. That first year, he hosted a company cookout at our house. Employees' kids swam with Natalie and me in our pool, and everyone stayed until dark. It was a great event, but we never hosted another one. Over the years, though, in lots of small, subtle ways, Dad made it clear that the company was his private domain, *his* company. He limited our contact with the employees and rarely entertained them at our house. He never invited Mom, Natalie, or me to the office during business hours. We went shopping in the garment district every few months, but Mom never dropped in, announced or unannounced, to say hello. When Natalie had looked for her first job, no one mentioned Baszile Metals. So instead, she'd sold pearls at Marineland, shoes in a boutique, and gelato for an Italian guy who had been sweet on her.

Even though we never visited Dad's office, his city and business lives came home to us. Every now and then, when I'd answer the phone in the early afternoon, women I didn't know called our house asking for Dad. In salt-tinged voices seething with anger, the women always called him Barry, not Mr. Baszile. I replied in a stony tone I'd perfected and asked the women's names. They never gave them or left the messages I offered to take. Sometimes, they'd hang up when they heard me, other times they'd linger on the line without saying a word.

News of these phone calls caused arguments between my parents and made Dad even more protective about all of his business for a while. Then things would seem "normal" until the next phone call. I kept answering the phone but stopped counting or mentioning the calls to anyone. I got the message anyway: Dad's business was none of my business and would not supply my first job. I was going to have to look for something outside of Palos Verdes.

I drove twenty minutes down the hill until I reached the nearby city of Torrance. My four older cousins who lived in San Diego were veteran fast-food workers, and I thought of the colorful and alarming stories they told about their adventures as I reached fast-food alley, the intersection of Hawthorne Boulevard and Pacific Coast Highway. The jolly, fat kid in the checked overalls welcomed people to Bob's Big Boy. I went there after the football games or movies. *No way,* I thought, *I couldn't apply there.* Across the four-lane street twinkled the yellow star of Carl's Jr. Near another corner, the Jack in the Box clown flashed his toothless grin. A Taco Bell was about a block away.

As I sat at the light, a red and white bucket spun like a globe as it towered over a squat brick building with tinted windows. I'd passed the building at least once a week for thirteen years but had never really thought much of the face plastered on the side of that giant bucket. The bespectacled, white-haired colonel wore an all-white suit with a black ribbon tie and smiled down on the passing cars. I had seen him in commercials thousands of times oozing his warmth and Southern gentility. Harland Sanders just might have been the whitest man in America. Then I saw the ten white letters on a red sign that spelled salvation: Help Wanted.

Okay, so a black girl walks into Kentucky Fried Chicken looking for a summer job . . . Where was Eddie Murphy when I needed him? If he'd had said it in a *Saturday Night Live* sketch, the audience would have been howling before the punch line. As I slammed the Nova's door and walked across the parking lot, I wasn't laughing. Mingled with the smog, I caught the familiar scent of eleven secret herbs and spices. *Denise Huxtable would never do this.*

The herb-tinged smell of grease filled the dim, cavelike interior of the franchise and flooded my mind with memories of our Friday trips to the drive-in. Natalie and I would cradle the steaming bucket of chicken and bags as we made our way across town. Once Dad parked and arranged the speaker in the window, Mom would dish out the coleslaw, potato salad, and a drumstick. I ate with a spork as we watched the cartoons and previews and sipped my orange soda—a rare treat—from a Styrofoam cup. By the time we returned home, the car and my pajamas smelled like the colonel's original recipe. Our family nights no longer looked or smelled anything like that. Joyful nights of family togetherness had disappeared.

Now, at sixteen, I stood at that empty counter desperate, praying for a break. Everything was brown and crafted from a man-made substance. Green plastic plants hung from the ceiling. Grease and dust had congealed into a sticky, clumped mess that gave each leaf its own furry coat. Streaks of water, cleaning solution, and bits of food clung to the wood-grain Formica tabletops and caught the fluorescent light. Countless rear ends had rubbed the sheen right off of the plastic benches and chairs. Even the light seemed dingy. Nothing glistened, nothing gleamed.

A brown polyester-clad cashier walked through the swinging kitchen door. Beneath the standard-issue cap hung honey blond bangs that grazed her tweezed eyebrows. Deeply tanned, I knew she must spend lots of time at the beach. Her lips and cheeks were decorated in shades of frosted pink. Her name tag read Mindy, and she provided the only hint of sparkle in the place.

"Can I help you?" she said. Her voice had a pleasant rasp mixed with a melodic quality that contrasted with her petite frame. She spoke in surfer speech but didn't sound at all ditzy.

"Ummm, yes," I stammered. "I saw the sign. Are you accepting applications?" I asked.

"I guess," she said, staring at me.

Mindy disappeared into the kitchen and didn't come out for a long time, so long I wondered if she was waiting for me to leave.

"I haven't seen you around, do you go to South?" she asked when she came back with an application. South High School was a few miles down the road, and the students maintained a pretty serious rivalry with Palos Verdes High School. The black kids who attended South were as few in number and as conspicuous as the ones at my school.

"No, I go to PV," I said.

Mindy's eyes narrowed; she made a disgusted sound in her throat. I could feel her suspicion. South High School kids con-

Jennifer Baszile

sidered PV kids stuck-up, spoiled brats. They were often right. But the typical snooty PV kid was also white. Maybe my brown skin helped overcome Mindy's distaste and temper her disdain for all things PV. After all, a black PV girl was nearly an oxymoron anyway. Maybe my request for an application was just another piece of the puzzling girl in front of her. She kept staring.

"Okay," she said, finally sliding the application over the counter. "Here's the deal. You can fill this out, but you need to talk to Luke and he's not here right now."

"When will he be back?" I asked, trying to mimic her surfer manner.

"He's sort of . . . whatever," Mindy said with a dismissive wave of her hand.

"That's cool," I said. "Thanks."

I returned the next day and handed my typed application to Mindy. *A typed application?* I was such a goof. I waited even longer than the previous day. Mindy never reappeared, even though I could hear her voice in the kitchen. Out walked a tall guy somewhere in his twenties whose name tag read Luke. He had narrow, birdlike shoulders and chapped lips. He kept his weight on the balls of his feet and it created a bouncy walk.

"Jennifer?" This guy sounded just like a really stuffy, nasal version of Jeff Spicoli from *Fast Times at Ridgemont High*. He wasn't pretending. I tried not to burst out laughing. I remembered what Mindy said about this guy and tried to seem laid-back.

"Hi." I put out my hand.

"Oh," he said, looking slightly surprised as he shook my hand, "hey."

He took me into the empty dining room, and my forearms stuck to the table when I sat down.

"So you go to PV, huh?" he said. "That's cool."

"Yeah," I said. "It's okay." I tried to keep an even tone and flashed a smile.

"Well, here's the deal," Luke began. "Right now I am looking for someone to work afternoons and some nights till closing."

"Okay," I said, "I can do that."

"That's cool," he said. "Let me show you around."

Around? The interview was over before it began. I guess I'd been hired. We walked through the swinging door and entered the kitchen, white walls, stainless steel countertops, and a clay tiled floor that looked a million years old.

"I can only start you at minimum wage because you don't have any experience," Luke said as he bounced, "but me and Mindy can train you on the registers."

"That's great," I said. My heart leaped with relief.

"When can you start?" he asked.

"As soon as possible," I said.

"Great," he said. "Come by tomorrow."

"There's just one more thing," he said as he exhaled in a long breath. "Would you mind making the biscuits when you start your shift? It's no big deal—just a mix, some buttermilk, rolling them out, and cooking them and stuff?"

"Sure." I was so busy trying to sound perky, I almost missed the hint of hesitation in Luke's voice.

I walked to the Nova with a brown pair of polyester pants, a matching shirt, and a floppy KFC cap slung over my arm. I felt strange—mostly relieved to have found a job.

Biscuits? Had I just committed to make biscuits all summer? I had never made biscuits in my life, not even from a mix. We didn't ever eat them at home. I doubted that Luke had asked me to become a biscuit maker because I was black, but I couldn't be sure. On second thought I guessed that the fact that I was black had made Luke more reluctant to mention the task. The summer ahead was growing stranger by the second. The season of chicken and biscuits had begun. Welcome to Kentucky Fried Chicken.

My summer weekdays unfolded on two opposite ends of a surreal spectrum. I spent my mornings as a debutante in training. I worked as a kind of candy striper at Orthopaedic Hospital, the largest children's medical center of its kind in the nation. I pushed craft carts through waiting rooms crammed with cast-wearing kids and down wards where patients laid on their stomachs as they received treatment for spina bifida. I tried to be cheerful as I volunteered there, even though there was nothing voluntary about it.

Since Natalie's middle school days, Mom had dreamed and schemed about our participation in a debutante ball—white ball gowns and opera gloves, the deep curtsy and the waltz. Mom wanted it for our whole family. But Mom didn't opt for the all-black cotillion, which she thought just slapped a smiling face on LA's history of discrimination. Instead, she became the first and only black member of a group called Las Madrecitas, the Ladies Orthopaedic Hospital Auxiliary on the Peninsula that sponsored the Evergreen Ball.

In the same way that Miss America contestants stressed the scholarship dimension of the program, Las Madrecitas emphasized the hospital service part of the debutante ball. But just like everyone knew Miss America was about beauty and swimsuits, everyone also knew that Las Madrecitas was all about the Evergreen Ball and the fancy dresses. Still the work requirement appealed to Mom's life experience.

My freeway driving ban forced me to catch rides with Las

Madrecitas members and their daughters who were also trying to complete their service hours. These girls weren't my friends, although some were nice enough. On the ride home, the girls would review their plans to lounge by their pools or meet friends at the beach. When they asked about my plans, I gave vague responses and prayed that I didn't smell like fried chicken. I never mentioned my afternoon activities or the fact that as soon as I returned from the hospital, I'd change into the brown polyester uniform, hop in the Nova, and spend my afternoons making biscuits and slinging chicken.

From the moment I announced my new job, Mom and Dad congratulated and encouraged me. To an outsider, their enthusiasm and my summer activities would have seemed perplexing contradictions, but not inside my family. There it made perfect sense. Only people who understood the world my parents had come from, and the world that we all now inhabited, could look at a black chicken-and-biscuit-slinging debutante without irony.

Hard work was a fact of life; anything worth having required hard work and, most times, a fight. Mom was three years old when her father was killed. She forgot most of the details about her father. She couldn't recall his elaborate funeral and the thousands of attendees or the story that ran in black Midwestern newspapers. She did clearly remember the day shortly after the funeral when moving men cleared all of the luxuries from their house—the piano, carpets, carved furniture—and left them with nearly nothing. Mom and her sisters sat around holiday tables talking about "double-timing," the advance degrees they pursued alongside raising kids and their teaching jobs. Double-timing was not just the pace at which they worked at everything, it was the pace at which they lived their lives and raised their children. My mother prided herself on her work ethic and often said that she could "outwork" anyone. That's what made her such a dynamic community volunteer: she was relentless, tenacious.

Every black girl, even a debutante in training, needed an intimate understanding of work. It was a matter of survival. Hard work was the only reliable insurance against hard times. Chances were better that a black girl would face hard times than she'd have lots of occasions to waltz. Hard times had been such a part of my parents' lives, they wanted to know for themselves, as much as they wanted us to know, that Natalie and I could survive them. I never heard my parents forbid us to take any legal job because they considered it too menial or "beneath" us. Her first year of college, Natalie took a job cleaning dormitory laundry rooms—mopping floors, clearing lint traps, wiping detergent stains off the machines. The black women who worked full-time in janitorial services harassed and berated Natalie and emphasized every mistake she made. When Natalie complained to my parents, they told her to suck it up, work harder, and keep the job. Natalie could have gotten a job in the library for the same or better pay. But my parents needed to know that no matter how far their daughters might fall, we could work our way up. Operating at these two ends of the spectrum wasn't easy.

I fit right into the Kentucky Fried Chicken menagerie of oddballs. The coleslaw lady had worked there for years. She had curly, gray hair and a thick, older woman's body, but she giggled like a girl. She mumbled disjointed phrases and then broke into cackles for no reason I could ever understand. Coleslaw lady, entranced by the hum of the grinders and slicers, seemed to merge with the cabbages and carrots. I never found the courage to ask her about the stumpy finger on her right hand.

I knew next to nothing about the mysterious cult of young guys who worked the fryers, not even their names. My cousins, the fast-food veterans, had warned me about the fryers, and the guys who worked at KFC fit the mold precisely. The fry station was the hottest, most dangerous, and most foul part of the kitchen, the realm of steaming grease. The hot oil suffocated the skin. The fryers got acne craters on their hands, faces, and even their backs. According to my cousins, it took only one glance or a single whiff to spot a fryer. The weirdest people—the fire-bugs, young guys who liked knives a bit too much, and the adults too desperate to complain—all became fryers. You needed quick reflexes, a taste for danger, or a thirst for isolation to become a fryer. Between batches of chicken, these guys sat on the curb behind the restaurant and smoked. I never exchanged more than a single word with them. I just smiled and passed as quickly as I could.

I chatted with Mindy between customers. We had very little in common, and maybe that's why she told me about living
with the dad who adored her but was clueless. Mindy never got
in trouble for all of her partying, and although she thoroughly
enjoyed all of her adventures, she seemed to resent the lack of
parental discipline. After she told me hadn't seen much of her
mom since she'd left the family, Mindy threw a couple of pills in
her mouth and gulped soda. She never told me what they were
and I never asked. She popped things in her mouth at least once
every shift.

Luke was another mystery Mindy solved for me. He was such
a laid-back guy, I had him pegged for a beach rat, never the man-
ager type. According to Mindy, Luke's dad was a self-made franchise mogul who was as intense as he was impatient. He allowed
Luke to run this branch of the family empire since Luke's most
recent troubles, which seemed to have included dope. If Luke
screwed up, his dad threatened to cut him off.

But the more I revealed about myself to Mindy and Luke,
the more of a mystery I became to my coworkers. I always
showed up on time and did what Luke asked without complaint. I made the biscuits at the beginning of my shift, add-
ing buttermilk to the rest of the powdered ingredients in the
industrial mixer. Then I rolled out the dough, cut it into circles,
and popped them into the oven. It never took much thought
or concentration to make decent biscuits; the food scientists
at headquarters pre-measured everything so that a goat could
do the job. I mopped the dining room and the kitchen, washed
biscuit trays, cleaned fingerprints off the glass door. I kept busy.
I worked in a way that they couldn't understand. Was the job
punishment for bad grades? What was I doing with the money?

Was I working for a cooler car? They couldn't understand how my parents could forbid me to buy a new one. I never even told them about my hospital work in the mornings or breathed a word about the Evergreen Ball. I tried to engage their questions about my work to avoid the other, deeper set of questions that I couldn't answer any better. *Why was the black biscuit-making deb-in-training the only one who accepted the offer to take home a box of free leftovers?*

Driving down Hawthorne Boulevard, threading my way parallel to the Pacific Ocean and then through the darkness of Palos Verdes Drive West, the familiar smell of warm chicken and steaming biscuits filled the car. When I got home, Dad was working late, Mom was at a charity meeting, and Natalie was off with friends, so I had the house to myself. I turned on the television, got a plate. I concentrated as I cut my biscuit in half, slathered it with a pat of butter and the grape jelly I'd brought from work. Although I ate on a ceramic plate, I never used metal utensils from home, just the plastic knife and spork I'd packed. My first bite of tender fluffy goodness filled me with a rush of relief. Everything faded away. The steam made the butter and grape jelly ooze, and each chew and swallow eased my sadness and confusion. I'd rip strips of center breast meat with my fingers and pop them into my mouth. I'd alternate between original recipe and extra crispy. Then I'd eat more biscuits, so many that I lost count. Every night, I ate until I was numb.

At one level, the chicken and biscuits were the opposite of the meals I'd eaten most of my life. Other than at the drive-in, we weren't a fast-food family. When we ate out, we did so at one of two places: Chinese or fancy restaurants for pre-theater dinner. But we only ate out occasionally. Dad's resistance to eating out was a matter of thrift as well as taste. I had been raised on homemade food created from scratch. Dad detested prepared foods, canned or frozen; they didn't taste or feel real to him. He made a few exceptions: Albert's Quick Grits, Jiffy cornbread.

But there was also a lot of fear around food that I could taste and feel. Dad's childhood memories of shortage and hunger informed the way that he cooked for us. Meals always featured a piece of meat prominently arranged on a plate—hamburger or steak, a chicken breast, or a pork chop. Having eaten his fill of rough cuts as a kid, Dad refused to eat any more of them or serve them to us. It wasn't the quantity of the meat, but the meat's prominence that mattered to Dad. He always bought quality cuts that didn't require hours of stewing to remove their toughness. Dad also outlawed recipes that appeared to stretch meat: casseroles and pasta dishes.

Dad's fried chicken was one of my most favorite foods in the world. Seasoned in the sink, shaken with flour in a paper bag, fried in cast-iron skillet in our family since we'd lived in Carson, Dad's fried chicken was the real thing. Dad's fried chicken, sometimes bearing an extra dark spot from uneven turning, wasn't perfect, but it was wonderful. He didn't even need eleven herbs and spices to make my mouth water. But as terrific as Dad's fried chicken tasted, I could also taste our loneliness.

That summer, as I became more confused and life in our house grew more tense, I relied on the nightly chicken-and-biscuit binge. In our house, food was the surest and most consistent sign of Dad's care and engagement with us. He cooked every weekend of my life; he simply never let our family go hungry. It was a kind of crucial stability, a way that I could track his connection as he withdrew from us in other ways, stayed out late during the week, said less and less around the house. I needed my own anchor to make it through the week. I didn't swallow alcohol or gulp down pills. I stuffed my face with free food and gained twenty pounds.

The weeknight binge food was manufactured Southern hospitality, fake and only as authentic as the factory where the chicken was slaughtered and the powders mixed and boxed for the biscuits—just what I needed and longed for. It was all I had. For once in my life, I wanted to feel the goodness in every bite without variation or complication. The seduction of the biscuits was the predictability, the reliability. I didn't care about it being premixed; in fact, the dependability encouraged me to eat one biscuit after another, night after night, shift after shift. The artificial flavors were irresistible. No matter the day or the hour, the food tasted the same down to the baking soda finish on the biscuit. It was perfectly intoxicating goodness without any of the despair.

By the end of the summer, I'd stuffed myself so much that I couldn't bear the smell of anything from work. I could no longer pretend that my family's striving had been easy. In fact, it felt more lonely and difficult than it ever had. Time was making the lives we were living seem more stressful. The strong fabric of our family was beginning to fray. Biscuits and chicken weren't changing that fact.

chapter eleven

MY FATHER'S DAUGHTER

IN THE NINE MONTHS since I'd gotten my license, the Nova had given me a new way to stay busy on Sundays, the most anxious day of the week. Sundays never felt restful, so I woke up early and at 9:40, I pulled out of the driveway and drove down Palos Verdes Drive West bound for St. Peter's by the Sea, the Presbyterian church in which I had been raised. I was a high school junior and had attended the church for fourteen years. I sat five or six rows from the back of the sanctuary, on the right-hand side of the church, our family's usual spot. No one made me go to church, and many Sundays, I attended without my parents, who were faithful but not devout and warned against the perils of too much religion and not enough work. The church was so familiar to me that I didn't feel awkward sitting alone, and I waited for the service I knew by heart to begin promptly at ten.

For the next hour, inside a cavernous modern stone and blond wood sanctuary, I sang hymns from memory, placed my own money in the offering plate, and passed the peace. Walking back out through the tinted glass doors, I ended the service with a sense of relative calm. Even if I chatted with my youth group pals or the husband-and-wife team of youth pastors on the patio as I drank a cup of milky sweet tea, I was always home and changed by noon.

In the early afternoon, the rich smells of Sunday dinner wafted through our house—baked chicken or fried fish, steamed cabbage or stewed collard greens, sweet corn bread or boiled rice. The sound of smooth jazz from KKGO-FM blared through the intercom system. Dad played it so loud it was impossible to watch television, and I couldn't listen to my own albums, even if I turned the intercom's volume all the way down. I knew better than to complain or ask Dad to lower it. Mom usually worked in the garden all afternoon. Tending her plants helped keep her out of the house.

Dad usually finished cooking all the food and cleaned the kitchen by three o'clock, two hours before dinner. When he turned off the radio, he sat in the yellow leather chair and stared silently at the television. I tried to make sure I'd cleared out of the downstairs by then. The Sunday descent was about to begin, and I knew better than to hang around much longer. The trick was to stay out of sight and distance myself from the looming darkness as much as possible. Dad's last rites of the weekend, the ones he used to manage his anxiety about having to go back to work, never masked the tension that ran through our house like a fault line.

As usual, Sunday dinner was delicious but somber. We all focused our attention on the television as we chewed. Even Natalie, home for a weekend from Berkeley, fell right back into the routine. Clanking forks and the occasional "please pass" or "excuse me" punctuated the silence.

The source of the silence remained the same. Dad's work-week squeezed us like a vice. The typical workingman's angst mingled with the pressures any business owner faced to meet payroll, monitor cash flow, and manage debt. Those dinners were more memorable for the fear than the food.

But by February 1986, things had gotten especially grim. The aluminum markets of the 1980s had been soft; no one knew how long the drought caused by high inventory, sliding prices, and weak demand would last. No one knew how quickly or how much the market would recover. All of this intensified pressure for contracts and forced distributors like Dad to cut all the fat from their bids. There was no doubt about it: the past few years had been really tough.

When Dad began his career as an aluminum salesman, people told him that some customers and businesses simply would refuse to buy metal from a black man, no matter what company he represented. Since he'd opened Baszile Metals, even though people had become less direct in their refusals, some still refused. But as a business owner, rather than just a salesman, the rejections meant even more and affected him deeply. Knowledge of these refusals colored everything. In strong markets, Dad had to be more charming, more competitive on price, more prompt in his delivery just to compete and stave off the worry about what buyers might think but wouldn't say. The market dive made all of the usual pressures worse. The way his face bunched as he talked to Mom about a lost bid or a conversation with a client reminded me of the way his face looked when people had defaced our house. More and more often since Christmas, Dad had distorted his face as he mimicked the condescending tone and slowed speech that competitors or even well-meaning acquaintances used when they tried to get Dad to admit the hopelessness of his situation. "Barry, there's no way." Or "You're just going to have to face facts." Repeating statements like those at the table always fanned Dad's anger.

Dad never complained about being a black man, but he couldn't disguise its particular perils. One recent Friday while Dad got his weekly car wash, he went to use the bathroom. When he walked out, a swarm of LAPD officers surrounded him, their drawn guns pointing at him. He complied with their order to raise his hands and he cooperated as they frisked him. The officers ran his license. They told Dad that any black man driving a Mercedes had to be a drug dealer. It was easier for them to believe that Dad was a criminal than a businessman. They didn't apologize when they let him go.

On Sundays, I could tell time by Dad's anger, it was so familiar. By dinner's end, as Dad prepared to pick up these pressures and worries he'd tried unsuccessfully to leave in the streets on Friday night, it was obvious he wanted to flee. Sunday evenings made Mom quiet. Natalie tried to make herself disappear. We all bowed down before Dad's funk; we'd been doing it for years. Me? I was just frustrated and sick of it. I usually headed off to youth group back at church, which would keep me out until nine.

On this Sunday, I had decided to skip youth group for no particular reason except that I had been feeling down in the dumps. Nothing had happened; it wasn't as though I faced Dad's kind of pressure or could pinpoint it. So that night I retreated upstairs and planted myself in front of the television. I flipped through the channels watching snippets of programs. I had an hour to kill before *60 Minutes,* one of my favorite shows. I managed to stay upstairs through Mike Wallace's cover story and Morley Safer's segment, but knew I wanted a bowl of ice cream for the last story and Andy Rooney's commentary. Going back downstairs was a gamble. I wanted to avoid Dad, but I also craved the ice cream. My biscuit binges had given me a taste for a sugar high when I felt low. I charted my course as I walked down the stairs. I'd pass through the family room, just scoop the ice cream in the kitchen, head through the kitchen's rear door and the dining room, and be back upstairs before the end of the commercial break. I wouldn't even pass back through the family room or eat dessert at the table. I didn't want to linger.

I walked toward the family room and at first the mood of the room didn't appear much different than at dinner. Natalie and Mom sat on the couch, Mom flipping through *Architectural Digest.* As I stepped into the room, Dad rose from his chair. An empty wineglass sat on the floor. The chair still held the outline of Dad's body.

He stepped into the narrow space between the television and the coffee table, the space I hoped to hurry through on my way to my ice cream. We traveled in opposite directions but crossed paths right in front of the television. I tried to cast my gaze down but couldn't do it in time, and he caught my eye. Dad smiled without humor.

"What's your problem?" Dad asked. He stood right in my face, leaving less than a foot between us. I could feel his breath and tried not to look in his eyes. From the smell of things, he'd had more than a few glasses of wine and his tone was more menacing than playful.

In sixteen years of Sunday nights, I'd become pretty familiar with Dad's arsenal of tactics to try to distract himself. They were all variations on one theme: sugarcoated bullying. I could never pinpoint what might provoke him, because the trigger changed all the time. Dad had lots of ways to do this, but all of his tactics involved questions. One favorite was "Have I touched you yet?" Dad's eyes twinkled with venom, and he smiled the same way he did when he used to summon his anger to his whipping hand that held the belt. He'd throw his hands behind him, hunch his shoulders, and thrust his chest out. His breath blew on my face. I had to stand there, eyes fluttering, and take it. He didn't stop when my body began to tremble. He stood so close that I couldn't move my head, and if I looked down with my eyes, he would cock his head and bend down and look up into them. Total control. In those moments, he never hit me, or even touched me, but he showed me that he could. Even without the physical sensation, I knew the feeling of Dad's blow. Only the well of tears in my eyes and the crack of my face in terror made Dad stop. Then he'd act as though this had been a game and walk away disgusted by my tears like I wasn't able to take a joke.

Every now and then, usually when he had had a bit of wine, Dad would back someone into a corner until they told him what he wanted to hear. He'd done this sort of thing since I was a little girl and he did it to all of us, even Mom. If Mom fell asleep on the couch, Dad would creep over to where she sat, get beside her, then wave his hand over her face. Then right into her ear, he'd bark, "Let me see the whites of your eyes."

But I was his target this time and his question hung heavy

in the evening air. At that moment, I knew I should've stayed upstairs.

"What's your problem?'" Dad said as he stepped to the right and blocked my path.

I stayed quiet and stepped back left. Dad tracked that step too, almost like we were dancing.

Of all the petty provocations, I hated "What's your problem?" the most. The question twisted everything because it arose out of nowhere, never in response to a comment or a complaint. It felt intrusive and off-base. There was no logical escape route because I hadn't done anything. I didn't answer because I hadn't uttered a word. I was trying to make my way to the kitchen and upstairs before the end of the commercial.

"Do you have a problem?" he said as he moved his face even closer to mine, twisting it from side to side.

Mom and Natalie were sitting on the couch, and I knew without even looking that they had heard the question and were holding their breaths waiting for Dad's next move.

"What's your problem?" He gazed at me wine-eyed, his bottom lip slick with his most recent sip of Chardonnay. He'd pinned his shoulders back to close the space between us. I could feel the tension in his body. He felt wound up, for what I didn't know.

"Come on, Dad," I said, half pleading, half ordering. I wanted this to end. I wanted to get Dad off my case. Screw the ice cream.

"I don't have a problem," I said. It's what I always said when he taunted me with this question, the answer most likely to get Dad off my case. It was the one he wanted to hear, just as "because I wanted to" was the only acceptable answer to the pre-spanking question. It was the one that would end this little confrontation on the spot and let him go back to his wine. It wasn't true, though, and Dad's menace stoked my anger.

"What's your problem?" he said. No space between us, his stomach brushed me. He stared down into my face.

Whenever Dad made me his target, I usually flash froze everything inside myself. The fear and the sadness were always too much. Instead of feeling those things, I focused on the cold within me. For as long as I could remember, Mom and Dad forbade my anger. They compared my life to theirs and told me I was not entitled to feel angry, and so I did my best to deny my anger and keep it from surfacing. Most times, I managed to suppress it, but the bullying question brought it closer to the surface than almost anything else, and so I found my own anger in these incidents even more frightening than Dad's anger. Exhausted by years of this funk, struggling with sorrows of my own and a bad sugar craving put me in no mood to indulge Dad. As he stood in front of me, I let my anger take over, as much to soothe as to distract me.

"Stop," I said, trying to keep my voice neutral and firm despite my annoyance. This had never been funny, but now my own anger began surging. I looked into his face for the first time as I spoke the words. Then I stepped back.

"What?" Dad said as he stepped closer to me again. He threw up his hands as if he could not imagine what was wrong. "I just want to know, what's your problem?" The ticking of the *60 Minutes* stopwatch on the family room television told me that this had gone on for the entire commercial break. Harry Reasoner introduced his story.

"Okay, Dad," I said. I hoped he heard the dismissal in my tone and my annoyance at this crap. *Game over.* It was time for this to end. I decided to walk and see what would happen.

Again Dad backed up with me for a step and then planted himself in my path. This time we just stared at each other. *Why did I always have to yield to this? Why did I have to cower when Dad got in my face?* As these questions flashed in my mind, the weight of my resolve bore down on me.

I'll just go through the kitchen and back upstairs. I took a half step forward and faked left and then shot past him on the right. My move surprised us both, but I bumped his shoulder. The bump infuriated Dad as much as my evasion. He expected me to yield, and I was breaking the rules, refusing to submit, denying him what he expected. I had ruined his game. But it had never been a game to me.

He grabbed my left wrist.

I kept walking.

He shouldn't have touched me.

I yanked my arm, but he wouldn't let go.

"Stop," I said. My voice sounded low and hard, even to me.

Dad tightened his grip and twisted my wrist a bit, as if he expected me to turn around to face him.

I didn't.

He wrenched my wrist across my back until it nearly touched my right shoulderblade. The pain pulled me back toward him.

Everything was changing so fast. We didn't give each other time to react.

"Do you have a problem?" he hissed over my shoulder. I could smell the Chardonnay.

Nothing separated us. I'd heard the question too many times that night and I had lied for too long. I swore I could feel Dad's racing pulse in the soft flesh between his index finger and thumb because he clutched my wrist so tightly, his hot breath brushing my neck as I tried to pull away from the pain. He'd posed the worst possible question one too many times.

"Fuck you!" I spat the words before I could stop myself.

As I stood there, pictures shuttered through my mind. Then I looked down at Dad's opened hand and stared at the pale scar on his right thumb.

Dad worked sugar cane as a boy. After the yearly harvest, they set everything afire to make way for the new crop. Once, as he stood and watched the fire, a raccoon darted out of the burning rows. Dad had left his shotgun at home but wanted to catch the raccoon anyway. He chased the coon all around the field and cornered the animal in a rotting log. Dad reached inside with his right hand. The coon had no outlet and did the only thing it could: it caught Dad's thumb between its teeth and ripped open the flesh right down to the bone. He gave up on catching the coon. It took a long time for the wound to heal and he kept the scar forever. Somewhere in the decades since then, Dad forgot the lesson the coon taught. Maybe it was the most important lesson from his bad, old Lousiana days. If he'd remembered, or looked at his thumb, things might have been very different for us that evening.

Dad jerked my wrist across my back even harder and the pain shot through my arm and up my shoulder. I didn't care.

I shoved my left elbow into his diaphragm and felt Dad's surprise. I had to protect myself. Outweighed by more than a hundred pounds, five inches shorter, thirty years younger, I was just a girl. We stood mere steps from Mary Dean Ballard's picture and the coffee grinder. Dad's menace encircled me. There was no place to run. I was headed for my own rotting log. If I didn't show Dad he couldn't intimidate me whenever he wanted, he would do it forever. I never wanted to believe that I would have to fight this way in my own home.

The man who confronted misguided teachers and corrected parents who lied about something in my feet; the man who taught me how to fight children and win, even if they outnumbered me, had become a bully himself. The man who defended me when his brother called me the Other One stepped into a space he forbade anyone else to occupy. The man who taught me how to stand up for myself, the man who told me to think and act for myself now tried to dominate and enclose me for no good reason.

I spread my feet to bear the pain as Dad twisted my wrist even harder and then wrapped his other arm around my collarbone, LAPD chokehold–style. He didn't constrict my airway, but my breathing quickened. I kicked Dad with the heel of my sneaker. He forced me to my knees, still holding my wrist. I scrambled like a spider on the slippery floor and lost my balance. In an instant Dad had flipped me onto my back and spread my arms out on either side of me.

"Get off of me!"

Dad draped his chest diagonally across me so that I was pinned. For the first time in my entire life, someone had put me on my back in a fight.

I turned on the big engine inside me, the one that my parents warned me about and made me fear, and fought. I burrowed inside myself as some deep part of my brain triggered my limbs. No matter how much I flailed my legs, I couldn't reach Dad. I lifted my body and Dad's torso a few inches off the ground. If I conceded anything, if I fought with any less that my entire being, I would be pinned the rest of my life, from the inside.

The next moments blurred with my shrieks and curses. I

unleashed my fury. I was taunting Dad. Part of me welcomed this fight because it brought to light what had made me sick trying to hide.

What's my problem? I'd followed every suggestion, taken every correction and criticism and implemented them without any challenge. I was a good student, completed my homework without so much as a prompt. I studied for my SATs. I held leadership positions galore—vice president this, treasurer of that, and gave Dad so many reasons to be proud of me. I drove myself to Sunday morning worship, sang in the teen choir, attended youth group on Sunday nights, even helped organize a silent auction to raise money for our youth mission project. I was a good girl. I didn't make my parents worry for a single second. I didn't drink or take drugs, ever. I never snuck anywhere or came home late. I never pushed the boundaries. I was a nice girl. I was the perfect daughter, the envy of their friends.

I thrashed my head from side to side. I strained to lift one arm. One good punch to his temple, that's all I wanted.

What's my problem? I didn't confide to even my best friends the details of Dad's city life that I had pieced together. I had grown to hate the sound of a ringing phone but politely answered his angry street women. I did my best to protect Mom from the phone calls, never asked her to explain the arguments I overheard. When kids in youth group shared their family struggles and requested prayer, I kept my mouth shut. I braced myself for the day Dad would come home, pack his bags, and leave all of us behind. I never told Dad how much his recklessness hurt and frightened me. Dad grinned with delight and feigned modesty as people called our family the real live Huxtables from *The Cosby Show.* We never admitted what was underneath.

"Fuck you!" My frothy spit covered Dad's face and infuriated him.

He stretched my arms apart like a convict getting frisked. I yelped as my shoulder pulled slightly out of the socket, but I never stopped fighting or screaming. The big engine revved and shifted into an even higher gear—rage, the emotion I most feared. I tried to ignore this searing pain I felt everywhere. The lower half of my body remained free and I tried to hoist my legs and back off the ground to overthrow Dad. I couldn't do it.

"Calm down!" Dad shouted in my face.

All the strength had left my body and so I strained and scrapped with the force of my mind. I sputtered and heaved, thrashed anew, and showed Dad the depth of the fight left inside me. I remained pinned. We both knew the truth. If he'd eased his grip a second earlier, I might've run into the kitchen and grabbed a knife. Even though I hadn't landed a single punch, I had made it clear that if I got the chance, I would kill him. He couldn't let me up.

I cursed, strained, and cried until my veins bulged and my limbs shook. My chest heaved.

"Calm down."

Every time I felt the least bit of strength, I tried to overthrow Dad all over again.

"Calm down."

I just couldn't connect with the words. For all of the times Dad claimed he knew me better than I knew myself, I think I shocked Dad as much as myself.

"Calm down."

The only other time we had even approached this place was the second time I had to get blood drawn, when I was five years old. I was so frightened that the phlebotomist and Mom couldn't restrain me. Dad had to bring me back the next day. He clamped me in his lap, grabbed my arm, handed it to the phlebotomist, and held it steady even as I screamed and squirmed. He wouldn't let me go no matter how much I yelled. He told me to calm down, then slapped my leg to focus my attention. It worked because I had trusted him then. I finally did calm down and let them take my blood. I hated needles after that but never had to be restrained again.

Dad might have slapped my face to focus my brain and body on his words, but he didn't dare release my wrist to administer the slap. He finally stopped saying anything and rode the wave of my resistance.

But this was different. I didn't trust Dad in the same way. Maybe I'd lost all my trust in him. He'd attacked me for no reason. Dad just lay there. Then he waited even longer. My rasping breath and the sound of the television were the only two sounds that filled the room. Finally I stopped moving and didn't say another word. I just wept. He let go of my arms and waited a few seconds, still pressing his weight on me in case I was faking. But I was too tired. Then, when he felt sure I wouldn't lash out again, Dad got to one knee.

"You just don't know when to stop!" Dad yelled.

In one way, it wasn't true. I stopped myself from speaking up all the time. Even if I couldn't stop myself from making mistakes, I always stopped myself from evading a legitimate punishment. I never questioned, pleaded, let alone protested, being sentenced to a spanking or some other kind of reprimand. I didn't quibble over details or try to defend myself. Whenever I got caught, I sat quietly, my countenance filled with remorse, and described my offense as honestly as I could. I answered whenever Dad summoned me and never made him call me twice. Sure, I squirmed and screamed with the lick of Dad's leather belt on my butt and thighs, but only because it hurt. I always yielded to justice and discipline.

But in another way, it was true. When attacked, I didn't know when to stop. If I wouldn't surrender in a fight outside my house, what made Dad think I would be willing to cave at home? As long as Dad pinned me, I wasn't going to stop fighting. I needed to show Dad, and myself, the high cost of his petty victory. Dad and I needed to know that no matter who else turned on me, even when the source of my greatest safety became the architect of my greatest fear, I would *always* protect myself. My opponent might be physically stronger, but the strength of my will would even things out. Every bone in my back ached. I had been pressed on the parquet squares for so long I wondered if the floor bore my impression. A moment later, Dad let me up but remained on his knees huffing and glaring at me. I remained on my back for another moment, looking up at Dad, trying to steady myself and feeling lightheaded. When I sat up, I sobbed again, staring at the floor pattern, beyond exhaustion and weary with despair.

Dad didn't know when to stop either, and that was most of the problem. No one ever made Dad stop doing anything, no matter how out of control the rest of us felt. Not ever. And Dad rarely stopped himself. Even though I certainly hadn't beaten Dad, some small part of me thrilled at the depth of the fight inside me. At least I'd made Dad pause. He would think hard before he asked me another shitty, provoking question like that again.

"Jennifer, you've gone too far," Dad said as his eyes brimmed with a new fury. Maybe Dad hated me; the glare in his eyes suggested that he did. He hated what I'd shown him about me. Maybe he also hated what I had shown him about himself. Fear pinched Dad's face. Anxiety filled his eyes. Maybe my labored breathing and sobs pressed the full measure of my frenzy back on him. I showed him that I possessed my own version of the fury that he struggled and failed to contain in his own life. Maybe he was as struck by my rage as I was. I knew I'd scared my father, maybe for the first time in either of our lives. Maybe he thought that my life hadn't been hard enough. Until that moment, I don't think Dad knew just how much he'd taught me, just how much we felt in common. I don't think he realized that my California girlhood had instilled as much rage in me as his Louisiana boyhood had instilled in him. Maybe of all the things he detested, for as much as he worked to make it that way, he hated me for that more than anything.

"You've just gone too far." Dad remained on his knee. All of the restraining had winded him. He still couldn't quite catch his breath. I had made him work harder than I'd thought. He stood up and leaned slightly forward as he rested his hands on his thighs. With a final heaving sigh, Dad steadied his breath.

All my screaming had strained my voice, and I couldn't speak the words in my head. *Fuck you.* I began to feel the adrenaline crash and knew that if I uttered a word we'd be back on the floor, or worse. I remained silent.

"You've gone too far." Dad spat the words over his shoulder this time, as he stalked into the entryway. He didn't dare stand in my presence another minute. He understood how much we needed to be apart. He understood in a totally new way that he needed to protect me from all that *he* felt. He pounded his heels on every step and then slammed his bedroom double doors.

Fuck you. At least I'd give myself the last word in my mind.

I pulled myself into Dad's chair. The leather cooled the ball of fire inside me. I wiped tears, sweat, and snot. I shivered as a strong breeze blew through the open screen door. Wind chimes tinkled in the evening breeze. Every part of me hurt. I looked at Natalie and Mom crouched together in the farthest corner of the couch. I began to snivel and gasp, trying to settle myself. I just kept waiting for someone to say something.

Neither of them moved. I kept waiting for the familiar questions. *Jennifer, are you okay? Jen, are you hurt?* No napkin to wipe my face. No bag of ice for my throbbing wrist. Nothing. We all sat there.

"I just can't believe what I've just seen," Mom began. "I mean, I really just don't believe it."

Here it comes, I thought. The shock only stalled their concern for me. *Mom's really going to give it to Dad.*

"Jennifer," she said, pointing her finger at me, "you have lost your mind!"

My mouth froze.

But my mind traced the pattern of all the things Mom hid from Dad. Mom tucked smoking pots of burnt rice and mangled teakettles in the backyard garden. She camouflaged mildewed laundry by drying it anyway and then putting it away in the linen closet. She stashed bags of clothes from clearance shopping sprees in the trunk of her car, a corner of the garage, or the back of her closet. She concealed things for so long she often forgot all about them.

Mom also hid herself. I replayed her silence during my fight moments ago. Mom didn't intervene when Dad pestered me. She never urged him to leave me alone as he invaded my space. She hadn't distracted him as he tracked me. She hadn't insisted that he stop as he wrenched my arm or forced me to my knees. She just sat there, hidden. She hadn't said a word. She knew him far better than I did, his patterns and contours. But tonight, as things spun so far out of control, she left me entirely alone to protect myself. I finally named what I had sensed for so long, the stench of Mom's fear. She was afraid of Dad. She hadn't stopped Dad because she feared him.

"You were out of control," she continued.

She spoke some other words, but I'd stopped listening and just started wailing on the inside.

A huge and terrifying breach opened up between Mom and me. She'd ditched me. She'd chosen Dad over me and, in that moment, I realized that she always had, and always would, defend him. All of the charm she used to dazzle the community, all of her wonderful snapshots in the local paper for leadership, all of her brazen challenges to store managers and real estate agents became hollow to me. Mom didn't confront Dad directly maybe she thought it would make him angrier.

"Yeah, Jen," Natalie said.

I'd hoped Natalie would defend me, see my side, but her two words told me all I needed to know. Even though we'd shared so much and had become so close, I couldn't expect Natalie to understand. She was the Pretty One, the popular girl, the home-coming queen who never had gotten into a fight. Sure, Dad taunted her, but somehow it never escalated. She always managed to evade confrontation, to charm her way out of it. How?

I wasn't really sure. Everything about her seemed attractive and yielding, so no wonder she wouldn't understand. She mostly managed to stay out of Dad's way, off of his bad side. Maybe that's why she defended him, because she thought that if she could do it, I should be able to do it, too. The Pretty One and the Other One parted company.

"But what about Dad?" I whispered as I looked down at the floor. "What about him?"

The vein in Mom's forehead bulged and split her face like a melon.

"This is your fault." Mom pointed a shaky finger at me. "You pushed your father too far."

I was drowning in sorrow now because they couldn't see how different things could have been for all three of us. If Natalie and Mom had defended me, I wouldn't have been pinned on the floor. If either one of them had piped up, told Dad to stop, he might have listened. But even if he'd pinned me, Dad couldn't have taken all three of us down. Natalie could have held one of his arms, Mom could have shouted at Dad to leave me alone or jumped on his back. But it hadn't happened that way. They'd just sat there and watched.

"Go upstairs," Mom began. "Go upstairs right this instant and apologize to your father."

Nothing inside me worked as I plunged lower than ever before. I couldn't have sunk any faster if Mom had attached weights to my ankles and thrown me over a cliff. Neither my mind nor my muscles could catch up. I couldn't brace myself. So I just kept falling.

Even with Dad out of the room, Mom wanted him back, however she could get him, whatever it cost me. She wanted me to bow at the altar of Dad's fury and submit. It was easier to shove a cork in me than to control Dad.

"Apologize to your father." She hissed each word, pausing as her body nearly shook.

The weight of my despair pressed my chin onto my chest. All on its own, my head started wagging like a pendulum. Back and forth it swept until it created its own momentum. As I shook my head, I stared at Natalie and Mom, faces and bodies I'd seen all my life, people whom I thought I'd known best of all but realized I didn't know as much as I'd thought about what really mattered.

"Listen, little girl," she said as she poked the air with her finger, "get yourself upstairs and say you're sorry right now."

Little girl? Mom was trying to pin me with words rather than her small, quivering body. She was trying to shrink my spirit to make me conform. *Little girl, weak girl:* it was a wish as much as an insult.

Back and forth, I swung my head, trying to hear something other than her words.

"What?" I was crying again, broken.

"You heard me," she said. "You've got to apologize to your father now. Tell him you were wrong and that you're sorry."

My pendulum swept back and forth.

"No," I said.

"Apologize!" Mom thundered.

"That's not right," I said over and over again.

"You better apologize, Jen," Natalie said. She was pleading, which told me how much all of this frightened her. She could feel it, the ripping apart of our family, and more than anything she just wanted it to stop. She was begging me to put the lid on

Dad's anger. Sure, she urged me to apologize because it was the way that these breaches usually got repaired—one of the three of us backed off or backed down, never Dad. But the "better" in her instruction told me the truth of where I stood: on the brink of family exile.

This wasn't like the *Fair Winds* Inquisition, learning kids' names to prove my blackness to Mom and Dad; I had to go upstairs and grovel to prove my loyalty to the Baszile name. These stakes were the highest of my life. This wasn't about being locked out of a cabin. This was a matter of being locked out of the family. Even I knew that I couldn't afford that. I didn't have anywhere else to go. I couldn't walk to my grandmother's house or call an aunt to pick me up. I didn't have anyone or anything else. Natalie was right. I had better go upstairs and apologize.

My chin quivered and I didn't cry when I told Dad I was sorry that I cursed at him. It was a thin, half-assed apology that we both knew I didn't mean. Dad sat there smoldering in his chair, staring at the television, and would not look at me. He repeated again that I'd gone too far. I suctioned my tongue to the roof of my mouth to get through my new wave of anger.

The apology I offered Dad that night didn't really thaw out the chill in our relationship for a long time. Maybe it was because of the way that I apologized.

In the end, my reconciliation with Dad came more easily than the one I had to make with Mom. My apology hadn't resolved anything. I remained wary of Dad. If we unexpectedly crossed each other's paths, we stepped wide to avoid each other, no brushed arms. "Excuse me" wasn't enough anymore. We passed each other in silence, didn't hug or kiss. He also laid off all of his bully questions. I spoke to Dad as little as I could, and he didn't have much to say to me either. As conspicuous as these gestures and avoidances felt, they served a purpose: things hadn't escalated any further. I steered clear of Mom, too. Natalie had gone back to Berkeley and made it easier for me to tuck my anger into a corner of my mind.

I stayed out of sight and in my room nearly all the time, not just on Sundays. I didn't confide in my friends, even when they asked me what was wrong. I just couldn't talk about what had happened. I knew better than to act petulant and pouty. I tried not to feel too much of the hurt and disappointment that the fight brought me. I tried not to feel anything at all.

I invented a new fixation: planning my departure from California. I didn't harbor a teenage runaway fantasy. I didn't want to hang out near Hollywood and Vine for a few days and come back home. I didn't want to escape. I wanted to leave. Everything about the place became unbearable. I didn't envision storming out of the house. I'd done the big fight, the tears, the screaming. I decided California wasn't the place for me. I despised the crystalline ocean and the sparkling skies. I hated the dusty hillsides as much as the meticulous lawns and carefully pruned gardens. Crowded freeways and empty streets irked me in equal measure. No version of California that I knew made any sense to me. Mine would be a quiet, permanent departure that barely rippled on the surface of family life. The state's borders choked me and I wanted to be free.

Beneath my California departure fantasy, lay an aching hurt I could barely admit. I allowed myself to despise the state because despising my family, even after what happened, felt so hard.

Along with my Golden State departure, I planned to divorce myself from needing other people. Dependence on my parents and Natalie had weakened me in the critical moment. Dependence and love had propelled me up the stairs to offer a liar's apology to Dad. So rather than continue to focus on my need for my family, I began to train myself not to want or need anybody. If I couldn't depend on my family, then that left me to myself. I would be friendly, but I wouldn't allow myself to be dependent. It hurt too much to be disappointed.

There wasn't room enough in the state for my family and me.

Almost every night, I walked down the LAX Jetway in my dreams and boarded a plane having packed only a small suitcase. No one, including the flight attendant who ripped my boarding pass, had a face. No one accompanied me to the airport or waved me good-bye. I didn't speak to a single soul. I just left. Where was I headed exactly? I never knew where the plane would land, but I'd always see the same image just before I fell asleep or awoke: my smiling face walking down another Jetway and into my happiness. All I needed to do was leave California and never return.

At school and during the rest of my days, I meticulously cut and polished each facet of my plan like a precious stone. Every afternoon I checked our mailbox before I headed inside the house. My PSAT scores had been good enough to flood our mailbox with flattering letters and brochures from colleges and universities. I threw all of the California packets in the trash can without even opening them. All of the Texas and Arizona packets went the same way. I pored over the booklets and tried to envision myself inside the glossy campus photos. I didn't know which college I would attend, but the greater the school's distance, the more it appealed to me. I kept a box in the corner where I'd stored Rosa Parks's costume while I mourned Harriet Tubman. In it I filed the brochures alphabetically and flipped through them whenever I needed a boost, which was nearly every day.

{ chapter twelve }

MY SUMMER OF LOVE

PEOPLE WHO SAW THE inside of my left arm often remarked on the dark circle on the underside of my wrist. They assumed that the cigarillo-sized patch of darker brown skin was a birthmark and marveled at its symmetry. If they stared at much longer, I reflexively covered the area with my right thumb. It wasn't a birthmark, and I didn't like to answer questions about it. If someone really pressed, I'd explain that it was a scar and change the subject. Most people who questioned me knew so little about how black skin scarred that they didn't understand the serious injury that the mark represented. Nearly no one outside my family knew that I'd gotten that scar from the worst burn of my life.

I'd loved fire as a little girl, especially campfires. I tried to dance like the flames, waving my arms and legs, trying to keep pace. When I was three, mesmerized by the shape of the flames and the staccato popping of the bonfire at Pismo Beach, I twirled ever closer and closer until I lost track of the heat and the danger. I fell to my knees and tipped into the fire. The heel of my hand landed on a burning-hot rock. After a trip to the emergency room, countless bandages, and a peeling, oozing hand later, all that remained was the scar. It never got smaller or faded. Whenever I felt deeply anxious, I imagined the scar throbbing and would try to rub the pain away. As I plotted my departure to college and tried not to need anyone in my family, I almost constantly rubbed my wrist. All of my rubbing couldn't erase the thick tension that lingered in my house.

A month after the fight with my father, April 1986, I retrieved a thick, white envelope from the mailbox and assumed that it was another college pitch brochure. I didn't bother to lift it from the bottom of the mail pile and carried it into the house. As I set the stack on the secretary under the telephone where we always put the mail, I separated it from the bills and cards addressed to Mom and Dad. I was about to wash my hands and get a snack when the envelope's upper left corner caught my eye. The return address read LEAD, Leadership, Education and Development, and when I realized what it was, my heart began to race. LEAD was a business enrichment program that exposed "minority kids" to corporate careers. I'd applied to it earlier in the fall. For a month, kids entering their senior year of high school would gather at the country's leading institutions to study business through the case study method. Natalie and another girl I'd met at the math program always raved about LEAD and the great people.

I usually found business fascinating. I kept tabs on the stock market and understood the basics. I paid attention to national economic indicators on the nightly news and read corporate news in the paper. The blood oath I'd sworn never to return to fast-food labor had gotten me through the essay portion of the application. The enduring stench of chicken and biscuits had drawn me back to the old typewriter where I plucked out letters on the forms. LEAD hosted its programs at college campuses throughout the country. The fight with Dad had compelled me to select the programs farthest from California and propelled me to the local post office where I'd mailed my application right before closing.

Please, please, please, let this be an acceptance letter, I thought as my heart pounded with anticipation. *I can't stay home this summer! Get me as far away from California as possible.* I gave myself a major paper cut as I sliced through the envelope with my index finger.

Get me out. Get me out. My eyes darted through the salutation and the congratulations about surviving in a very competitive applicant pool.

Where was I going? Which institute? How far away would I get? When could I make my break?

Michigan. Go Blue! I had been assigned to the University of Michigan Institute. No, it wasn't Massachusetts, where Natalie had spent her summer at Babson. But then again, I'd always wanted my own experience. I had no idea what Ann Arbor, Michigan, looked like, and I almost didn't care. The University of Michigan did the trick for me. I pumped my arm in victory and smiled to myself.

Just then, I heard the creaky hinges of the garage door opening and then heard Mom's heels on the steps. I placed my acceptance letter on the table and tried to act casual as Mom walked into the family room. She wore one of her volunteer meeting outfits and carried an armload of papers. Her makeup was freshly applied and perfect, her hair still teased.

"Guess what?" Despite my intention to be cool, the thrill of my letter overwhelmed me. "My LEAD letter came today. I got into the program at Michigan."

I handed Mom the letter and watched her scan the page.

"Congratulations, Jen. That's great," she said. She seemed really happy for me, and her warm tone thawed some of the frost I'd been feeling toward her. She hadn't pulled me aside to discuss the fight with Dad since she'd ordered me upstairs to apologize. Through the gleam in her eye, I also detected a hint of relief at the idea of getting me out of the house for a month. The fact that the program covered virtually all of my expenses only sweetened the news. Everyone won. I'd get a nearly free, prestigious, and enriching experience; Dad would get some peace; and Mom would get some quiet. I began the LEAD countdown that afternoon.

The LEAD letter reduced my wrist rubbing almost immediately and made everything else about the remaining weeks of the school year more bearable. My school friends planned to attend band camp or language immersion programs, but I tried not to make a big deal about LEAD. The college application process was already straining the bonds of some of my friendships, and I didn't want to hear any more talk about my slam-dunk chances for admission because I was black. These conversations had never gone well, but they had taken on a nastier edge recently. So I described LEAD as a summer business program and left it at that.

Jennifer Baszile

I spent June checking items on my to-do list. Call Mr. Lyde
to schedule appointment for relaxer touch-up at the end of the
month? Check. Take trip to the drugstore to restock my toiletry
bag? Check. Keep quiet and out of the way at home? Check. Get
the suitcase from the garage and wipe it down? Check. Wash,
press, and pack everyday outfits? Check. Select dressy outfits for
corporate field trips and church? Check. Last visits with friends
before we all scattered? Check. Pack hair rollers, scarf, blow-dryer,
and curling iron? Check. Plane ticket and boarding pass? Check.

My relief overwhelmed me as the plane finally climbed
through the clouds to Michigan. With every hour and every mile
I put between myself, my family, and California, the calmer I
became. I had dodged another summer of chicken and biscuits,
and I wouldn't have to see Natalie, Mom, or Dad for a month.
What exactly was I about to walk into? I had no idea. It didn't
matter. I didn't care. Anything was better than where I'd been. I
picked my Samsonite off the baggage carousel and loaded it into
the waiting shuttle van. I was headed into my future, trying to
put the past behind me as quickly and as thoroughly as I could.
I just stared out the window and rubbed my wrist.

I'd never seen a town like Ann Arbor, a strange mix of Midwestern humility, hippie throwback, and college casual. With book-
stores and record shops to browse in my free time, new streets to
wander, I would loose myself and forget California. I marveled at
the trees, bursting with leaves. California summers unfolded in
shades of drought-induced brown. The University of Michigan
consumed Ann Arbor, and it was impossible to recognize where
the town ended and the school began. The buildings looked old
and yet everything felt new to me.

As I stood in front of the dormitory, anxiety overwhelmed my relief. I knew how much the first few hours could set the tone of a summer experience. Two summers before that one, I'd met three other African American girls on the shuttle van ride to the Mount Holyoke campus. We became instant friends by the time we pulled up to our summer math program dormitory. But while we took our suitcases from the back, a white woman wondered aloud to her husband what we were doing there. "Those must be the scholarship kids," he'd said. The succeeding weeks presented offensive variations on that infuriating theme. My black girlfriends and I formed a tight-knit group that was barraged with questions: Why do you guys eat every meal together? Why do all of you hang out together all the time? Do you dislike white people? That experience had unraveled, and I had nearly punched a girl who called us niggers near the end of the program.

Shaking that memory, I lugged my suitcase through these new doors and into the cinderblock lobby. I was damp with sweat by the time I reached the elevators. I hoped for a quiet program, free of conflict. I didn't need to have the best summer of my life, just a better one than last year. One decent month, I prayed, that was all I needed.

A wall of must hit me as I crossed the threshold into my room. I opened the window and door to try to create a breeze. A gust of humid air blew dust balls across the floor like tumbleweeds. I would have the room to myself, so I slung my suitcase on a bed and began unpacking. My tiniest movements echoed off the bare walls just like the words streaked through my mind: quiet and decent. I repeated the words as I made my bed. Someone knocked on my door.

A short, stocky girl bounded across my room with her hand

out. I shook it as she introduced herself. Her name was Maria, she said, her own room was a few doors down the corridor from mine. She was from Phoenix, Arizona. Her rapid-fire English told me Spanish was her first language and the one I guessed she still spoke at home.

Maria and I walked from the dorm to the program orientation. Every now and then, we interrupted our easy and steady stream of conversation to consult the campus map. It was a hike from the dorm to the business school campus. Maria was terrific and we had a lot in common—our interest in student government, our plans for business careers, strict parents. Maria punctuated the conversation with warm laughter that put me at ease. She was really smart but didn't take herself too seriously.

When we got to orientation and saw the throng of kids milling around, my pulse quickened. I'd participated in scenes like this one lots of times, with everyone flashing smiles tinged with hesitation. Maria had met everyone in a few seconds. I said hello and introduced my way around but was more reluctant. I also detected another kind of excitement surging through the room, but I couldn't put my finger on it. I was as interested in it as I was in learning everyone's names. The noise level in the room continued to rise as more and more kids arrived.

A distinguished older man walked into the room, trailed closely by two eager young people, and I took a seat beside Maria. We sat in the second row behind a bank of desks that stretched the length of the room. The professor offered an eloquent but sonorous speech about corporate leadership and the program's goals. Then we all introduced ourselves even though we'd each propped little printed signs with our names on the desk in front of us. I listened but couldn't concentrate. We'd come from almost every corner of the country. The program was roughly half guys and half girls. As I looked around the room, I couldn't help but marvel at everything. I paid attention with only half of my mind because the other half was busy trying to figure out why my heart was beating so fast.

These kids were anything but quiet. They were exuberant and really funny. Animated conversations exploded around the dining hall table at dinner, and I lost myself in the frenzy of conversation. We laughed as some kids told hilarious stories about their first airplane rides to get to the program. These kids challenged all of the categories I'd brought with me from California. The BHA categories fell apart: some of the guys played varsity sports and took advanced placement classes; there weren't really any BAPs in the group, and none of these kids wore the frightened, beleaguered expressions that I saw so often on the faces of black PV kids. Besides, not everyone in the group was black, and it was fascinating to listen to the differences between Mexican American Spanish and that spoken by Puerto Rican kids. Just as strange was the brand of state pride that some kids mixed with ethnic or cultural allegiance. Demanding parents, rigorous classes, our favorite songs—we covered it all by the time we returned to the dorm and the guys headed off to their floor.

Music blasted into the hallway as girls darted from room to room, chattering, sharing pictures, and getting to know one another. I walked into a bathroom filled with girls preparing for bed. Every girl carried a washcloth along with her towel. None of us walked into the bathroom barefoot, and half of us wore rollers and scarves, but we didn't feel like aliens. By the time I dropped off to sleep, my cheeks ached from smiling so much.

I kept thinking about the other mysterious element that sharpened my excitement. The first week, Maria and I met for breakfast every day and then took our same seats near the front of the room. I took notes, listened to the lectures, and participated in the seminars. Then I solved the mystery and realized what was setting this summer experience apart from so many others for me. At seventeen years old, this was the first time I sat in a classroom without any white kids. Our professor wasn't even white. In the first few days, sitting among those kids trading insights and knowing how lively they were outside the class made me feel my usual isolation in a new way. Being the only black kid in the class had been the norm for me since first grade, ten years. More than just the stares I received during history lessons or the compliments about the quality of my vocabulary, sitting in that Michigan seminar room, I felt the perpetual loneliness that had defined so much of my intellectual life. But by the end of the first week, as I scanned the room, the burden that I usually carried eased. The only one, the minority: my load shifted and receded. Here I wasn't such an anomaly or a freak. There were lots of other kids like me.

Minority had always sounded and felt like a dirty word for so much of my life. I had grown accustomed to cringing on the inside when I heard it. *Minority* was just a matter of *quantity*, yet it so often implied inferior *quality*. We didn't have any tests to take at LEAD, but I didn't need scores or grades to know how sharp these kids were. I always knew we existed, but the ease with which these kids displayed their intelligence was the miraculous thing for me. They didn't cower or act embarrassed. They were really intense, and I loved it. *Minority* had always sounded like damaged goods, the upper cut of insults. At the end of the first week, a chasm had opened between the way people said *minority* and the way I felt it.

The first Sunday morning I woke up early and greeted Maria at the sinks. She headed off to Mass. I went on my way to a nearby Presbyterian church. My mind had been sorting through new experiences for seven days, trying to process one surprise after another. I needed to get a hold of myself, order my mind to the extent that it was possible. A familiar ritual in the still strange town seemed a good place for it. The church looked ancient compared to St. Peter's—this one was all dark wood and stained glass. I saw more white people at the service than I'd interacted with all week. Even though my worship community usually looked this way, I thought about the contrast through the sermon. I sang most of the hymns from memory and enjoyed the service well enough. But after it was over, I wanted to get back to the dorm to my friends and to the excitement that I found irresistible.

A few hundred yards from the dorm, I saw Maria walking beside a tall, familiar figure. They walked along another path that would intersect with mine. I recognized the long, deliberate strides and bent head. It was a guy from the program named Rick. I knew nearly nothing about him except that he was from New York. I kept my pace steady but knew our paths would meet.

"Hey, Maria, how was Mass?" I asked.

"Mass was fine. Rick and I bumped into each other on the way out. How was church?" Maria asked.

"Hi," Rick said to me. He spoke in a thick Long Island accent, his voice slightly husky, but he never said a lot. Rick cleared his throat all the time but didn't seem shy.

"Hi, Rick. Church was fine."

We walked in silence for a few minutes.

"So what do you think of the program so far?" I asked Rick. He wore his curly, black hair cut long enough to see the clear pattern of his loose curls. He had perfectly clear skin the color of gingerroot. His broad forehead and almond-shaped eyes tilted down at the outer corners and gave him a slightly somber expression.

"It's good. You?" he replied as he glanced at me.

"Yeah, I really like it," I said. "You know, the case studies are really fun." *The case studies? Fun?* I decided to stop talking so much because I knew I sounded goofy. I let Maria fill in the rest of the silence as we rode the elevator to our floor.

I had promised to call home every week. I was having my best Sunday in a very long time and didn't want to interrupt it with a sober conversation with my folks, but I couldn't put it off any longer. Without me at home, I hoped Dad was having a better Sunday than usual. Our conversation turned out to be brief but surprisingly pleasant. Dad sounded cheerful as he described Sunday dinner. I knew it probably tasted great, but I couldn't say I missed it. Dad asked about dorm food and I didn't lie. It sucked, but I didn't really pay much attention to food or overeat the way I did at home, and those were new developments. I had nothing new to numb, so I didn't want to stuff my face. I couldn't explain that to Dad and Mom because I could barely explain it to myself. Mom asked about the program, and I told her that I planned to read my case studies beneath a tree and then find some other kids for more fun later. I could hear the jazz playing softly in the background at home. I didn't have any questions to ask about California because I didn't miss anything about it. I promised to call the next Sunday and got off the phone.

In the middle of the next week, Maria and I were hanging out in her room.

"You know Rick's been watching you, right?" Maria kept her head down as she tried to sound casual. She knew me well enough to anticipate my shock.

"What?" I said. "No way." My face instantly flushed.

"Yeah," she persisted. "He looks at you in seminar all the time."

Rick? Looking at me? Maria knew everyone and watched everything, so I had to accept what she was saying even though I couldn't believe it. *When did he look at me? How had he been looking at me?* I participated in class, raised my hand, but that was because I found the material interesting. Maybe Rick looked at me because he thought I talked too much.

"But he always hangs out with the guys," I said, as though it mattered. "He never says much." *Rick?* He was quiet in class. He joked with his friends in the dining hall but seemed an economical talker.

"Well, he may not say much," Maria said with a smile, "but he's *totally* been checking you out."

Could I have been so clueless? There was a huge difference between watching in annoyance or in interest; my guy friends at home had showed me that. I knew nearly nothing about Rick, so I wasn't going to get all dorky and excited just because of what Maria said. I'd been burned too many times. I remembered the phrase I read all the time in business: "Past performance is no indication of future returns." Those words filled me with hope and I swelled with expectation. Things with guys, this guy, might be different. But the thought frightened me. I couldn't take more disappointment. *It was probably a fluke,* I told myself. *I'd probably shown Rick something he didn't like. No guy had ever watched me do anything.* Still, as much as I wanted to protect myself from getting hurt, as much as I had tried not needing people, I couldn't suppress the glimmer of hope I felt. Things might be different, even better. I didn't want to overreact, just to get disappointed. I tried to forget what Maria said. But I couldn't.

The next morning, I took my usual seat beside Maria and looked down as soon as Rick walked into the room. He was with his buddy, a tall, toffee-skinned guy named Will who always wore pristine white sneakers and sweatsuits despite the heat. Will was from Atlanta, which might have explained his heat tolerance. They took their usual seats near the end of the back row.

I tried to focus on the seminar and act normal. *Don't look back there, stay focused. He's not looking at you.* The words raced through my mind for half an hour. I swiveled in my chair, crossed and uncrossed my legs. *Sit still, stay focused.* I tapped my pencil and rubbed my wrist. I couldn't get hold of myself. I forced my attention back to the discussion, but all I wanted to do was look. This had to stop. I raised my hand just to distract myself. Words came out of my mouth as the argument continued inside my mind. *He's not looking at you.* The more I tried to face front, the more looking back at Rick tempted me. I had to know.

Okay, fine. Look but don't get your hopes up. Don't let Maria see you, I told myself. With my head down, I tried to casually twist my chair in Rick's general direction. A brief glance that blurred everything, and then I whipped my head around and faced forward again. I couldn't have acted more guilty if I were shoplifting. *Had Rick been looking?* I had no idea. I took a deep breath and tried it again. This time, I tried to position myself perfectly and snuck a peek without detection. I bent my head and peered over my shoulder, raising my chin until he came into view. I knew his head was raised this time, facing the front of the room. Then I looked at him for a long moment. At first, he continued looking at the lectern and the professor. *See,* I told myself, *Maria's wrong. He's not looking at you.* But at the very moment I finished the thought, Rick looked right at me. He smiled shyly, almost reluctantly, hitching the right corner of his mouth slightly higher than the left.

Overwhelmed with shock, I couldn't smile back. Now that Rick had looked at me once, I had a new set of problems. I had to know *how* he was looking at me. *Was he looking at me because I looked at him first?* I didn't want him to think I was staring at him, so I faced front again. But after a few minutes, my curiosity overwhelmed me.

I looked again. Rick met my glance instantly. He didn't turn away when our eyes met. He smiled ever so slightly, but there was some other expression on his face that I didn't know him well enough to identify. This guy wasn't glancing at me, he was looking at me and wanted me to know it. Rick held my gaze and wouldn't let it go. I couldn't move. His eyes were forceful and insistent. The center of my stomach fell through the soles of my feet. I couldn't take my eyes off him. I had to look at him as long as he looked at me. Rick didn't waver for an instant. No one had ever looked at me that way.

Maria was right.

Bodies crowded my sight line before I knew it and Rick vanished. Break time. I had no idea what I had just done. I couldn't move or focus, and my body was exhausted and thrilled at once. I heard everything and nothing. Maria called my name, and it sounded as though she stood across the room, rather than right next to me. I sputtered a response but didn't tell Maria what had just happened. *What had just happened?* I wasn't sure.

I had no idea what to do next. I had never done this before. I walked to the bathroom to try to release some of the energy surging through my body. I could feel my heart racing. I said a prayer of gratitude for deodorant and air-conditioning as I felt the dampness in my armpits. My shocked face stared back at me in the mirror. There wasn't much time left in the break. Getting up and out of the room had been a great idea, I realized as I reached the seminar room door, but now walking back felt like the worst prospect in the world. *Oh, great.* I hurried into my seat and kept my eyes on the floor. *What next?* I couldn't keep trading looks with Rick. Could I?

By lunchtime I was a mass of anxious distraction. My hands shook, a glass nearly slipped out of my hand at the soda fountain. I wasn't the cool girl who'd flirted with guys lots of times. I was the other girl, the unsteady one for whom all of this was new. Balancing my tray required all of my concentration. I did and didn't want to watch Rick. Would Rick sit next to me? What if he didn't sit next to me? The intrigue put my senses on high alert. I was trapped by indecision. If I ignored Rick, he might think that I had lost interest in him. If I paid him too much attention, I might frighten him away.

Rick fell in step beside me as I walked back to the seminar. He'd timed it perfectly to look casual and coincidental and, thank goodness, I didn't jump. It was a smooth move that I really appreciated. But his presence raised the air temperature ten degrees. Nothing felt cool. Maybe Rick saw my struggle or maybe he just felt more confident in these situations—I didn't care. The halting way in which he said hello told me he felt a bit nervous himself. I marveled at Rick, walking there beside me in silence for a moment. He really took chances. I took a deep breath, opened my mouth, and said a silent prayer of gratitude that coherent words came out.

To my ears, everyone else in the afternoon seminar sounded like adults in a *Peanuts* movie, all garbled and confused. I turned around occasionally and found Rick waiting to meet my glance every time I did it.

The next day, I watched Rick play basketball in an entirely new way. I knew that he and some of the other guys played college students, and had glanced over at them in the gym without paying particularly close attention. But since our encounter yesterday, I stopped a fair distance from the court where I wouldn't disturb him and watched him more closely. When I did, I nearly lost my mind. Rick focused all his attention on the game. He wore loose-fitting shorts. His tube socks stretched across his marvelously developed calves. His sweaty shirt clung to his pectoral muscles and broad shoulders. Physically, his boyhood was finished. He had a grown man's body. He played defense with precision and waved his arms to deflect shots. When he ran for the ball and began to dribble down the court, all his natural confidence showed in his game. The way his thigh muscles rippled and tensed as he took his three-point shot made me gasp. As little as I knew about basketball, I recognized the sure efficiency in his moves and admired his elegant jump shot.

Talking to Rick was even better than watching him on the court, and by the third week we talked all the time. He had a sexy mind, incisive. His sly wit appeared unexpectedly and made me laugh out loud. After I began to relax a bit more, we developed a rapid-fire, witty banter sometimes that showed me how much he admired my mind. Other times, we put our heads closer together and talked in hushed tones in the moonlight. We talked about our lives at home, but we mostly kept each other present in the moments we created together. No one had ever said or shown me so much admiration and care before. The more we talked, the more Rick challenged all of my assumptions and promises to myself.

But for all of his intensity, Rick remained physically reserved. Between weekly Mass, regular confession, and his altar boy training, Rick was respectful. More than anything else, I *really* wanted Rick to kiss me. Everything between our bodies had become so intense that the most minor graze of fingers, feet, or legs made my whole body shiver. The strength of our connection was almost too kinetic. But I also didn't want him to kiss me because I knew that I wouldn't stop myself. I had no idea how to hold in everything being with him made me feel—pretty, smart, funny, on fire. I loved and feared my surging passion.

The last night of the program, Rick and I stayed awake all night, and I lay with my ear on his heart. We said so few words because there was everything and nothing to say about that moment. I felt too much to cry or allow sadness to overshadow my exhilaration. We had already agreed to write and call. My attraction to Rick had saved me. He helped me feel my way out of the emotional exile I had imposed on myself before I got too comfortable with it, before my resignation to loneliness became any more familiar. He was kind to me.

The boy with the charmingly heavy Long Island accent showed me that I didn't have to settle or lower my expectations. He answered a set of questions I had been too hurt and too frightened to fully form. He showed me that I deserved fluttering excitement. He showed me that I even attracted admiring stares from the handsomest and smartest boy in the room. He showed me that, yes, a boy like that could like a girl like me. He proved there was more than what Palos Verdes offered me.

{ chapter thirteen }

SEPARATE LIVES

THE REPORTER AND PHOTOGRAPHER arrived at our house one Saturday in late February. They were from the *Daily Breeze,* the newspaper that circulated through the southern cities of the Los Angeles basin. The paper dubbed the area the LA Gold Coast, which included the four towns of the Palos Verdes Peninsula, the beach cities, and the working-class communities more inland that reached to the border of Long Beach. Even though I didn't know the story's angle or why the reporter had chosen to interview our family, I knew what to do. All Mom had to say was "fix up." I wore my argyle sweater and purple pleated wool skirt. I curled my hair and placed gold hoops in my ears. After lining my eyes with blue pencil, I added mascara, a dab of blush, and some powder for shine control. I made sure to apply lipstick because I knew that's what Mom wanted. When it came to newspaper coverage, the Baziles had become seasoned professionals.

I also knew why Mom and Dad agreed to participate in the article. They lapped up publicity like thirsty lions during the dry season and never declined a feature. Mom's picture ran in the *Palos Verdes Peninsula News* all the time for her volunteer work—a familiar head shot accompanied descriptions of her work with a multicultural organization she'd helped establish, candid shots captured her beaming face at dinner dances, others featured her participation in Black Heritage activities. The camera always found her. Dad's business profiles, featured in city papers and in trade journals, hung on the walls of his office. He always rehearsed his sales figures and the story of his ascent from food salesman to business owner. Natalie's collection of clippings and features was no less formidable. Her reign as homecoming queen, announcements of various prizes and awards she'd won, her presentation at a debutante ball—all were folded into a scrapbook. I'd grabbed a few headlines over the years and had recently added new ones to the stack: September 10, 1986, the *Daily Breeze,* "Junior Auxiliary Names New Officers"; December 1986, the *PV News,* "Bazile Presented at Deb Ball."

On the chilly afternoon we talked to the *Daily Breeze* reporter, we sat in the family room as the photographer set up in the living room. Mom and Dad told the version of our story that they always told. It was the one of unbounded achievement, easy accomplishment, and harmony. Dad talked about Bazile Metals and the $9 million to $10 million in sales from the previous year. He described our Christmas trip to Asia. Mom told the reporter that living in Palos Verdes felt "like being on the top of the world." It was the story that enabled us to keep all the other versions of ourselves hidden. We concealed those things from the reporter because we tried to keep them hidden from ourselves.

I knew the routine by heart and when it was my turn, I knew what to say. When Mom began talking about the senior class trip to Europe, I piped up, a trained parrot reciting my lines. I wouldn't take the six-week European tour, I explained, "because they're going to many of the places I've already been." I moved the parts of my mouth and fired my brain like a well-oiled robot, hardwired by years of indoctrination and relentless pressure to make my family and me seem perfect.

As much as my body remained in Palos Verdes that day, my spirit and my mind had already migrated east. Really, I had never fully returned from LEAD. I poured all of my energy into my relationship with Rick. My heart and the deeper parts of myself existed on the pages of letters I wrote and received. We exchanged letters all the time, and I'd rush home to check the mailbox. If I got a letter or a mix tape, I'd run upstairs, close my door, and come alive. What we shared on those pages kept me going until we spoke on the phone and I floated away. I allowed myself to fall in love for the first time and it felt wonderful.

I couldn't hide the change that Rick and Michigan had made in me. I didn't even try. I stopped talking but wasn't surly. I kind of drifted through my Palos Verdes life in an automatic and hollow way. So Mom and Dad weren't surprised when I explained my plan to go east for college. I was focused on getting out, keeping busy until that day came. They didn't ever ask whether I was trying to follow Rick; they could see that my desire was even bigger than my affection for him. Signs of the shift appeared everywhere in my life.

I considered myself a long shot for Ivy League acceptance. My grades were good but not great. I was accomplished as a student leader and knew I could handle the work. I just needed to convince admissions to admit me. When I found out that on-campus interviews were possible, I asked Mom and Dad if I could schedule them. I knew that other kids would have stronger transcripts than me. I had to show interviewers my heart and my determination. With Mom and Dad's okay, I arranged an October interview and overnight visit at Harvard, campus tours of Brown and Yale, and an interview at Columbia and was accompanied by my parents. After a glorious day at Columbia—and a great interview—Mom said, "All of these schools are wonderful. Just don't pick Columbia, not the one in New York City."

I heard those words but didn't pay much attention because we were headed to Penn Station to meet Rick's train. Seeing him again was thrilling, and Mom and Dad got a chance to know him over dinner. He was centered in the way that I remembered, made lively conversation with my parents, but always paid plenty of attention to me. Just sitting next to Rick was fantastic. I could tell how much he impressed Mom and Dad by the way that they kept glancing from him to me and smiling. What wasn't to like? Rick embodied all the qualities they respected: he was studious and well mannered, handsome, and ambitious. By the middle of dinner, everyone relaxed, and even Dad acted more at ease with Rick than I had ever seen with any guy either Natalie or I had introduced to him. Rick, Dad, Mom, and I spent another two hours together in the car. We all joked together and Rick held my hand in the dark as we drove down the Long Island Expressway to Rick's house.

When we arrived in Rick's driveway, he thanked my parents for dinner and led me inside his house. His parents were out, and Mom and Dad had agreed to let us spend a little time alone together. They had never done anything like that before, but they also understood how much Rick meant to me. As I rode back to our hotel after saying good night to Rick, I folded myself back up and tucked my feelings into the envelope of our relationship.

Back in Palos Verdes, I had focused on the completion of my college applications. Mom, of course, expressed her own version of interest in my college application process. First, she handed me an ROTC application and tried to insist that I complete it. The army? I had never expressed even the faintest interest in military service. My connection to Rick and the glimpses of the wider world had ended my marching days; I'd spent enough time on the front lines. So I told Mom no.

Then Mom ordered me to apply to at least one historically black college. We had battled for weeks over that one. Mom thought Howard University would be a good place for me. She didn't invoke the Hall brothers' postslavery education at Tuskegee or the general principle of paying homage to the black college tradition. If she'd made the order in the name of family legacy or historical solidarity, I might have applied. Some of my BHA acquaintances and LEAD friends were headed to black colleges and I was happy for them. Maybe if it had been my idea, I'd have embraced it, but I felt too much of the *Fair Winds* in her insistence. I didn't need to learn any more names to prove anything to Mom and Dad about how black I was. Besides, what had we moved to Palos Verdes for? The demand revealed Mom's second thoughts about integration. If I agreed to apply, I'd have done it only to convince Mom of something that had nothing to do with me. So I just didn't fill out or mail the application.

By the gusty afternoon when I sat staring into the *Daily Breeze* photographer's lens, I felt empty and exhausted. We looked fantastic, the reporter and photographer assured us, just perfect. We posed in our living room decorated in tones of taupe and peach. An oil painting of a European village square and the upright piano no one ever played framed us. Natalie and I, both wearing skirts and sweaters, sat knees pinned together in the corner of the elaborately tufted couch we used only for company. Mom wore a red sweater decorated with an abstract black, yellow, and purple design in the center. She sat cross-legged in a chair beside us. Dad's red tie popped against his pale blue short-sleeved dress shirt that revealed the muscles in his forearms and biceps as he rested his hands on the back of the couch and leaned between Mom and me. Crisp tan slacks completed his outfit. Natalie looked closer to tears than joy to me, as though beneath all of the perfection she felt miserable. Time after time, the flash blinded me and I grew even more vacant and glassy-eyed than usual. I stretched the corners of my mouth into a full smile but kept my thumb on my wrist for the entire shoot.

On Sunday, March 8, 1987, the article appeared, and Mom and Dad pored over every word of the article, cooing over our picture, delighting in the sound bites that had made it into the paper. The article, titled "Separate Lives: Three Families Miles Apart Living in Different World," ran on the front page of the Life/Arts section and covered two full pages.

Seeing the article, I realized that there was a lot I didn't know about it, but that was nothing new in my life. This was the sixth story in a series focusing on the contrasts of Gold Coast life. A text box on the far right of the page explained that this article explored the "economic diversity to be found in the area, from affluence, to yuppward mobility to hard-luck lives." Until that moment, I didn't know anything about the other families featured. Then I felt sick.

The top third of the page featured Bill and Lisa Couey, a couple in their thirties who posed with their blond toddler and infant sons in a Buick station wagon surrounded by streaks of light, the time exposure effect of moving cars on Pacific Coast Highway. At the University of Southern California, where they met, he'd rushed Beta and she was a Tri Delta. They fell in love, married, and now lived in a comfortable Manhattan Beach home they planned to upgrade. He worked as a cameraman and drove a Porsche. She was a former flight attendant who worked part-time in a dermatologist's office. They described themselves as "just the average Manhattan Beach family."

Beneath the headline on the far left, a smiling pecan-skinned woman, Danella Caldwell, rode on the seat of her seven-year-old son Amantu's bike while he pedaled through an alley near their apartment. The clear sky twinkled the shade of a robin's egg, but Amantu wore gray knit gloves on his hands. Ms. Caldwell liked red as much as Mom. She had a red clip in her hair, a sweatshirt of the same shade, and matching red plastic glasses. Amantu wore a red sweatshirt and jeans like his mom. The caption beside the picture explained that Ms. Caldwell was a single mother who lived in Inglewood, the gang-ridden community where Mom used to teach school. "I never have what you call peace of mind," the caption quoted her as saying.

Our picture sat at the bottom center of the page. I marveled at how different Natalie and I looked compared to our parents. Mom and Dad both appeared excited and poised in their pride, their eyes shone with vigor. Natalie looked haggard around the eyes, weary, and on the verge of despair. My blank expression telegraphed emptiness and fear. Beside our photo, the caption read "the Baszile family of Palos Verdes Estates . . . are living what they call the American dream."

I found it strange that black people took up two-thirds of the pictures and the story when we didn't take up two-thirds of the Gold Coast. There were people far wealthier than our family in Palos Verdes. Where were the Korean, Japanese, Hong Kong Chinese, Taiwainese, or Japanese American families? Where were the white families? What about the family who'd escaped Iran? So why'd they pick us? How did we end up profiled?

The text of the story only deepened my dismay. The notion

that it described three families was a lie. It really profiled two kinds of black families: the right kind and the wrong kind. Ms. Caldwell and Amantu were trotted out as the rule for black people. She described her financial struggles, her reliance on public assistance. She explained that her older son, my age, was serving time for a robbery conviction and how that fact spurred her struggle to protect Amantu. She drove him to school and never allowed him to play outside, only through their security door.

My family represented the exception, and I hated that day as much as I had hated so many other days we'd lived in Palos Verdes. But it only seemed that way because we presented the slip-covered version of our family. We didn't expose the true fabric of our family when it was just the four of us. We had trapped ourselves beneath a thick layer of yellowing plastic, and we never let ourselves breathe. We never aired out and were beginning to stink.

No one mentioned our first appearance in the paper, the 1976 article featured in the *Palos Verdes Peninsula News*. The "Go Home Niggers" incident certainly didn't make it into the final text of the story. But in many ways, I was still that six-year-old scrubbing the cherub. I was still the seven-year-old fighting her way to a second-grade portrait that wouldn't pass Mom's or Aunt Frenchie's muster.

In the article, Dad counted himself fortunate because, he said, Nataile and I had "bought into his values." Which set? The Monday-through-Thursday set? Or the Friday-through-Sunday set? The truth was that I bought into both sets. I bought into those values because I knew nothing else. Besides, Dad was a great salesman. Out of habit, I did what he and Mom expected, what I had come to expect of myself without much examination. As much as it had paid off, no one asked me whether I considered it a worthwhile purchase. I had only begun to feel how much that purchase had actually cost me and I had not yet calculated the expense.

I scanned the article and heard the echo of a reprimand for Ms. Caldwell as clearly as the backhanded compliment that the article paid to us. Community and class supposedly separated our two families, but the line was thinner than anyone wanted to admit. Ms. Caldwell was a decade younger than my parents, but her oldest son and I were the same age. She was from Cincinnati, Mom from the Township. But if we'd been standing together on Aunt Eva's porch on an early summer day, or in a public park, we could have passed for members of the same extended family— Auntie Danella and Cousin Amantu—rather than the two ends of the Gold Coast spectrum.

The reporter failed to ask us the most important question: Why all this relentless achievement? The truth was that integration had been a long, hard slog, painful and shot through with contradictions. At home, Mom plotted to "outwhite the white folks" as she put it, which made my achievements both a spear and a shield. "The first black" usually preceeded Mom and Dad's descriptions of our achievements. It wasn't just that I was the student body president, it's that I was the first black one. It wasn't just that Natalie was a homecoming queen, it was that she was the first and only black one. But maybe people had gotten so used to the phrase that they stopped hearing it and lost track of the aggression in it. I never did.

So when the article quoted Mom's claim that I'd been involved in "the very best that the community had to offer," it was accurate but unclear. We had pursued the best the community had to offer because we were met by its worst offerings when we moved there. Rage and fury fueled my parents' intrepid drive for achievement as much as ambition did. My achievements were weapons, the tools of conquest that they used in the long siege against prior generations of exclusion and refusal. We'd been hunkered down for a very long time. Mom explained that she loved Palos Verdes, not just for its beauty but because it was "not a community of inherited wealth." The reporter didn't know it, but she was speaking well-rehearsed lines she always fed reporters: "Most people are very similar to us, no matter their ethnicity," she continued. My girlhood had shown me the differences with my peers and neighbors more than the similarities. I had never felt like all the other PV kids; my girlhood had been anything but colorless. My participation, or my achievements, weren't interchangeable with those of my peers.

I found Mom's last claim disturbing because it was a shaded version of the truth that was less than honest. I could only explain it in terms of an image that flashed through my mind as I read the article: the gray lips of the cherub in our front yard. I couldn't hear the frequency of the words it spoke in my mind, but I knew without hearing that they were words of truth and distress; from the day the vandals had shaded it with black paint, the statue had never stopped speaking to me.

What we couldn't describe and what the article couldn't convey was the color of our fear. I was accomplished and had managed to avoid most of the adolescent and teenage pitfalls with this strategy, but this was more than mere garden-variety discipline. In truth, my compliance and achievements were about fear and rage. I had become numb to my Palos Verdes life. But the problem for me was that we had sacrificed feeling for achievement, and I wondered if it was a trade-off we had to make.

Mom and Dad knew more about the truth of black American life, and Ms. Caldwell's experience, than they admitted. The truth was that segregation and discrimination had erased "the middle" for black people. It never had existed for the Basziles and the Caldwells. LA papers and local news programs covered the funerals of diligent black students caught in the cross-fire.

No American law had ever been passed to prevent the Coueys from doing anything. No one greeted their arrival in Manhattan Beach with painted words of hate. Those facts and our feelings about them, hidden from the reporter and from me at the time, explained so much of my girlhood. If Mom and Dad hadn't worked so tirelessly to get out of Louisiana and Michigan and never return, we would have been trapped by segregation or factory work. If they hadn't undertaken integration and achievement as the cornerstones of our family life in California, we could have been the Caldwells' neighbors. We just would have deferred the slog for another generation.

The American dream? Over and over in the article Mom repeated the phrase. From where Mom had come, she'd surely achieved her American dream. She'd overcome so much.

Dad had fulfilled his American dream, too.

As I continued reading, I felt less and less sure of what the idea of the American dream meant for me. I could feel but not name the emotion that underwrote our quest for achievement as well as our manipulation of visibility. The article talked about the self-esteem that defined our family and Mom's positive thinking, but no one mentioned that beneath those things lay consuming fears of poverty, failure, exclusion, and rejection. I wished Mom and Dad would have told me their stories to help me carry the burden of integration and face the challenges of the life we were trying to lead. If I'd known more about what we were all feeling, then maybe I wouldn't have felt so haunted and afraid all of the time.

What was my dream? I wondered. More than anything else, that was the most pressing question in my life, the one I ached to answer. I knew we traded in the currency of achievement, but in one way it felt like fool's gold. I had lost track of what mattered to me, if I'd ever had hold of it in my life. It was time to leave this one-dimensional life of mine and create a new and separate one for myself.

A few weeks after the article appeared, private college decisions for regular admission began to arrive. Harvard, Brown, and Yale rejected my application. The thin envelopes were not entirely a surprise and I didn't take the no too hard. My Columbia interview had been my best and longest one. I'd loved the classes and the campus from the instant I walked through the gates in Morningside Heights. Besides, the school had no math requirement to graduate. My math skills had proved so dismal that I knew that the college and I were a match. My hands trembled as I opened the thick envelope and screamed in the street at the congratulations offered me in the acceptance letter. All of my planning, all of my hoping, all of my wishing had led me to this moment.

My acceptance shattered the veneer on my old self. My dream? The answer to that question began to unfold the afternoon Columbia offered me admission to the class of 1991. That was the day I stirred myself from the deep sleep I had imposed since returning from LEAD. I woke back up to myself. More than Ivy League prestige, Columbia offered me anonymity and the chance to get to know myself. The dispassion of New Yorkers thrilled me. I would choose rude people over the rude surprise of secrecy any day. No one in New York knew or cared anything about the perfect black family we tried to convince everyone we had been. Seated beside strangers on the crosstown bus or standing on the subway platform, I would be alone.

"Let's just wait a minute," Mom said when I told her. "What about Berkeley?"

She made the same case that she'd made since the day I'd been admitted to the state's flagship institution. But it all sounded like I was being slotted into Natalie's life rather than my dream. It was a perfectly fine and acceptable version of my future, except for the fact that it was neither fine nor acceptable to me.

But Mom wasn't willing to say what was true: she was worried about the cost of Columbia. She had a practical point. Columbia dwarfed Berkeley's in-state tuition costs. I could live in the condominium my parents had already purchased for Natalie and cut the room and board expenses even more. Berkeley was the practical choice. But I knew that practical would cost me too much. I'd spent enough time being practical. Remaining in state and doing what was better for the family pocketbook was the wrong thing to do.

Underneath all of that, what hurt most was the fact that Mom so often positioned herself between me and my desires and tried to redirect me. Why couldn't I just want something else? Why weren't my desires good enough? Why wasn't I good enough?

I couldn't give Mom the final word on my future. Now was the time to fight in a different way for what I knew was best for me. I couldn't afford to let Mom talk me out of another thing. It had to be my version that prevailed this time, no concessions and no apologies. I couldn't stay in California. I'd come too far, worked too hard to stay alive. If I remained, I knew I would be miserable. Rick and LEAD had shown me I didn't have to be.

So I ran upstairs and dialed the phone. Standing there punching the numbers on the phone's keypad, I knew that Dad was my last chance, that he might be the only person who would really recognize my desperate need to get out of California for good. I didn't even think about what might happen if I failed.

"Good afternoon, Baszile—" the voice on the other end of the line began.

"I need to speak to Mr. Baszile right away," I said before the receptionist finished her greeting. My heart pounded. This was no time for politeness or pleasantries.

"He's in the warehouse, Jennifer," the woman said. "Would you like to leave a message?"

"No," I said. "Would you please page him? I'll wait." This had to be settled now. I wasn't going to defer my life for another moment.

As I listened to the hold music, my mind drifted to one of the few stories Dad told from his boyhood, the story of how he left the South for the last time.

When Dad turned sixteen he asked his mother's permission to finish high school in Port Arthur, Texas. Compared to Elton, it was a bigger and better town, a place with a stronger high school. Dad's uncle Madison and aunt Josephine, who loved Dad like their son, had already invited him to stay at their house. So for those two years, Dad worked alongside Uncle Madison on weekends and attended school during the week. On the night of his high school graduation, his mother and the rest of the family traveled to see Dad cross the stage as the first member of the family to receive his high school diploma.

But Dad didn't stand still after he crossed that stage. In fact, that night, after pictures and warm hugs all around, Dad walked right out of the South for good. Even though he had a better education than anyone in his immediate family, and more opportunities, it wasn't enough. He had already packed his few belongings in a cardboard box and headed for the bus station. He arrived in California and began another life. He never returned south except to visit.

"Barry Baszile," Dad said.

"Dad, I just got into Columbia. I want to go. Mom's trying to talk me into Berekeley—"

There was silence on the line for a second, and then Dad spoke the words of my salvation.

"You can go," he said. "We'll find a way to send you."

Dad knew I needed to get out of California. Maybe he wanted me to leave to make his life easier. Whether he said yes more for himself than for me, or vice versa, it didn't matter. I was sure he said yes for both of us.

Maybe he finally understood that integration had been as hard on me as segregation had been on him.

My heart soared and tears welled from a deep place inside me.

"Mom!" I called downstairs. "Pick up the phone."

Dad repeated himself to Mom.

"But Barry," Mom said.

"Janet," Dad said. His tone said everything. He had the last word that day and I was really grateful.

She didn't offer much in the way of protest, and for once I was glad that she yielded to Dad.

That day the best version of our family showed up, won out, and prevailed. I think that as much as anything else, Mom and Dad tried to be the people in the newspaper. They conformed to the image that they projected in the article even more because maybe they knew I wasn't going to. They knew that I needed a separate life in order to survive.

Very little about Palos Verdes mattered after that phone call.

By graduation night, I barely felt anything except relief that it was over. On the night of my high school graduation, as my friends and nearly the entire class boarded the bus for Grad Night at Disneyland, I turned my back on my whole life and went home. I opened my graduation presents surrounded by my grandmother and Aunt Rose, Mom, Natalie, and Dad. I received a blue trunk, a family photograph from the Evergreen Ball, and some cash. It was enough to get me where I wanted to go.

My days as the black girl next door had come to an end.

Acknowledgments

The journey to this memoir began when I realized the absurdity of trying to be a professional historian without engaging my personal history.

Amazing people nurtured me along my way. Elizabeth Alexander, Hazel Carby, Tisha Hooks, Casey King, and Carlos Miranda provided much needed encouragement at the early stages of this project, which coincided with a turning point in my life.

Each time I saw her, Essie Lucky-Barros helped steady my hand on the plow.

Jonathan Pitts-Wiley, as amazing an artist as he is a man, helped me find my voice as a writer. His open heart, keen eye, and generosity sustained me and made this book possible. As we discussed words and ideas, I discovered a true friend.

Bernadet Pitts-Wiley felt the spirit of the book and extended to me a kind invitation to read at Mixed Magic Theatre, the warm and welcoming community she and her husband, Ricardo Pitts-Wiley, have created. An author couldn't wish for a better debut.

Thanks to the entire Bolden family for their love and prayers.

Every working mother needs to be blessed with someone like Roxie, the gifted teacher who has cared for the most precious gift in my life when I had to work.

Babz Rawls-Ivy, Briana, Gregory, Khalil, and Margeaux Ivy filled my heart with laughter as I completed the book.

My agent, Robert Levine, possesses clarity that has made me

a braver woman and a better writer. His associate, Kim Schefler, always encouraged me.

Cherise Davis, the kindred spirit who bought the book for Touchstone, believed in my story from the beginning and became a wonderful friend. I was fortunate to work with Amanda Patten, the patient and compassionate editor who helped me bring the project to fruition. Lauren Speigel and the entire team at Touchstone always made me feel welcome.

My family and I have walked a daunting path together. My love for them exceeds everything else. Thanks to my mother, Janet, whose fortitude and sacrifices sustained all of us. I appreciate your struggles even more now that I am a mother. My father, Barry, always encouraged me to tell my story. Natalie and I have shared strong bonds as sisters, friends, and writers. She is my other brain. She answered the phone whenever I called. Natalie's talent as a writer and her love for me inform this work.

Caleb is the bright spirit who remains my inspiration.

The Black Girl Next Door

This reading group guide for *The Black Girl Next Door* includes discussion questions for enhancing your book club. The suggested questions are intended to help your reading group find new and interesting angles and topics for your discussion. We hope that these ideas will enrich your conversation and increase your enjoyment of the book.

FOR DISCUSSION

1. Why would Jennifer's classmate's father make the claim that "black people have something in their feet to make them run faster than white people"? Is this perpetuation of a myth rooted in racial ignorance, jealousy, or malice?

2. When young Jennifer senses falsehood in this claim, she feels compelled to expose the classmate's father and her teacher. What is the significance of a child challenging an adult? Is it easier or harder to fool a child?

3. Baszile writes that in her family "integration was a form of competition." What do you make of the Basziles' strong drive to surpass and exceed expectations? What triumphs come out of this motivation? What tensions does it create?

4. How did you respond to Jennifer's imitation of her grandmother? What purpose does parody serve, and when does it go too far?

5. What does Grandmother Rose mean when she tells Jennifer's mother that her children are "just like perfect little white girls"? Is this a compliment, and if so, to whom? Is the goal for Jennifer's parents to preserve or escape their black identity?

6. Discuss the theme of alienation in the memoir. Why does Jennifer think of herself as "The Other One," and how does this shape her personality and the choices she makes?

7. Jennifer's Aunt Frenchie keeps a scrapbook for every member of the family, paying tribute to their accomplishments. Jennifer suspects that there's more to the story, though, and asks, "How much were her albums and photos a mirage?" Do you believe Frenchie's process of selective documentation serves the family well? Is it representative of their story through the ages? Does suffering and failure deserve to be remembered alongside success?

8. Jennifer loves the photographs of her ancestors her mom displays in the house, particularly the one of her great-great-grandmother Mary Dean Ballard. She says the pictures, "made me feel less isolated. I was a daughter and a sister, but I had also become a great-granddaughter. For the first time, we had ancestors to watch over us, which made it seem as though I could feel the roots of our family tree." How strongly do you feel rooted in your family's lineage?

9. Why is Rosa Parks a more acceptable hero for the school parade than Harriet Tubman or Frederick Douglass in the eyes of Jennifer's teacher and mother?

10. Jennifer undergoes a few major transformations in the story—one at the department store cosmetics counter, and another when she gets her hair straightened for the first time. Why is the lure of a "new and improved" self so strong? Who creates the ideal for Jennifer? For young women today?

Printed in the United States
By Bookmasters